Social Development

Social Development

Challenges Faced in an Unequal and Plural Society

M.S. Gore

RAWAT PUBLICATIONS
Jaipur • New Delhi • Bangalore • Guwahati • Kolkata

ISBN 978-81-7033-756-0

Reprinted, 2016

Published by
Prem Rawat for Rawat Publications
Satyam Apts., Sector 3, Jawahar Nagar, Jaipur - 302 004 (India)
Phone: 0141 265 1748 / 7006 Fax: 0141 265 1748
E-mail : info@rawatbooks.com
Website: rawatbooks.com

Delhi Office
4858/24, Ansari Road, Daryaganj, New Delhi 110 002
Phone: 011-23263290

Also at *Bangalore, Guwahati* and *Kolkata*

Typeset by Rawat Computers, Jaipur
Printed at Chaman Enterprises, New Delhi

Contents

Preface

This book brings together some of my papers published earlier in two separate books entitled *Some Aspects of Social Development* (1973) and *Social Aspects of Development* (1985).

Initially, social work curricula did not have much content dealing directly with social development. In fact, the word 'development' was used for many years to refer primarily to economic development. This might seem surprising since, in India, the idea of conscious efforts at development began with the projects initiated by William Myers in Uttar Pradesh in the early 1950s which were called Community Development Projects. But, the emphasis was on introducing progressive methods of agriculture and other economic activities with a view to raise the living standards of the rural population. These projects were experimental in nature and naturally few in number. The Ford Foundation had supported these projects and soon they attracted the attention of the Government of India.

When the government entered the field they extended the number to some 50 odd projects spread over different states in the country. Soon, there was a demand for extension of these projects to all states. A somewhat diluted version of these projects, called the National Extension Projects, was introduced and extended to many more districts in the form of specially carved-out 'development blocks'. Persons deputed from the

Revenue Department largely headed these projects. This was natural since they were the ones closest to the rural areas and had adequate rural administrative experience. But it was soon realised that the traditional administrative approach was not best suited to nurture developmental projects in which the people's initiative was at the core of the experiment. One needed people who could elicit this initiative.

It was also perceived that an exclusive focus on agricultural or economic activity was self-defeating. All other economic activities needed to be attended. It was further realised that if villagers were to be involved in the development activity, they needed to be better informed about the projects as well as their own problems and how to cope with them. It was also appreciated that economic developmental efforts could not go far without positive action in the fields of health and education.

The awareness that the fast rate of growth of the country's population would nullify the benefits of any growth in the economy brought in another important dimension that showed that a near exclusive focus on economic goals would not achieve the goals set for development and that the community as a whole and its social life aspects needed to be attended to.

The concept of social development as different from economic development arose out of the many discussions at the annual national conferences on Community Development and National Extension Projects as also out of the discussions in many international meetings under United Nations auspices.

The schools of social work had been uncomfortable with the exclusive emphasis on economic goals right from the beginning but their voice began to be heard only after wider opinion had come to realise the futility of a wholly economic development effort. But, the schools of social work had difficulty in defining what role exactly the social workers could play in the community development effort. Their graduates would be too young and relatively inexperienced in administration to occupy the post of the Block Development

Officer and there was for some time no other post where they could utilise their social expertise. Some of them took up the posts of Social Education Officers but the role of this officer remained vague for a long time and there was often frustration among those who occupied these positions.

The schools of social work were themselves trying to ascertain what role they could play in this newly identified field of social development. They had to define what social development meant and what role social workers could play to promote such development. They had to think of what new courses they would need to formulate and what fieldwork experience they could provide to their students to make them useful. Social work itself was traditionally relief and rehabilitation oriented and focused on the specially disadvantaged sections of the community, except in the area of community development. Social or community development as a national programme required that they learn about the needs of the community in general and identify areas where they could be useful. The Indian Association of Schools of Social Work, as also the International Association of Schools of Social Work, held many meetings to clarify and work out a role for social work in the broader field of social development.

Many of the papers brought together here were prepared for these national and international meetings and deal with the effort to build a bridge between social work and social development.

But I was myself interested in the broader philosophy of social development and its linkages with the concept of human rights and the fundamental rights enshrined in the Indian Constitution. The United Nations were also concerned about defining the scope of social rights as different from political or civil rights of an individual. The International Council of Social Work held a special meeting at Helsinki on the subject of human rights.

There are altogether 19 papers in this book. It is possible that there is some repetition of views between papers since they were written for different audiences at different times.

As I wrote these papers I was trying to clarify my own ideas on several themes and there was in my mind certain tentativeness about my views. Not all the papers deal with social development as a concept. Some of the papers deal with different aspects of the process of development and with the different groups in the population that need to be mobilised. One continuing concern in writing these was how this field was relevant to social work practice.

It is not unlikely that what I have said in some of my papers is not any longer a new perspective. But these subjects were very much discussed and formed a part of the discussion on social work and social development when I was active in the field. In the 1950s and 1960s community development was at the core of many discussions, whereas in the 1970s family planning and family welfare had moved to the centre stage. Today, it is the right of the underprivileged groups to fight for equity that holds attention. But all these are part of the broader field of social development and still have a relevance.

I am also aware that there is a counter-perspective to the very concept of development. The South American sociologists, who argued that the concept of development as visualised by the capitalist world is itself exploitative, articulated it best. I have not dealt with it directly. But my preoccupation has been with discussing and elaborating the concept of development in a liberal society which recognises that inequities exist and is concerned with how to minimise them and what role social workers can play in it.

M.S. Gore

1

The Concept of Social Development

THE BACKGROUND

Before the Advent of Freedom

Most countries of the Third World gained their independence in the late 1940's and early 1950's of the last century. Prior to independence, all these countries were poor and underdeveloped though they differed a great deal from one another in the degree of their poverty, in the stage of their techno-economic development, and even in the legitimacy of their claim to nationhood or to their historicity as a people with a unifying and continuous tradition. They were generally characterised by high birth and death rates, low expectancy of life at birth, low rates of literacy and by education limited to a small elite. Their primarily agrarian economies were subsistence-oriented except in some sections where the European masters had developed plantations of tea, coffee and rubber or where, as in India, a small local response had developed to the demands for cotton, oilseeds, sugar and tobacco from local as well as foreign markets. Small new towns had developed and mud roads connecting them to the villages on the one hand and the larger metropolitan cities on the other had been laid down. The small towns served as centres of

---

Public lecture delivered under the auspices of the Department of Social Work, University of Hong Kong on February 19, 1972.

administration and as collection centres for agricultural produce; they provided high school education and served as locations for lower and middle-level courts established by the alien rulers. These rulers had also laid down the major arterial routes of a railway system and developed a postal system using canoes, horse-carts, buses and railways as means of surface transport. In all these countries, alien rule had been a modernising influence affecting their traditional legal, economic and military systems; in some of them, alien rule was also the first unifying influence which brought different ethnic or linguistic groups together. In India, alien rule was accompanied by new systems of law and administration, by changes in education, and by the arrival of Christian missionaries. There was also the enlargement of internal and external trade. In India, the nationalist movement grew largely out of the impact of ideas and institutions introduced by the British. On the whole, the modernising influence exercised by foreign governments, traders and missionaries was more readily perceptible in the economic, political, legal and educational institutions. The familial and religious institutions proved relatively less amenable to sudden change; the social and religious movements which arose in response to the challenge of western ideas tended, on the one hand, to reinterpret and defend established practices and, on the other, to make a plea for new modes of adaptive change. They prevented the development of a breach in the continuity of social and religious traditions.

This was not uniformly the experience of all countries under colonial rule. Generally, it may be possible to say that the simpler cultures of Africa accepted social and religious change more readily than the more complex cultures of Asia. But, even large-scale conversions of whole tribes to Christianity did not always mean a change in their basic religious belief. Sometimes it meant only the substitution of a new deity for the old one with the existing complex of beliefs and worship remaining largely untouched. This was also the case in India where large-scale conversion of the lower castes and untouchables took place in certain areas.

Since education was limited to a relatively small, urban elite, the new ideas that it introduced remained on the surface, accepted in part and as per convenience by the urban dwellers. The extent to which the urban elite in different countries served as agents for communicating these new ideas to larger segments of the native rural and urban population varied considerably from one country to another and even within a country from one region to another. The variations between countries were the result of several factors, not the least of which was the existence or otherwise of a major cultural tradition which bound the different segments and strata of the native society together through a system of interlinked, if not universally shared, values and through the existence of a literary class whose one of major functions was to interpret the tradition of the group to every new generation. Wherever such a tradition had existed—as, for instance, in India—some members of the urban, educated middle-class thought it their responsibility to communicate their changed or 'modern' values to others atleast in their own stratum and to those immediately below it. This they did by writing, public speaking and through the establishment of associations for the special purpose of propagating their ideas. But, even in these countries, 'modernisation' was a weak force which penetrated society unevenly and influenced most, the economic and politico-legal structures and least, the social and religious framework.

The Post-Independence Situation

I have dealt with this pre-independence situation in the countries of Asia and Africa because it will help in understanding the type of overall, societal goals they set for themselves prior to and after independence. Prior to independence, the goal was primarily political, viz., the attainment of freedom. Different parties and political leaders gave a different substantive content to the idea of freedom and what it would help achieve, but on the goal of freedom from alien rule they were generally united. On attainment of freedom, many of the countries have experienced political strife and instability and between them witnessed governments which are as varied as monarchies, military dictatorships, parliamentary democracies and people's democracies. In most cases, the political problems arose not because the new rulers tried to implement their pre-independence promises nor because they had failed to do so. The strife has been primarily due to the fight for spoils among the rival political leaders, sometimes within the same party. Occasionally, the strife has an ideological colouring, but for the most part it can be related to tribal loyalties and to rival ethnic groupings in many of the countries in Africa and Asia. Those who are in power have sought to use the demands of national security as a base for unity and consolidation but without a corresponding readiness to make the concept of a nation more meaningful to the less privileged groups in society.

Whatever the ideological hue of the governments in Asia, they are all faced with a common social and economic reality. The countries are poor with varying proportions of 30 to 40 per cent of their populations living below the poverty line. Poverty in their case means not only relative deprivation but also the lack of the rudimentary requirements of life—adequate food, clothing and shelter. In spite of poverty and the low level of industrialisation, most countries have witnessed rapid population growth and a firm trend of city-ward migration of rural peoples. The growth in population was due to the reduced death rates resulting from systems of public health that had been developed earlier by the colonial rulers. Today, more than half of the world's population lives in Asia. The migration to cities has resulted from the failure of the outmoded agricultural technology to support growing populations; the present percentages of urban population are relatively low—only about

10-20 per cent, but already, the absolute number of urban dwellers in Asia and Africa closely approximates this number in the developed world.

The countries are poor, but the poverty is not distributed uniformly. Typically, the countries are characterised by great inequalities based partly on the traditional hierarchical structures of caste and race and partly on the varying abilities of different groups to utilise the new opportunities that arose in administration, commerce and incipient industry during the colonial period. Inequality breeds further inequality and most countries have witnessed a widening of income disparities since freedom.

The levels of education are low, with India having among the lowest percentage of literates in its population. Only a small proportion of the child population above the age of six attends schools regularly, though many more are enrolled. The proportion of girls who attend school is universally lower. Over the last two decades both these proportions have increased considerably. The system of high school and college education is primarily geared to office jobs and a few white-collar professions. In many countries, the system of university education is not fully stretched.

Housing is inadequate whether in the rural areas or in towns and cities. But, the problem becomes specially acute in cities where the individual cannot do much to rectify the situation for himself. He does not have the land nor the materials, nor the know-how to use urban building material. City legislation forbids unauthorised construction as well as unauthorised occupation of open land. In the larger cities of Calcutta and Bombay, over 70 per cent of the people live in single-room accommodation. About 16 per cent live on pavements and as squatters on open land. The water and sanitation services are woefully overstretched.

The welfare services for handicapped groups are almost non-existent. Governments generally take the position that voluntary agencies should provide them. In India, social security provisions protect only workers engaged in organised industry and in government service. This leaves over 90 per cent of the workforce outside the scope of such provisions. The provisions themselves are inadequate and do not cover unemployment risk except for a brief period. There is no system of family assistance or assistance to dependent children.

Most of these problems have been defined as problems following from the paucity of economic resources. And, the solution sought is the increase in the gross national product (GNP) through massive programmes of industrialisation and modernisation of agriculture.

But poverty as well as prosperity have their own social and psychological correlates. Developing countries have to attempt simultaneously to undo those attitudes and values which, while they made poverty bearable, impede development and they have to create new values and institutional frameworks that will be conducive to growth. This is a perspective that is only recently gaining acceptance.

The Economic Growth Approach and Problems

To the extent that economic development requires a physical infrastructure of roads and communication, the need for it is easily recognised. Further, the need for education, interpreted as investment in human capital, has also received verbal support and has even led, sometimes, to indiscriminate expenditure of large sums of money on perpetuating or extending a system of education that is unsuited to meet the needs of economic development. The model of economic development, followed by most countries in the first decade of freedom, was such that it seemed to assume that larger financial inputs, with some relatively marginal organisational and technological (i.e., know-how) supports, would lead to increased production in all sectors of the economy. The factors relating to motivation for savings and hard work, the factors impeding labour and occupational mobility, the generally low standards of health and nutrition affecting production and productivity, the fact of rapid population growth and its tendency to nullify the beneficial consequences of economic growth were considered relevant but secondary in their immediate significance for the process of economic development. Sometimes, it was assumed that given the necessary financial and technical inputs, the other conditions would follow by way of adjustments in people's attitudes, ways of thinking and habits.

However, economic development, like every form of development, demands a price. One form this price takes is the acceptance by people of an economic discipline involving, simultaneously, hard work and a readiness to postpone immediate gratification. This discipline to work hard and to effect savings may be self-imposed, as in the case of the Puritan entrepreneurs with their this-worldly asceticism about which Max Weber wrote, or, it may be a discipline externally imposed as in countries where the state tries to mobilise resources through taxation or direct physical controls. Even where the discipline to save exists—as it did in the case of the Puritan entrepreneurs—it always imposes great hardships on the common man. In the countries of Western Europe and the USA, during their early stages of industrialisation, the hardships took the form of long hours of work, low wages and non-recognition, if not suppression, of workers' rights. The European countries which industrialised in the 19th century did not have to come to terms with the strength of organised labour and they had the added opportunity of reducing the hardships of their own populations by passing on some of the burden to their overseas colonies which provided cheap raw materials for industry and later large markets for finished products. The United States did not establish colonies, but it could tap the vast resources of an expanding frontier and used cheap imported slave labour in its plantations.

The strategy of economic development which was available for Western Europe is not available for the newly independent countries. While industrial labour in these countries is not as strongly organised as in developed countries today, it is yet strong enough to exert some influence and it is becoming sufficiently aware of its own rights not to accept the proposition of higher production in the present for the promise of higher wages in the future. While labour may not always resort to strikes, it can still withhold cooperation by 'going slow', by delays and by high rates of absenteeism which are various forms of sulking, non-cooperation or just plain indifference.

Moreover, the developing countries cannot pass on their burden to other countries as the colonial powers did. It is true that in large, subcontinental nations, in the early stages of development, a kind of intra-national 'colonialism' develops in the form of regional imbalances in economic development. But, there are clear political limits to such a development in democratic societies. The countries which are now poor have to achieve higher levels of development in a world where they can neither look to expanding frontiers nor to other poorer countries which can be colonised for supply of cheap agricultural product or cheap labour. They also encounter a situation where the aspirations of the poorer segments of the population are high and rising. Though the people are illiterate, the process of political education during the struggle for independence has given them some idea of what they can legitimately demand.

Quite apart from the political factor, it is also true that the gross poverty and low levels of nutrition cannot generate the necessary motivation or the physical fitness for hard work and higher production. The strategy of development which assumes that worker motivation can be taken for granted or that workers will routinely respond to the rationale of 'ultimate' benefit for themselves or of prosperity for the abstract entity of the nation is a strategy that is not likely to succeed. The idea that distributive justice is something that can follow as a second step after economic growth has taken place is found not to have worked well in the developing countries. In the larger developing countries of Asia, the annual growth rates achieved by the economy have been generally low. In India, it has been between 4 and 5 per cent at its best. The inflationary pressures are high and the prices have risen by more than four times their level in 1950. Attempts at economic development in the context of social and regional inequalities inevitably imply greater sacrifices and deprivations for the poorer section of the population. They will resent this unequal burden and the political framework will face major challenges in maintaining law and order because this resentment will express itself in varied forms of unrest—strikes by industrial workers, riots based on communal or ethnic tensions (where particular groups serve as scapegoats), protests and strikes by students who are poorly motivated and involved in the education system, and food riots during periods of extreme stress. In democratic polities, opposition parties will cynically exploit this situation even though they may themselves offer no radical alternatives. Even non-democratic political regimes may find it difficult to achieve developmental goals in the context of gross inequalities.

It is against this background that the concept of the primacy economic development has had to be reconsidered. Most developing countries in South Asia have a planning machinery which has been in existence for about two decades. Planning during the first decade, i.e., in the 1950's, was characterised by this emphasis on economic development with a secondary place given to social services and with only a marginal allocation for social welfare services. While the planning for economic objectives was goal-oriented and sought to create certain types of infrastructure in a time-bound programme, the planning of social and welfare services was *ad hoc* and geared only to an expansion of existing services. The social plans were not articulated with economic planning nor were they specifically linked to the social goals—e.g., secularism, equality and democracy in the Indian context---in such a way that the operation of social services would lead closer to the goals. Social service programmes were not subjected to criteria consistently derived from these goals.

SOCIAL DEVELOPMENT

The Concept

The re-examination of the concept of economic development has led to its broadening into the concept of social development. The United Nations and its many associated agencies have had a great deal to do with the gradual adoption of this new concept by the developing countries. The concept of social development is inclusive of economic development but differs from it in the sense that it emphasises the development of the totality of society in its economic, political, social and cultural aspects. In this sense, social development planning is not concerned with planning exclusively for social services, any more than it is with the exclusive planning of economic growth. There are many areas, apart from social or welfare services, wherein the 'social' perspective has a relevance. Prominent among these are relating to population policy, policy relating to urbanisation, industrial location and environmental pollution, policies relating to regional development, policies of income growth, income distribution and land reform, policies governing administration and people's participation in planning and in the implementation of plans.

Social development is thus not a plea for a larger allocation for social and welfare services, though such allocations may be justified on other grounds; it is really a plea for an integrated view of the scope of development which should embrace development in all its varied facets. Such a view would not result in a plan for economic development which is expressed only in terms of financial and raw material allocations but would indicate simultaneously the political, social-structural and cultural goals, and infrastructures that are necessary both as a means to achieve economic development, and as ends in themselves. A social development perspective cannot permit of propositions in which economic development comes first and is later followed by steps to ensure distributive justice through a modified incomes policy or through provision of an extended network of tax supported social and welfare services. In this sense, social development----as distinct from economic development---involves planning for simultaneous development on many different flanks.

But social development means something more than merely socio-economic, political and environmental development. It is not simply an effort to provide *ad hoc* growth targets in each of the separate sectors of planning. This type of social developmental planning has existed in all developing countries. Most of the national development plans provide for economic, physical, infrastructural, educational, health and welfare targets of growth or expansion. Social development planning requires the perception and delineation of the nature of inter-relationships between the different sectors. As stated earlier, social development is an integrative concept and this integration depends upon a clear enunciation of the values and the type of society toward which planning is to be undertaken.

Models of Development

Developing countries have before them several models of development and they may follow one of these either as a result of choice or circumstance. It is customary to identify and group them in terms of the dichotomy of capitalist and socialist models of development, though, in a strict sense, classical capitalism cannot be reconciled with planning. Actually, the terms 'capitalist' and 'socialist' are not as distinct in their meaning and implications as they used to be. There are atleast two different dimensions along which these terms are interpreted. One of these dimensions is provided by the extent to which the economy is controlled by the state. Today, after the depression of the 1930's and the Second World War, there is hardly any government which leaves the economic forces in the country to operate freely without some measures of state regulation. But, there are differences in the patterns of state regulation. At one end is the pattern where regulation is effected through legal and fiscal measures in an economy which is otherwise considered to be open or free for the exercise of private initiative. The other end is the one where the economy is directly controlled through state ownership and leaves no role, or only a very minor role, for private enterprise.

The capitalist-socialist label was traditionally expected to reflect also rejection or acceptance of the concept of social justice and the right of individuals to be provided social services equally without reference to their ability to pay for these services. The stereotype of the socialist state holds out the hope that all citizens will receive equal opportunity for personal development irrespective of race, religion or parental income. Even where the socialist states have given up in practice the ideal of a complete equality in rewards for all types of work, they are still committed to the idea that the disparities in income should be minimised.

In actual fact, the adjectives 'capitalist' and 'socialist' do not help to neatly divide countries either in terms of the minimisation of inequalities or in terms of the adequacy of social or welfare services freely available to the citizen. Some of the Scandinavian countries, which are not socialist in the sense of their adopting a system of state monopoly of ownership of the means of production, have minimised income differentials to a greater extent than the socialist states and offer a wider network of social and welfare services to ensure equality of opportunity for individual development and advancement.

Apart from the capitalist-socialist differentiation, there is the other dimension of a democratic-totalitarian polity along which states are differentiated. The democratic state may have either a capitalist or a socialist economy, though in the old stereotype, capitalism and democracy on the one hand and socialism and totalitarian rule on the other necessarily went together. In the world today, one can see countries which combine these two pairs of characteristics in different ways. Besides the capitalist-democratic and socialist-totalitarian countries, there are some totalitarian-capitalist states which maintain a facade of democracy but effectively deny the basic civic liberties to their citizens, and there are others which are aiming to develop a democratic-socialist polity. The choice of the 'socialist' or 'capitalist' models of development—however inadequately these are defined—will tend to influence the types of social services that are planned, the percentage of population covered through them, the legislative measures that the government may take to strengthen or weaken labour organisations, the types of incentives that may be offered to entrepreneurs, the definition of policy relating to distribution of essential commodities and even the relative priority given to the production of luxury and essential goods.

The Model and the Compromises

The developing countries, which are universally poor and have in most cases a colonial history, had made certain ideological commitments during their struggle for freedom. Politically, they were committed, at least initially, to a representative democracy and economically they were committed to work for improving the lot of the common man. The economic goal did not always commit them to any one system—capitalist or socialist—but it left them with enough initiative to undertake regulatory legislation of any degree of restrictiveness. In course of time, some of the countries have developed economies in which both the state and private entrepreneurs have a role. Some other countries have called themselves socialist though, as of the present, they have acted only to nationalise foreign owned industrial and business enterprises without necessarily legislating against all private enterprise.

Even on the political front, many of the developing countries have not been able to sustain their democratic framework. Parliamentary forms of government have given place to presidential forms which in turn have sometimes given place to a rule by a military junta. The constitutional proprieties are sought to be maintained by a great deal of sophistry but otherwise under the pressure of internal strife and sometimes, external danger to national security, governments have found it necessary and convenient to take on more and more powers whittling down, in the process, the freedom of the individual citizen.

However, all governments in underdeveloped countries are under pressure to maintain a pro-common man posture. This implies not only a statement of long-term goals of economic development, but also the immediate provision of some measure of social and welfare services to raise the level of living of the common man. This, in its turn, may imply that if any economic discipline has to be imposed to engender a higher rate of savings, the burden of such economic discipline exercised through direct taxation will fall more heavily on the middle and upper income groups who alone can make the sacrifices. These sacrifices are necessary not only for the somewhat marginal contribution they can make to the total available resources in the country but also for their symbolic value. However, in the absence of efficient enforcement and an adequate distributive machinery even for essential commodities, the burden of direct taxes is often passed on to the poorer sections of the population through the mediacy of inflation, tax evasion and the emergence of a parallel economy based on 'black' or unaccounted income.

Need for Austerity

The discipline that a government can impose on society is based only partly on the use of the stick; it depends also on the spontaneous acceptance of the need for such discipline by the people. The law of the land provides the government with the stick that it needs, but it will gain the moral authority to use the stick only when those in authority, whether in government or in administration, themselves lead a life conforming to the norms of economic discipline. The people will accept their deprivations more willingly---in the interest of the nation (!)---when they find that those in power practise what they preach. Conspicuous simplicity on the part of the rulers and their readiness to punish the delinquent promptly, irrespective of the class origin of the delinquent, is essential for establishing the credibility of a government's austerity measures requiring people to make sacrifices.

In a poor country, the net addition that can be made to the quality of life of the common man or to the total resources available for development as a result of the sacrifices made by the well-to-do will always be limited. This means that there is a simultaneous need for considerable ingenuity on the part of the planners for identifying patterns of development which are labour-intensive rather than capital-intensive. Expenditure on buildings, on prestigious but functionally non-urgent machines, equipment and gadgets, on imported cars and expensive furnishings would have to be reduced. Ways may also have to be found for multiple utilisation of physical plants and other facilities which are bound to be in short supply.

People's Participation

As already stated, the willingness of the people to accept sacrifices without allowing them to warp their lives depends upon the credibility of government's performance and on the lead given by the elite in society. This willingness also depends upon the degree of people's participation in the process of planning. While the broad or strategic decisions of overall planning and planning in relation to capital-intensive projects may have to be taken at higher levels of national and regional government, there is a great deal of planning and implementation that can be left to people at the local level. In the highly stratified societies of Asia, participation by the common man in any deliberative process is difficult to achieve.

There are major hurdles in ensuring such participation in societies which are highly stratified and are culturally divided into different ethnic communities. In some of the Southeast Asian countries, the existence of large national minorities—the Chinese and the Indians—has complicated the task of ensuring effective political participation by all groups. In India, the existence of religious minorities and the claims of regional-linguistic loyalties have created difficulties at the national level and the differentiation based on caste has vitiated local, regional politics. Not uncommonly, ethnic differentiation of the types mentioned above coincides with economic stratification. Effective political participation by different groups is difficult to achieve in this context.

The very low percentages of literacy and education in the general population also present a major difficulty in communication and participation. The elective democratic polity is based on certain assumptions of relative homogeneity and a commonality of interest in the electorate. The absence of such homogeneity poses problems of national integration and the low levels of literacy and education make for serious difficulties in communication except at a very gross level. Both these factors are obstacles in the way of motivation for participating in political and decision-making processes except in the form of voter participation during elections to legislatures. The lack of political participation by the mass of people is the cause and consequence of poor mobilisation of the people in governmental programmes of development. It is said that in countries with a single-party regime, this work of mobilisation is done by members of the cadre working among the people and setting up new deliberative structures of workers' committees, neighbourhood committees, etc. This they are probably able to do in the context of cataclysmic changes brought about by civil war, the emergence of charismatic leaders during this process and also the reordering of political power relationships in the community. But, a great deal is also due to the effective physical force that can be exercised by a government which does not have to seek a popular election and which wholly controls the media of mass communication.

Problem of Motivation

The challenge of social development is not so much, or even primarily, a problem of mobilising money resources but rather a problem of motivating and mobilising people. Poor countries have by definition a paucity of material resources and while a certain amount or proportion of them must necessarily be found, borrowed or commandeered, a good proportion of them would have to be substituted by human labour, enthusiasm, ingenuity and creativity. In such mobilisation, equality and democracy are not only desired end-states, but also necessary means and instrumentalities in the present.

The problem of motivation and mobilisation of people runs through the whole spectrum of social development programmes. It is a necessary part of all efforts at economic development and also of efforts to ensure utilisation of all services.

As pointed out earlier, economic development calls for hard work and for a capacity to save, to forego immediate gratification and to make sacrifices. This, in turn, demands a change in the perception and the values characteristic of a given culture. If the sequence of hard work, greater production, saving for reinvestment and achievement of higher levels of production is to be seen in practice, it requires a certain approach to life characterised, on the one hand by economic rationality and, on the other, by a type of non-rationality which makes hard work a virtue or an end in itself. Similarly, when people belonging to different castes, different language groups and different tribes have to live together in urban communities and have to be welded into a new entity based on the concept of nationality, there has to be a change in their attitudes toward one another. Such a change involves acceptance of new loyalties, and the subordination, if not rejection, of older ones. The value of secularism provides the basis for this change. For the individual, the value is its own justification, though, for the nation, practice in conformity with it may seem to serve a function. Again, industrialisation requires man to accept a way of life based increasingly on science and technology. He finds himself under pressure to explain his own attitudes, evaluations and choices on grounds of science and rationality.

What is true of motivation for economic development is also true, in a different sense, in the area of social service development. While services cannot be provided without material resources being available, services will not be utilised unless people are motivated to use them. If family planning services were fully utilised even to the extent that they are available in India, they would themselves make a major contribution to national development by restricting population growth and reducing the number of mouths to be supported by each family out of its meagre income. Education services are not fully utilised in the rural areas and it is estimated that less than half the children enrolled in the first year go on to complete the five years of primary school. Sanitation and preventive health measures cannot be fully imposed. People will not use latrines even where they exist and will not easily adopt more hygienic practices of disposal of faecal matter. Parents do not bring their children for vaccination and do not participate fully in general programmes of immunisation when they are organised. Where public sector industry has sometimes provided good housing to its low-paid employees, the latter have tended to sublet the additional space and convert it into extra income, in the process, overloading and bringing down the quality of the services and amenities provided.

The fuller utilisation of available services demands a change in values, attitudes and behaviour patterns. For example, the acceptance of family planning involves a change in the quality of the husband-wife relationship requiring greater communication and an attitude that sexual intercourse is an end in itself, a change in the value set by the society on the child-bearing capacity of woman, a de-emphasis on the birth of a male child and an understanding and acceptance of the fact that, in the context of limited incomes, fewer children mean greater provision and opportunity for each child. Parents will not send their children to school, support them through a period of years and deprive themselves of the chance of an additional income unless they value education in the abstract and also see its relevance in their own lives. People will not change their personal sanitary habits unless they have learnt to see the cause-effect relationship between unclean habits and ill-health. They will not willingly accept vaccination for their children so long as they think that small-pox epidemics result from the wrath of the village deity.

The problem of motivating and mobilising individuals for hard work and for making their contribution to the community and the problem of motivating individuals to fully utilise available services are not as different as they may seem. We are inclined to look at one as the contribution that man makes and at the other as a benefit he derives, but both depend upon the values and beliefs he holds. Social development involves and is contingent upon the establishment of an appropriate system of values.

On the other hand, it should be equally apparent that the values and beliefs of people are also related to the objective conditions of life. They will not use the services offered to them unless they see the use for them. At the level of subsistence and poverty at which most people in developing countries live, what they ask for is work, food, clothing and shelter. Without adequate work and food, lack of education and protein and vitamin deficiencies in diet do not appear as problems. To the houseless, lack of shelter is a problem, not lack of privacy. The levels of aspiration of people are subdued under conditions of extreme poverty and they aspire only for what they see as possible of achievement.

This means that while there is a clear need for the creation of a social infrastructure, it is important at the same time to give careful thought to the order of priorities, the specification of standards and other matters of policy which will ensure a fuller utilisation of the services brought into existence. Also, it is necessary to remember that even in the implementing of economic policy there are certain social dimensions that have to be borne in mind. The integrating principle is provided by the concept of equality and social justice.

SOCIAL POLICY ISSUES

Distributive Justice

The first priority in any poor country is of course to seek economic growth; but this growth is to be measured not exclusively in terms of the GNP. It has to be measured also, and among other things, in terms of additional jobs created. This may mean lower productivity per person but on the other hand if the economy grows without corresponding increases in the number of jobs, the country will have to bear the cost of supporting unemployed persons through programmes of social assistance of one variety or the other. A job-oriented economic development programme has the advantage of maintaining the self-respect of the individual. From this point of view, even subsidised programmes of producing hand-spun and handwoven textiles are better than any system which reduces the recipient of state assistance to the position of a social dependent because he is considered to have individually failed to find a job and make a success of his life.

The other important social guideline for economic growth is that it should be regulated in a manner that it reduces economic disparities. Disparities can be between persons, groups or regions. In all cases, however, the tendency is for those who are already advantaged to add to their wealth and improve their relative position. Rich persons, rich communities and rich regions generally tend to grow richer. This happens because they are better motivated and better equipped to benefit by the facilities that government can offer, they have capital resources which they can mobilise, they have better education and technical skills, they are more familiar with the rules and procedure of government and know how to manipulate them to their advantage. As a result, the benefits of public supported programmes of social and economic development often go to the better off sections in the community. But, the goals of social equity demand that economic policies be so devised and operated that the poorer and weaker individuals can have access to opportunity and are helped to benefit by them. This may involve concessions and modifications of qualifying clauses to counter the initial handicaps suffered by certain groups. This is, however, not merely a question of stating a broad policy. It calls for detailed, operational guidelines and a continuous monitoring of results.

Large-scale investment of public funds for promoting economic growth is always accompanied by inflationary pressures. If the interests of the poor have to be protected, the state must organise an effective distributive system through which essential commodities will be made available to the people at regulated prices. In the absence of such a system, and in the context of the perennial shortage of most commodities in developing countries, available goods will be cornered by hoarders and sold for the highest prices they can fetch. This will affect the poorer sections of the population most adversely.

Strategies of location of industry can also do a great deal to prevent the imbalances in growth that normally result from a simple calculation of profitability. While the criterion of 'profitability' must be maintained—for, in the last analysis, that is the index of efficiency of operation—consideration must also be given to the principle of ensuring balanced growth in different geographical regions. This problem has a special relevance to large countries of subcontinental dimensions. Regional distribution of industry can also be an instrument of a population policy directed at a better distribution of urban growth and urban migration

Population

Equally important for economic growth, but vital even from a purely social point of view, is an effective programme of checking population growth. The programme cannot gain acceptance only on grounds of national interest. It must find legitimacy and meet needs in the life of the individual citizen. But, even at the level of calculation of economic gain, the programme cannot achieve a major breakthrough until the current income levels of peasants improve making it unnecessary for them to depend upon every marginal addition that even young children can make to a family living at a level of bare subsistence. Children also mean security in old age—a much needed assurance in a country which offers no other form of security. Besides, though the life expectancy at birth has increased in most countries of Asia, the rates of infant mortality continue to be high. These are estimated to be about twice as high in Asia and three or four times as high in Africa as compared with Europe. High infant mortality is a disincentive for the adoption of family planning. Improved child health services are a necessity even from the perspective of population control though in the short run they may accentuate the rate of net population growth.

Very few countries have given a priority to population control in their development plans and even fewer have shown any marked achievements in this respect. The rate of population growth in most Asian countries is between 2 and 3 per cent. In the USA, Canada, Australia and New Zealand, it is between 1 and 2 per cent.

Control of overall population growth is only one aspect of population policy, though in the context of the economic situation in developing Asian countries this has occupied most of the attention of planners. There are other questions of massive rural-urban migration, age composition of the population, spacing of child births, sex ratios in cities which are of great relevance from the point of view of their social implications. The changes in the age structure of the population have a bearing on education, available labour force and the proportion of dependents that have to be supported by society both in the younger age groups and among those who have ceased to be economically active.

Health

Health is another area where an overall policy perspective has to be developed. Western countries have developed a very expensive system of health care—whether this cost is borne directly by the individual or the state. The developing countries may not be able to copy the model. While clinical care will necessarily have to be provided, it is even more important to organise an effective, preventive health service. This is difficult to do. A person who is ill goes to a doctor and takes the medicine prescribed. But, a person who is not ill does not give the same measure of cooperation in a programme of prevention. Even from the point of view of the medical profession, there is much more prestige, as well as profit, to be had in the practice of clinical medicine, and little of either in preventive medicine.

Among preventive health services, those which ensure protected water supply and sanitation should receive high priority. These are the two strategic areas for prevention of disease in all age groups. Next in importance are the services for child and maternal health. The foundations of physical and mental health are laid in the early stages of childhood and adolescence. Whatever can be done to protect and promote the health of a child will serve his own individual interest as well as the interest of the nation. Good food is a basic requirement of good health. While developing countries may not be able to provide an adequate and balanced diet to all their citizens, they must still do all they can to provide it at least for the young. For the school-going population the school system can serve as a convenient delivery point for both health and educational services. A balanced meal provided to all children in the public school system should form part of a school health service. Additionally, services would have to be provided in the community for the mothers of young children and other children outside the school system.

Education

In the sphere of education an important policy question relates to the level of education at which major financial investments should be made. From an economic as well as social point of view it is of the highest importance that universal literacy in the adult age group and compulsory primary education for children between six and eleven years of age should be achieved. For a variety of reasons India has not achieved these targets and this is true of other Asian countries as well.

Considerable expansion at the high school and college level has taken place in India---including professional education for law, engineering and medicine. In countries with high income disparities and socially imposed stratification expansion of higher education benefits primarily the middle and the upper classes. Besides, if the rate of economic growth is slow, the production of college graduates and highly qualified professionals soon exceeds the effective demand that exists for them. This is what has happened in India as well as some of the other developing countries. Such lopsided development of education implies a waste of scarce resources and takes place at the cost of neglect of the needs of the poorer segments of the population.

A broadening of the base of the education pyramid at the primary and high school stages should be the first priority. Along with such broadening of the education base a qualitative change must also take place in the overall direction of education. In the present system, in India, school education is not organised as an independent stage in itself but rather as a preparation for college life. The emphasis is mainly literary and the individual completing his primary, middle or high school education is not equipped for any particular type of work. While primary education may necessarily have to be a general preparation, it could be more work-oriented than at present.

At the middle and secondary stages, definite courses for technical and vocational careers should be available to those who do not wish to continue to the stage of college education.

A fact that has become amply clear from the experience in India as also in the advanced countries is that equality of opportunity at the point of entrance to the educational system does not ensure effective equal opportunity for students from the lower strata of society. If the formal equality of access is to be converted into a real equality, the system of education would have to be given special supports that will compensate at least for the material and physical facilities, if not for motivational supports which are lacking in the case of students from the poorer strata.

Admission to higher education in the universities should be selective, and for those who qualify, there should be a state subsidy available. It is only then that the deserving students from the poorer families can expect to get the benefits of higher education.

Of considerable importance is the policy adopted with reference to professional education. In the professions of medicine, engineering, education and social work, there has been a tendency to make education long and expensive with the result that graduates of these institutions often place themselves out of the market while simultaneously the needs of the majority of the population are not met. Under these conditions, Indian medical graduates and engineers tend to migrate to other countries and our educational system in effect subsidises the cost of technical education for the more developed countries.

It is important that professional education be so reorganised that it equips students to fit into service delivery systems that exist in developing countries at various levels. It will be necessary to establish, and expand where they exist, the facilities for training of auxiliaries or aides who can work independently on simpler problems leaving the more complex ones to higher qualified professionals and specialists. This is true particularly for the health professions where the shortage of trained personnel is acute at all levels. This is also true for social work where in many of the developing countries, training facilities do not exist at the auxiliary level.

Administrative and Political Parameters

The acceptance of the values of equality, social justice and, generally, a recognition of the claims of the poor has important implications not only for the economy and the social services in a country but also for the political and administrative machinery of the state. As has been pointed out earlier, acceptance of the claims for distributive justice on the part of the poor increases the burden of sacrifices required to be made by middle and upper income groups. These sacrifices may involve acceptance of a wide variety of taxes, taxation at a high level and limitations on ownership of land and urban property. The socialist countries question basically the right of the citizen to own property in his individual capacity.

Can the state impose these sacrifices? Gunnar Myrdal, in his books *Asian Drama* and *The Challenge of World Poverty*, has raised this question in terms of his concept of the 'soft' states and the 'hard' states. As he points out most of the developing countries in Asia have accepted at the verbal level of declared objectives the responsibility of the state to meet the claims of the poor, but he finds that their political leaders have been unable to implement their promises. At the administrative level, he identifies the problem of corruption and nepotism which nullify governmental efforts to respond to the needs of the less privileged. But, the problem is more basic and has to be considered at the political level itself.

In a democratic context various interest groups are expected to organise themselves and fight for their programmes through the electoral and parliamentary machinery. But, the poor and the underprivileged do not have the financial resources and the skills required for building up organisations to serve their interest. Who then will provide the leadership for their cause? Is the commitment of the power elite to the declared social objectives sufficiently strong so that they will force through legislation and administer it effectively even when such measures affect their own interests or the interests of the groups from which they are drawn? If they are unable to do so, are they at least sufficiently committed to values of a democratic policy that they would allow to the poor a free vote and the effective freedom to organise themselves?

These are questions that are not currently answered. To the extent that we concede that the progress towards the removal of poverty and the equalisation of opportunity is slow we are admitting that the questions have so far been answered in the negative. Yet, there are one or two countries which are struggling to find answers to the problems of social development within the open, democratic polity and one must wait and withhold judgement.

Besides, there is no assurance that a non-democratic policy will succeed better in carrying through a programme of social development. The 'strong man' states have proved to be as vulnerable and 'soft' when it comes to adjustment of basic conflicts of interest and the imposition of a social and economic discipline on the country. The 'strong men' are often sitting on an insecure power base made up of narrow personal, ethnic or class loyalties. They are hardly in a position to repudiate the interests of those who support them. The political problem of social development basically hinges on the capacity of the poor, weaker segments of the population to throw up a leadership that will on the one hand organise and integrate these segments into a unified force and at the same time prevail as a dominant force in the political structure of the country—whether this structure is democratic or totalitarian.

2

Social Development, Social Welfare and Social Work

There is a great deal of ambiguity in the conceptualisation as well as discussion of the terms 'social development', 'social welfare' and 'social work' as is evidenced by the considerable time that is spent on defining these terms at the beginning of every national and international meeting on the subject. Since such ambiguity exists, it is necessary for a writer to specify the meanings that he attaches to these terms so that his subsequent discussion can be better understood.

SOCIAL DEVELOPMENT

In the historical context in which the term 'social development' has evolved it has come to imply economic growth with social justice. This is, in a sense, a negative and somewhat truncated view of social development, but I believe that it is historically true. Social development arose as a corrective to the preoccupation of national governments in developing countries with economic development or economic growth. This preoccupation was found, on experience, to be limiting and self-defeating. It was limiting because preoccupation with economic growth with no reference to its social parameters

---

Public lecture delivered under the auspices of the Social Workers' Association of Hong Kong on February 22, 1973.

tended to neglect the claims of whole segments of the population which not only could not benefit by such growth but tended, in fact, to suffer because of the increasing disparities between the rich and the poor, the normal and the handicapped, and the privileged and the underprivileged. The pursuit of economic growth without any reference to its social determinants was self-defeating because experience over the period of a decade and a half showed that economic growth could not be achieved without social change and the creation of the necessary social infrastructure. Economic growth was sought to be achieved through a programme of rapid industrialisation and improved agriculture. Even if the goals of industrialisation and improved agriculture could be achieved, they could not be regarded as ends in themselves unless they resulted also in a better quality of life for all citizens. The fact, however, is that economic growth cannot be achieved in isolation and without reference to social values or social goals.

The injection of the concept of social justice introduces this social value parameter. Even social justice has a somewhat corrective overtone, since it seems to suggest a restoration of balance after imbalance has already resulted. But, in the developing countries, it is undoubtedly the foremost social value so far as national planning is concerned.

The social change required for achieving social development implies, and is sustained by a change in the dominant social values. While no exhaustive list of these values and value changes can be provided easily one can easily identify some of the more important of these. Casteism, religious bigotry, a belief in the privilege of the few based either on birth or property will have to be replaced by a rational, secular and egalitarian system of values. No larger national community can achieve even a relative integration except insofar as the narrower, particularistic loyalties are subordinated to more universalistic norms. Attitudes favourable to hard work, savings, occupational mobility and the small family would also have to be generated. The acceptance of these values has implications for all policies and programmes of growth. Political unification, legislative and administrative measures for reducing economic disparities, a distributive machinery for essential commodities, a well-articulated population policy, a policy of regionally balanced development, an educational policy which simultaneously takes account of the need for social relevance and for an open opportunity structure in society, a health policy which emphasises prevention and ensures child health, a housing policy which imposes discipline on consumption of built up space and also develops more realistic standards for housing quality and finally a policy with reference to the needy, vulnerable and disadvantaged sections of the population are the various facets of social development which will reflect and sustain the new social values. Between them they describe the scope of social development.

SOCIAL WELFARE

The scope of social welfare is more difficult to define. The reason is that the area of social welfare activity has changed from time to time. It has identified new needs as societies have passed from the primitive to the peasant or feudal, and industrial stages. It has also happened that some of the needs and the problems identified by welfare workers have later on developed into independent problem areas served by new professions. As Pusic has observed, there is a residual or subsidiary character about social welfare activity "in the sense of doing what others are not doing, not yet doing or no longer doing."[1] The term 'social welfare' has been used in a restrictive as well as broad sense. When used restrictively, the term refers to the services oriented to the poor, the physically or mentally handicapped, the socially 'maladjusted' and, generally, the vulnerable groups in society. To begin with, these services had primarily an ameliorative or a relief goal. But, in course of time, with advances in psychology, behavioural science and material as well as behavioural technology, the preventive, curative and rehabilitative goals have also been added.

The concept of the 'needy and the vulnerable' has, of course, also varied from time to time. Apart from the poor, the handicapped and the socially deviant individuals, the term 'vulnerable' has been extended to include women and children, industrial workers and socially disadvantaged groups like the scheduled tribes and scheduled castes. It has been used to cover social security programmes, neighbourhood services for the urban poor, and adult and social education services in rural areas.

Sometimes used in an even more comprehensive sense, as in some of the international conferences, the term 'social welfare' includes all the areas of health, housing, education, cooperation, mutual aid, and becomes coterminous with the scope of social development itself.

The restrictive definition of the scope of social welfare suffers from the disadvantage that it tends to focus narrowly on the 'poor' or 'dependent' losing sight of the contribution that social welfare can make to promotion of overall development. On the other hand, equating social welfare with social development loses sight of the many different disciplines and areas of professional practice that make up the scope of social development. By doing so social welfare loses its particular identity and function.

To my mind, social welfare has always sought to serve the needs of the 'forgotten' individuals and groups in a society at any given point of time; it has done so largely within the framework of the society in which it has functioned but in doing so it has selectively emphasised certain values—charity, love, human dignity, equality and social right and de-emphasised certain others such as rugged individualism, competitiveness and survival of the fittest. Social welfare has thus been a force for change helping all the time the emergence of more humane values. The social context has determined the explicitness with which social welfare has been able to plead for, advocate, or assert the needs, the causes and the rights of the 'pitied', 'despised' or 'exploited' sections of society. As the *laissez-faire* model of the state gave place to the liberal and later to the welfare and socialist state, successively new values were legitimised and new patterns of meeting human needs emerged. One must admit that social welfare activities have not been the most important instrument for effecting changes in values and institutional structures of a society, but they have always pioneered in recognising new needs and have found ways of giving expression to the new values required to meet these needs. In the new developmental context, social welfare must on the one hand continue to offer special services to those in special need and must on the other hand show how by incorporating the principles of equality and social justice in the entire framework of society a country can in effect prevent the emergence of new problems of distribution and simultaneously provide the motivation fo: development.

Richard Titmus, in his address to the International Conference of Social Work (The Hague, 1972) on "Developing Social Policy in Conditions of Rapid Change: The Role of Social Welfare" suggested that one could probably identify three highly generalised models of social welfare. He called them: (i) the Residual Welfare Model, (ii) the Achievement-Performance Model, and (iii) the Institutional-Redistributive Model. In the first one the organised community takes no direct responsibility for the well-being of the individual citizen; the dominant theme is one of individual autonomy and self-reliance; one's needs are met within the family or through market mechanisms, and welfare institutions only enter where these mechanisms fail. This corresponds to the stage at which the *laissez-faire* concept of the state prevailed and welfare was largely undertaken as charity or philanthropy.

In the second model, the society accepts some responsibility for provision of social services in the areas of health, education and social security, but the dominant philosophy is that the individual should pay for them through contributions to security schemes, or, where they are offered selectively, the beneficiaries be selected on the basis of merit. This corresponds to the liberal-democratic state. The services are offered as social services through mechanisms of social security, pensions, unemployment insurance, contributory health insurance, etc. Basic education is available free to all, but higher education is available on payment or on assessment of special merit. The expectation is that the individual will strive and provide for himself. If he fails, the society may aid as and where necessary through welfare measures of public or private charity.

The third model accepts the cost of social as well as welfare services for every citizen as a charge on the public exchequer and provides services universally to all as also on a selective basis to those in special need. It accepts the right of all individuals to basic social and welfare services as a part of its concept of social justice and also because these services help prevent the disruptive effect of rapid change. Since these services are based on altruistic rather than competitive, individualistic values, they are likely to be more integrative. This approach to social and welfare services which seeks to ensure distributive justice through state supported institutions and programmes corresponds to the stage of a welfare or socialist state.

This third model of social and welfare services provides a bridge between the narrower and the broader perspectives of social welfare. It simultaneously recognises the need for some universal services available to the general population and some selective services for specially needy groups in society. They are both offered in the same attitudinal and value context. As societies move from the value of charity to the value of social justice, economic development as an exclusive preoccupation begins to appear redundant. The value that establishes the tie between the 'normal' and the 'handicapped' is the same value that legitimises the claims of the different interest and status groups in the population to a share in the resources of the community. The economic system, the social services system and the social welfare system are all linked by the same values, instead of the economic system emphasising the individualistic, competitive values and the social and welfare services emphasising the altruistic, philanthropic values.

To say that in the institutional-redistributive model, the three systems are linked by the same or mutually consistent values does not mean that the lines dividing their boundaries are unimportant. The systems and sub-systems call for different kinds of role competences from individuals who work in them. As knowledge advances, social life in one sense gets divided into more specialities, while at the same time new principles of integration are found to unify these specialities. But, at any given point of time, the different systems have different task orientations, they specify different role expectations and require different types of competence.

SOCIAL WORK

It is in this context that the relationship of social work to social welfare, social services and the economic system must be considered. Social work is one type of professional activity that has gained recognition as a profession only in the 20th century. It is not uncommon to identify professions by the problem areas in which they operate rather than by the function they subserve or the contribution they make to society. Thus, those who work with physically ill persons are called doctors, those who work with students are called teachers and those who work with the poor, the deviant or the dependent are called social workers. This is not a satisfactory way of characterising the nature and scope of a professional activity since not all those who work with patients are doctors nor are all those who work with students are teachers. Similarly, not all those who work with the poor or the handicapped are social workers.

Professions are better identified by the nature of the contribution they make (to the persons with whom they work), by the type of skills they utilise, by their knowledge base and work values. The contribution of social work is to enable the individuals, groups or communities with which it is concerned to function better in their social environment so that, on the one hand, they are able to grow and develop to their greatest potential and, on the other, by the same measure, are able to contribute their best to the society of which they are a part. Generally, the individuals or groups with which social workers are concerned are handicapped or underprivileged in some way, but this is not necessary. Social workers are as concerned with prevention of disabilities (physical, social or psychological) and with fuller development of individuals and groups as they are with remedial and rehabilitative goals. Doctors, teachers, nurses, physiotherapists are all concerned with rendering help and providing cures and rehabilitation with different types of problems. Social work shares this concern with the other helping professions, but its distinctive contribution is that it looks at the totality of a person's (or group's) needs and seeks to meet them either by rendering a direct service or through referrals and through collaboration and liaison with other professions. The social worker is concerned with varied needs of his clients. He is concerned with the bare survival needs of individuals, with their needs for physical care and rehabilitation, their needs, if any, for special education, for counselling, for intra-familial adjustment and with a wide variety of other needs. He does not have the skills or the resources to meet all these needs himself. He takes the help of other professionals, but through all the various phases of search and procurement of these types of help he keeps in touch with the individual and provides continuity and coordination to the rehabilitative process.

Social Work and Social Services

Having said that professions should be identified by the kind of contribution they make rather than by the broad area in which they work, it may still be conceded that there are specific problem areas and institutional settings with which each of the professions is more commonly associated. Doctors work in hospitals or clinics and are primarily concerned with problems of illness; teachers work in schools and meet educational needs; lawyers work in courts or in their chambers and represent their clients or advise them in matters concerning law as it affects the interests of the clients. Similarly, it is possible to say that social workers work primarily in and for welfare institutions and services. The scope of welfare services and programmes has already been outlined. The typical welfare settings are provided by residential institutions for dependent children, protective homes for young girls, family welfare agencies, community welfare centres, welfare extension centres, youth welfare activities, child guidance clinics, institutions providing social work education, organisation of relief programmes, administration of governmental welfare departments, etc. In the area of social welfare, social workers play a role of leadership, but they also work in settings other than those of social welfare institutions. For example, social workers in India work in industry as welfare officers, counsellors, case workers and promoters of family planning; they work in hospitals as medical social workers; they work in schools and colleges as student counsellors and school social workers. These latter are often referred to as secondary settings.

The role of the profession of social work in relation to health, education and housing is not unimportant or less relevant to the profession because these settings are termed 'secondary'. Secondary only implies that in these areas the major goals of the agency may be somewhat different from those of social work, and social workers are brought in only to provide special help or to help in special situations. The nature of service provided by the social worker in these settings is essentially the same as in the 'welfare' setting.

Another point that may be made about the relationship of social work to the area of social services—the secondary setting—is that here, since the social worker does not provide the leadership, his skills of working with other professionals are tested. Some of the co-professionals may be superior to him in the organisation, some subordinate in status and with reference to others his status may be unspecified. All these types of relationships create certain strains and it is not unusual for social workers to complain that the doctors with whom they work in hospitals or the heads of schools where they work as counsellors, do not understand or value the role of the social worker. Matters of relative professional status pose other problems and are compounded by the conflicts and insecurities in concrete institutional situations. But, despite these strains, the role of social work in secondary settings in industry, health, education and housing is gradually being recognised. However, in developing societies, such recognition is often marginal and restricted largely to the major cities.

SOCIAL WORK AND SOCIAL DEVELOPMENT

Case of Community Development

The relationship of social work to social development is still undefined and in an exploratory stage. In India, social workers have tried in the past to be involved in some of the programmes of social development with only partial success. In the 1950's, when the Community Development Programme (CDP) was launched by the government, social workers sought an entry into it but the only area where they stabilised themselves as an important professional group was the area of training, particularly, the training of social education officers.

The reason why the social work profession sought to enter the field were both practical and philosophic. It was felt that in a poor country poverty was the most important single problem. Any programme that sought to remove poverty by a simultaneous attempt at a change in the knowledge, attitudes and practices of a whole community was a programme to which social work, with its community organisation skills, could contribute. The setting in which the community development programmes were to be undertaken was the rural setting in which professional social workers did not have a great deal of experience. Even then, the schools of social work tried to reorient their regular programmes and also accepted additional responsibilities for undertaking the training of social education organisers to be able to make themselves useful. The practical reason why the profession wanted to enter the CDP was the scope that it offered for large-scale employment.

However, as stated earlier, social work could not stabilise its involvement in community development except in the training programmes for various categories of workers. The reasons for this failure were several. The profession was still young. Except for one institution, all the other schools of social work had come into existence only about five or seven years before the CDP was launched. The potential contribution of social work had yet to be interpreted to the community. Social work training was primarily oriented to problems of urban areas. The post-graduate trained social workers looked for jobs at the middle and upper levels in the hierarchy. Positions at these levels were considered primarily administrative and persons from the revenue and other administrative services were preferred. Finally, though the CDP was conceived as a programme of community change, in practice it tended to emphasise physical targets and the distribution of material commodities, and it generally focussed on agricultural development to the exclusion of all other aspects of development. Social workers had no special advantages of training or skill in this area over workers with other backgrounds.

The Social Education Officer's role, which was considered the appropriate one for social workers, was never properly defined and was somewhat inadequately rewarded. Social workers would have preferred to have the Social Education Organiser function as the main coordinator but that coordinative role had been given to the Block Development Officer. The Social Education Officer as a functionary hung loose in the organisation. He did not belong to the education department which had responsibility for school education nor did he have a distinct community organisation role. He tended to be in charge of a somewhat diffuse programme of social, cultural and adult education activities for which he had no ground-level supporting staff. In course of time, the redundancy of this functionary was recognised and some of the states abolished the post.

The contribution that the social work profession made to the training programmes in the community development movement was, however, an important one and helped to establish its interest in programmes of development. It gave rise to considerable rethinking among social workers about the role of social work in poor countries. Social work had been criticised for being overconcerned with the handicapped and dependant, oriented primarily to urban areas, and being dependent on institutional settings. Social work education in India tried to make marginal changes to meet the criticism by developing rural placements in fieldwork and offering a course or two on community development as distinct from community organisation. Basically, however, the problem was that the CDP emphasised, despite its philosophic stance, the material and technical inputs rather than the community itself. In such a programme one position from which a professional social worker could have made a major contribution was the position of the chief coordinator at the block level. Very few social workers got recruited to this position. The other position in which social workers could have contributed was that of the worker who worked at the level of individual village communities—the village level worker (VLW). But, the salary attached to this position could not possibly attract post-graduate trained social workers.

In many ways, though the VLW was a low level functionary, he could have made a material difference to the way the movement developed. But, considering the large numbers in which such workers were needed, they could only be recruited at low salary levels. This, in its turn, determined the basic educational background of the potential worker. Most VLWs were largely high school passed and there was no established programme of professional social work education at this level. In fact, some schools of social work at that time stood away from the newly created government sponsored training programmes for VLWs on the ground that no meaningful social work education could be given at the high school level. At that time formal social work education was only available a the post-graduate level. The training programmes for VLWs were organised either directly under the government auspices or in some cases by a few Gandhian institutions which had rural work experience and which even otherwise depended upon persons with lower levels of formal education for their normal work. While Gandhi was alive, his aura had attracted a number of highly educated individuals to work in rural areas, but even at that time the mass of 'constructive' workers came from amongst those who had barely completed school education.

What has been said above applies with some variation to the family planning movement and the role of social work in relation to it. Social workers have participated in the movement as instructors in training institutions, as research personnel and as administrators. A relatively smaller number of them has been involved at the field level.

The question of the level of education at which professional education is offered is of considerable importance. If the profession is identified by the kind of a contribution that it makes, then educating persons to make such a contribution demands also a certain appropriate level of prior educational preparation. What this level should be will vary somewhat from country to country but if professional social work involves at one end the skills of planning, administration and policy formulation or skilled case work and group work, and requires at the other end nothing more than the performance of routinised or simple functions of distributing commodities, then obviously it would be difficult to devise one single programme to provide well-motivated workers for both these types of requirements. You would have to think in terms of a series of linked but graded programmes of training and education and workers trained at all these levels would be doing a welfare and/or a developmental job.

Like most professions, social work has tended to shy away from the concept of varied levels of professional education and professional functioning where the functionary at each level would be called a social worker. But it is obvious that there is a need for functionaries at various levels. If the social work profession would like not to call all levels of functionaries social workers, the profession may find some other labels for them, but it is important unless social work is to lose all relevance in poorer countries that social work identify the contribution that it has to make to the preparation of functionaries at each of these levels and ensure that they are linked to each other through some system of academic recognition. In doing this it should also be recognised that in the preparation of social workers disciplines other than social work also have an important contribution to make.

National Service Scheme

It is not an accident, in this perspective, that schools of social work have been involved more meaningfully in the newly devised programme of the National Service Scheme (NSS) for student youth. The programme seeks to involve college youth in service activities for the community. The leadership is provided by college teachers and some students. The schools of social work have been involved in conceptualising and working out the details of the scheme; they have participated in organising training and orientation programmes for college teachers, and as the programme expands, they will be able to provide the social workers that will be needed for programme coordination in individual colleges and universities. The schools of social work have felt at home working with college teachers and college students and through them working in urban as well as rural communities. The social workers who may subsequently find employment as NSS coordinators in individual colleges will also be in their familiar institutional settings in which and from which to operate.

Social Work and Social Context

In any effort to relate social work to social development, a certain clarification of the role or contribution of social work in the development context becomes necessary. Traditionally, social workers have worked in the welfare field and it was not uncommon to define the role of social workers by saying merely that it consisted of meeting 'welfare needs'. Sometimes, the welfare needs were listed but often they were left ambiguous. It has been pointed out earlier that the welfare needs may be defined, in a relative sense, as the needs of individuals or groups who at a given time in a given society are considered handicapped, dependent or deprived. But, which individual or group is considered deprived or handicapped or in need of assistance depends among other things on the material resources available to the society, the level of knowledge and technology which would provide the tools for doing something about the need or handicap and, above all, upon the larger values that the society accepts. For example, poverty will tend to be defined in relation to the level of living of the vast majority of people in a given society. Also, if the standard of living of the people is so low that they face the problem of bare physical survival, it is unlikely that other problems, e.g., those of psychological strains and tensions, would normally get differentiated and identified in society for specialised treatment though such problems may also exist in that society. Advances in knowledge, particularly in psychology, have helped identify emotional needs which, when met adequately in the early stages of life, can ensure normal personality development and prevent the warping of individual lives. The recognition of certain situations as problematic depends also on the values accepted by that society. Slavery, serfdom and discrimination based on caste or race are not problems except insofar as the values of human dignity, equality and social justice are accepted. The relevant values in each case may not be universally accepted in a society but they have to be sufficiently widespread and legitimised to make the emergence and support of organised professional action possible.

Insofar as the material conditions of life and the nature of values characteristic of a society tend to influence the perception of a 'need' they also tend to determine the significance that society attaches to individuals who seek to meet that need. If the need so identified is considered important, either from a cultural, economic or political point of view, or if it is such that even the most privileged may at some time or the other experience it----e.g., the need for relief from illness and physical suffering----in their own lives, then the profession or occupation which helps in meeting the need will be rewarded well. For, such rewards, whether material or other, motivate individuals to join the profession and develop the specialised skills. Other 'needs' may be recognised but considered marginal or not recognised at all. And, in a few cases, even the articulation of some needs may be regarded as subvertive of the social orders.

What has been said above about professions generally applies to social work as well. Social workers have certain skills in human relationships, in modifying and changing individual attitudes and values, in communication, in mobilising community resources around 'welfare' needs, and in conceptualising a generalist role in relation to the varied and specific needs of individuals and groups. These skills are important or unimportant depending upon how the process of development is conceived. If development is based upon a material input-output model and if the human factor is conceived of passively as a responding, dependent factor, social work has no specific contribution to make to the development process. On the other hand, if development is conceived in human and not mechanistic terms, the social worker will have a meaningful role to play.

It should be said at once that the social worker can lay no exclusive claim to the various types of competence listed above not to the many others that would be needed to meet the challenge of social development. But social work can certainly claim to be one of the professions that provides some of the necessary skills and abilities needed for social development. It is from this point of view that an attempt should be made to outline the various tasks that social work can undertake—singly or with other professions—to promote social development. The following is one such attempt.

Development Tasks for Social Work

Social work must uphold and help to promote in its normal pursuits as also through special programmes undertaken for that purpose, the broader social values which are necessary for social development. The most important of these values in developing countries is equality. Since it cannot be asserted that all individuals are either alike or equal in their abilities, the acceptance of the value of equality means primarily the equalisation of opportunities for all individuals to grow to their maximum potential. Acceptance of the equal rights of all citizens reflects itself in a democratic polity. From equality is also derived the value of social justice, which argues the need for providing compensatory benefits to those who are otherwise at a disadvantage—socially, physically, mentally, economically or in any other way. From equality also can be derived the value of secularism insofar as it asserts that the fact that individuals belong to one religious persuasion or the other should make no difference in the opportunities available to them for participating in and contributing to national life. Equality also requires that universalistic norms keep the accessibility channels open to all who have the skill, ability, aptitude or talent required for particular functions in society. Secularism and universalism also derive strength from the value attached to rationality which in turn is strengthened by an acceptance of science and the scientific method.

Another value important for social development is the commitment to national unity. By its nature it is a restrictive—somewhat non-universalistic—value in that it seems to be derived from a certain particularistic attachment to the concept of a nation. But developing societies need such a commitment because in its absence what they may obtain is not a commitment to the world community but rather a relapse into tribal, casteist and religious loyalties. Important from the point of view of economic development are also the values of hard work, dignity of labour, and postponement of gratification or reduction of individual wants. Willingness of workers to move to places where work is available and, in this sense, a loosening of the village and linguistic region ties is also important for industrial development. Another important attitude is the willingness to accept change, i.e., adaptability to changes in work techniques and to differences in patterns of living. Such adaptability is necessary for those who migrate from rural areas to large cities with the processes of industrialisation and urbanisation.

A question has often been raised whether social work can really work to assert any system of new values except to the extent that these values are already accepted in some measure by influential elements in the community. My own view is that social workers can do a great deal for canvassing and extending values which have gained acceptance and support, even if only at the verbal level, from the elite sections of society. Even here, when they come up face to face against organised interests, individual social workers may not be able to find solutions in concrete situations though as a group through their professional organisations and through the use of communication media they can contribute to bring about a change. Social workers in this sense can promote social reform and undertake social action in a limited sense. I doubt, whether social workers as a professional group can participate in movements of social action which raise issues of law and order. Short of this and depending upon their ingenuity and skills of mobilisation, social workers can and should represent, argue for and press the interests of the disadvantaged. This is their work and mission. In this sense they will serve as agents for modifying and changing the legal, social and financial structures in the direction of equalising opportunity as well as rewards.

Social work should identify the dysfunctional consequences of industrialisation, urbanisation and the rapid development of market-oriented agriculture. In all these social changes it is always the poorer sections who suffer. They have neither the resources, the skills nor the staying power to withstand strain, to buy services or to utilise new opportunities. Social workers must be able to institute services which will smoothen the change by providing rehabilitative, re-training and community support facilities. Stabilisation of the labour force in their new urban surroundings, the promotion of population control, and the facilitation of land reform are important areas of social policy in which social workers may be called upon to help in a variety of ways.

Social workers must develop new services which will increase the utilisation of available social services in the areas of health, housing, education and population policy. Very often, utilisation of services requires not only attitudinal change, but some material facilities as well. Child care services can relieve women for greater economic participation and mid-day meals in schools may help stabilise school attendance, improve children's health and indirectly subsidise family budgets. Youth counselling and vocational information programmes can help young students to get more out of available facilities for vocational training. Social service projects for college students may help the middle class student to have a better appreciation of the problems that he studies in textbooks and will simultaneously help in providing voluntary manpower for social or welfare services. Programmes of continuing education can help urban workers to improve their job skills and promote upward mobility. They can help women to adopt better practices of nutrition, child care and housekeeping. They can help the farmers to keep abreast of the latest developments in better seeds, fertiliser mixes, pesticides, and methods of crop rotation or crop planting. Social workers have a role in creating these supportive services through urban and rural community self-help programmes.

If social workers are to help effectively in anticipating needs at different stages of development and in creating service structures to meet them, they must participate in the planning and policy formulation processes at the local agency, local community, village, district, state and national levels.

IMPLICATIONS FOR SOCIAL WORK EDUCATION

The implications of orienting social work to meet the challenges of social development flow over into the preparation of social workers themselves. Some of these implications for social work education are outlined in this section.

Inculcation of New Values

We have seen that one of the important tasks in social development is to encourage the emergence and stabilisation of certain new values. If social workers are to help in this process, they must themselves subscribe to these values. It need not be assumed that because social workers have had the benefit of a college education and have been exposed to urban influences, they necessarily subscribe to the new values which are important for a modern, developing society. On the contrary, we may find that the young entrants in the schools of social work are not very different from other educated, middle class young persons. They sincerely believe that they are modern and subscribe to new values, but they have never understood what the implications of some of these new values may be in their own lives. Castelessness is easy to profess, difficult to practise. Most of the young college graduates have no friends outside their caste, except in the colleges and schools. They have been brought up in the norms of their own caste, will marry within their own caste and also at the behest of their parents. They are unlikely to have entertained an untouchable in their homes and have probably had very limited contact with persons of other religions. They may feel sympathy for the poor but have had no opportunity to see their lives closely. They do not know how their servants live in their own homes and cannot imagine what the dimensions of providing equal educational opportunity for their children really are.

One of the first tasks that social work education in developing countries faces is to communicate to the dominantly urban student body the meaning of the new values which they have learnt as words but have not understood. Unless the social workers inculcate these values in their own life they cannot become agents of the change. This will require them to overcome prejudices which they do not even know they possess.

The inculcation of new values cannot be achieved through class lectures. It requires that students see examples to follow in their teachers. Additionally, guided observation and work experience as a part of supervised fieldwork are essential. The fieldwork agencies will have to be chosen from the point of view of giving students this learning opportunity.

Local Teaching Materials

At least as important as fieldwork and example by teachers is the role that locally prepared teaching material can play in interpreting the operative significance of new values in the national, cultural setting. Concepts of equality and individual dignity have to be understood not in the abstract or context of the American class or caste situation but in the context of the people and the social hierarchy of India, Pakistan, Ceylon, Malaysia or any other countries where the training programme is located. This applies not only to the larger social values, but also to the values more specific to the profession of social work. The need for teaching materials based on local experience and establishing continuity with the local tradition is urgent from every point of view.

Emphasis on Structural Modification

Another important requirement is the social work curricula be so designed that they enable the student to keep the broader issues facing the society constantly in their mind. There will have to be a distinct shift from an emphasis on individual readjustment to social structural modifications. While social workers will and must continue to work with individuals and small groups in the course of their professional careers, they must also be able to see the problems of these individuals and groups as part of the larger social, economic and political processes taking place in society. This will enable them to focus on community programmes and preventive measures as much as on the curative or remedial measures necessary for tackling the problems faced by their clients. This will call for a greater emphasis in the curriculum of courses which interpret the social, economic and political dynamics of the society in which they live and work. It will also call for greater knowledge of the development programmes and their operation. Time would have to be provided in the curriculum for knowledge on demographic problems and population policy, problems of industrialisation, urbanisation and urban migration, consequences of the green revolution, manner in which change has affected different segments of the population in different ways and implications of this differential impact. These problems will have to be viewed in their social, psychological, economic and political aspects. The interpretation must be such that the student does not give up the tasks of social work as meaningless or marginal, but is encouraged to think and devise ways of mobilising the community to solve the problems through acceptance of new values, institutional structures and services. He should become an activist and must for that reason develop the skills of writing, speech and action in the community.

Preparing for Policy Formulation

A thorough grounding in the socio-politico-economic dynamics of society is also essential if at a later stage in his career a social worker is to participate in the planning, administering and policy formulation relating to welfare services. If, however, he is to participate in the total social development planning, he would need a deeper understanding of the functions fulfilled by the different sectors of development and their resource needs. This insight he may gain with experience and opportunity but it would be facilitated if he can have the benefit of special training at some stage in his career. It seems unlikely that all the knowledge and the techniques required for inter-sectoral planning could be imparted as a part of the first social work education curriculum even at the post-graduate level. Preparation for planning and policy formulation requires not only a broad basis in social sciences but also a certain capability of interpreting factual data which have to be specially collected or culled from available records. Training in research, data interpretation and data utilisation is an essential part of a planner's skills. Such research may or may not be theoretically sophisticated, but it minimally demands the ability to work with aggregate data at various levels of the administrative or political units. It would be necessary to develop specialised training programmes for participation in social development planning. It is generally unlikely that the schools of social work with their present faculties will be able to provide this type of training.

Different Levels of Education

It has also emerged clearly from our earlier discussion that at least in developing countries there is a need for social work oriented personnel---whether you call them social workers or by some other name---at two or three levels of education. A single category of post-graduate trained social workers will not meet adequately the demands of the rural areas or even of the smaller, urban welfare agencies. It may be necessary to organise training at the post-high school, the under-graduate and the post-graduate levels. The important thing, however, is to ensure a continuity of values and basic approaches at all these levels and to devise a system of credits whereby a person who has obtained his first qualification can over a period of time accumulate additional academic credits and obtain a higher qualification.

Social work education will have to devise a more flexible system wherein social workers in employment can work toward obtaining their basic or higher level qualifications through short-term, full-time courses or longer duration, part-time courses.

Faculty Composition

The schools of social work would need to re-equip themselves somewhat differently in their faculties to shoulder some of the added responsibilities. Even assuming that the specific task of training personnel for inter-sectoral planning is left to other training institutions, the faculties of the school would still need to represent a better multidisciplinary mix than is commonly noticed in schools of the region. The schools should have at least one representative each from the disciplines of sociology, psychology, economics and political science. These specialists will have to be brought in on the basis of their known or potential interest in matters of social welfare and social policy. In the absence of such a commitment on the part of the social scientists serious problems of integration and community of interest may arise. The schools on their part must be able to give them professionally challenging work or else they will find themselves always on the margin and may not stay on in the institutions.

The schools of social work in the developed countries do not necessarily offer a good model for faculty organisation for schools in developing countries. More recently, though the programmes of the western schools have themselves tended to change and accommodate a wider variety of disciplines and interests, they have also sought to develop social policy as a special area of social work practice. But, there is much greater need for such a development in the developing countries, though, as in everything else, the paucity of suitable personnel and other resources in these countries is directly proportional to the need for them.

Community Role of Schools

Schools of social work in the developing countries have often bemoaned the absence of well-developed welfare institutions of the remedial type which could provide good fieldwork centres. They should have to meet their problem in two ways. First, they must pioneer and get the community to set up such agencies and services; simultaneously they must also see that their real need goes beyond the traditional pattern of welfare agencies and that they have to develop patterns of services in the open community and in relation to other development agencies and programmes. The very experience and opportunity to participate in building new services should serve as excellent fieldwork experience for students under training. Most schools in the Asian region have had to pioneer new services and to serve as unidentified field counsellors to existing agencies in the community.

Schools of social work must also strengthen their research potential and capability if they have to participate in social developmental tasks. Nothing persuades better than a clear statement of facts. But, often, the facts are not available. Much research in developing countries will have to begin at the level of fact gathering and presentation to highlight descriptively the problems that demand solutions.

Just as schools of social work may have to work for greater community consciousness to facilitate development of new services, they may have to educate the community in using professional services. One of the schools in India has a small but long-standing programme to promote the use of professional services in the field of child and family welfare. Even apart from this programme, it is true that the schools of social work have had to get recognition for their graduates and for the need for professional education in social work. This is true of all countries.

It should be clear from the above discussion that the schools of social work which aspire to train their students to meet the challenges of social development have a difficult role and that they need to have a second look at their curricula, forms of course organisation, faculty structures and conception of their own role in the community.

Social development is an ambiguous concept and a complex undertaking which involves different kinds of tasks in different countries whose only common denominator is that they are poor and technologically backward and want to be prosperous and advanced. Any effort to list out a single set of functions for social services, social welfare services and social work is bound to be unsatisfactory. I have tried to identify as many of the common elements as I could. It would probably have been better if I could have drawn on the experience of different countries in meeting this challenge, but I have avoided doing so; first, because I do not have the necessary equipment for such a task and, second, because I was afraid of getting lost in a maze of particular illustrations losing in the effort a conceptual analytical continuity of discussion. This inevitably has led to some abstractions and to some unwarrantedly generalised statements. I hope, however, I have succeeded in showing the links successively between social development, social services, social welfare services, social work and finally, social work education.

Note

1. Eugene Pusic, Review of *Social Welfare in a Changing World* by Elizabeth Wickenden, *International Social Work*, Vol. IX, No. 2, April 1966, pp. 46-47.

3

Social Work: Its Human Rights Aspects

While the origins of social work can be traced to the early beginnings of human society, the origins of the concept of human rights can be traced at least to those societies in which the rule of law, as different from rule by the whims of an autocrat, came to be established. But, the substantive goals pursued by social work and the nature of its activities have differed from society to society and from one period of history to another and equally the scope and content of the rights of the individual as recognised by society have also varied according to time and place. Even today, there is considerable variation between countries in what goes by the name of social work and certainly there is a great deal of difference in what the countries concede in practice by way of human rights to their citizens. It is, therefore, imperative that if a discussion of the human rights aspects of social work is to proceed intelligibly, it should be accompanied by a statement of the society and the period of history with reference to which the discussion is to be undertaken.

So far as human rights are concerned the point of reference is clear and specific. We are referring to the rights listed in the 30 articles of the Universal Declaration of Human Rights as

---

First published in *Social Welfare and Human Rights*: Proceedings of the XIV International Conference on Social Welfare, New York, Columbia University Press. 1969, pp. 56-68.

proclaimed by the General Assembly of the United Nations. While every one of the articles may not have equal significance for social work, the declaration as a whole, the fact of its existence, its tenor and some of its articles have a great deal of significance for social work values, goals, functions and practice. It will be my endeavour in the course of this talk to underline some of this significance and to do it with one question at the back of my mind: what are the points at which the pursuit of social work raises issues involving human rights?

THE DECLARATION OF HUMAN RIGHTS

The United Nations' Declaration of Human Rights is a long and complex document. Its 30 articles are spelt out in 50 paragraphs, all tersely worded. It is an affirmation of values, a statement of aspirations of world conscience on behalf of the common man and an indication of the direction in which the United Nations would like the nations of the world to move. It covers a wide range of rights and value affirmations. Besides, it deals with what are usually referred to as political and civil rights under a representative form of government: right to nationality, freedom of movement, and the freedom to seek asylum, freedom of thought and conscience, and the right to social security, to an adequate standard of life and to the opportunity for the free and full development of the individual's personality. It also affirms human dignity, equality and the right to freedom from discrimination and exploitation. Finally, in a very significant addition, it refers to the duties of the individual to his community in which only the free and full development of his personality can take place.

Relevance of the Declaration for Social Work

The relevance of the Declaration of Human Rights for social work lies mainly in the fact that it unequivocally recognises the worth and dignity of the human person and asserts that he has a right to "seek the free and full development of his personality".

Social work also proceeds from the same basic assumption that the human individual is worthy in himself independent of the material or social conditions in which he may be found and that it is important to provide him with every facility for the full development of his potentialities. Without the acceptance of this value much of social work activity would lose its meaning and sense of purpose and would look rather like a response based on the social worker's sense of sympathy or pity. While such sympathy and fellow feeling have been strong urges for social work in all societies and while they have been legitimised by religion and social usage, there is increasing recognition of the fact that by themselves they provide only one and a somewhat inadequate orientation to social work activity. The acceptance of the dignity and worth of the individual and the value of promoting his development is the other---and more important---orientation in social work today. In this acceptance, one finds a common emphasis in the Declaration of Human Rights and the values basic to social work.

Differences in Respective Approaches

However, even in this point of contact, there is a difference of approach---a difference which may appear inconsequential at first glance, but one which I believe is fundamental. In the Declaration of Human Rights everyone is entitled "to the realization... of the economic, social and cultural rights indispensable for his dignity and the free development of his personality" (Article 22). Social workers accept the free development of personality of their client to be a basic value, but they are not always, in every society, able to regard it as a right of the individual nor do the societies in which social workers function always accept the obligation to provide the individual with the opportunities for such individual fulfilment. The right of the individual to social security, to a minimum standard of life and to the provision of opportunities for free and full development---even within the means available to the state---has been recognised only recently and not in the same way by all states. Some recognise the right to work and pay, and to protection of minimal income in the form of social security, but they do not necessarily grant freedom in religious, educational, or civic matters. Some grant these latter, but do not concede the right to social security and income maintenance. Social workers have had to work in all these situations. They have sought to render services when no 'rights' were recognised and when no law existed for the provision of special amenities and services to individual citizens and in a greater part of the world they continue to work in these conditions even today.

Typically social workers operate with the concept of needs---basic human needs---rather than of rights. The concept of needs can often go beyond the rights that are recognised in a given society. In this sense, social work has a very different stance and approach from that which is suggested by the use of the word 'rights'. Rights give rise to questions of justice—or, at least of equity in particular social arrangements. If the basic urge of a worker is for greater justice, his stance tends to be more heroic and his action bolder. The social worker's urge is for healing alleviation and soothing and he tends to take on the less heroic, but no less useful, role of a constructive worker. The specific challenge he faces and the particular tasks he is called upon to perform are likely to vary from one society to another. The equation between human rights and social work is, I believe, also likely to change from society to society. It would be useful to explore this suggestion a little further by examining the relationship between human rights and social work in different types of societies.

Four Types of Social Contexts

All typologies are inadequate and typologies of societies are particularly unsatisfactory because of the complexity of phenomena that they attempt to summarise. But typologies help by throwing certain aspects of phenomena into bold relief for purposes of discussion. In the discussion of the relationship between human rights and social work it might be useful to distinguish between societies on the basis of two questions: (i) does a society recognise the obligation to provide its members with the freedom, the opportunities and facilities to achieve the maximum development they are capable of, and (ii) independent of its value commitments does the society have the material resources to enable it to provide the opportunities to its members? The two questions are too broad and vague to be made applicable to particular known societies. One may also say that it is never possible to make categorical distinctions of the type implied by the questions. It is difficult to characterise societies as having accepted or not accepted the whole set of human rights. They may recognise some without recognising others. Particularly, there is a basic distinction that may be made between the civil and political rights of the individual on the one hand and the right to social security on the other; societies which accept one do not always accept the other. Yet, I suggest, the questions are helpful in distinguishing between four types of social situations in which social work may be called upon to function. The consideration of the stage of economic development of a society becomes particularly relevant in respect of the rights of social security. We can first distinguish between societies which *in principle* recognise social security obligations toward their individual citizens and societies which do not. Each of these groups can be further sub-divided into those which have the means to accept the responsibility for providing these opportunities and those which do not have these means---or, in other words, societies which are economically 'advanced' and those which are 'backward'. Thus, we have societies which have accepted obligations toward their members and have the means to meet these obligations and those which have accepted the obligations but do not have the necessary means. Also, we have societies that do not accept the obligations though they have the means and those which neither accept the obligations nor have the means to meet such obligations.

Different Modes of Relationship between Human Rights and Social Work

The four types of social situations pose different types of challenges and should give rise to differences in goals, methods and dominant concerns among social workers.

In all societies, the basic concern of social work is to help individuals and groups to survive, to grapple with problems posed by their physical and social environments and to achieve the full development of their potentialities. The recognition or non-recognition of 'human rights' by the society in which they work provides social workers with a value context which may help or impede their efforts and so will the availability or non-availability of material resources. In this sense, the four types of social situations are likely to pose different types of challenges and give rise to differences in the goals, the methods and the dominant concerns characteristic of social work in each of them. I will attempt to follow up this possibility with reference to the rights to social security and standard of living (Articles 21 and 25).

In a society which has accepted the obligation of the collectivity to provide security to the individual and guarantee a minimum standard of life, social work can become one of the major instrumentalities of giving reality to the promise held out by the recognition of his 'rights'. If this society is economically advanced, the social worker will tend to be preoccupied with mobilising resources, diverting them to particular areas which he considers of primary significance, and raising questions of the most appropriate way to provide assistance to the needy. As he finds that the basic problem of physical survival is gradually overcome, he will identify problems of social and psychological adjustment, organise his knowledge, refine his methods and move towards the establishment of a profession.

In a society where these rights are not recognised social work will have to serve as a means of awakening the conscience of the society so that these rights come to be recognised. In the period in which the rights are not yet recognised by a society social work will have to mobilise resources on the basis of humanitarian and religious appeals and seek to provide for the minimum needs of at least the most indigent sections of the population. It is unlikely that a profession can crystallise at this stage where those engaged in social work can look to no adequate recompense for their efforts and will often be expected to first utilise their own means and materials before approaching others for help.

In societies which are economically advanced and have therefore the means to provide security, but have not formally accepted the individual's right to security, it is likely, though not certain, that social workers will find less resistance in their efforts to bring about a value change and to gain acceptance for the principle of the individual's right to social security. Social workers are likely to find it easier to evoke a response to their appeal for support in a society which has the material resources, even if it has not formally accepted the obligation to provide security to the individual. But, to the extent that such a society has not accepted the 'right' to social security, the social worker will operate in an atmosphere of paternalistic charity and philanthrophy as different from an atmosphere characterised by the recognition of the dignity of the individual.

The right to social security came to be recognised very recently in history and its recognition in most countries was associated with their increasing economic viability to accept the responsibility implied in recognising such a right. However, in the total world context, there are many countries today which are in principle responsive to the concept of an individual's right to social security, but do not have the means to formally endorse it. These are countries which have some of the most idealistic political constitutions in the world but they are without the means to make their promises viable. Social workers in these countries face a situation where policy makers concede the validity of their plea on behalf of the needy sections of the population but also simultaneously express their inability to help. This gives rise to an unreal atmosphere of lip sympathy for noble sentiments accompanied by an almost cynical inaction. In such a situation social workers are likely to be led to believe that their work in bringing about a value change has already been accomplished and that they have only to await the availability of material resources to be able to offer the services they consider necessary. But, the value change may be only superficial since it has never been tested out in action and the non-availability of resources may only be a spacious excuse for inaction.

Finally, there are societies which have neither accepted the obligations toward the individual nor have the resources required to meet them. In these societies, social workers are on their own. They are called upon to work at two levels—that of persuading the community to recognise the needs of some of its weaker members and that of proceeding to meet them with the limited available resources. The services provided are likely to be directed to the barely physical needs of food, clothing and shelter since these are the only ones that are likely to gain support in the community. Social work will tend to be done primarily under religious auspices and in a few cases with the help of individual philanthropists. Questions of human rights are likely to appear as somewhat remote to social workers and clients alike.

Limitations to the Use of the Typology

I have deliberately refrained from identifying particular countries or parts of the world as belonging to one type or the other—though in a loose fashion it should be possible to attempt such an allocation. I have refrained from undertaking such an identification not so much as a matter of strategy in an international gathering, but because I am conscious of the essential crudity of the typology that I have suggested. As stated earlier, one cannot easily group countries as having accepted or not accepted the whole list of human rights. A country may accept some rights and not accept others. Also, even in the same country, particular rights may be accepted with reference to one section of the population—on ethic or religious grounds—and not accepted with reference to others. This is likely to happen particularly in respect of the civil and political rights of the individual. This may seem to violate the very concept of 'human rights' since these rights, if they have any meaning at all, are in principle indivisible. Yet, in practice, no country has an altogether clear record in respect of human rights and countries do vary in the thoroughness with which they accept one set of rights rather than others and also in the evenness with which they succeed in making them available to different segments of the population. All societies thus live in proverbial 'glass houses' and, mixing metaphors, one may say that none of them can allow their members to lift and cast the first stone at other societies.

This situation suggests that one should seek to apply the typology not so much to whole societies but in respect of particular rights and particular groups in that society. It may even be that the availability or non-availability of means also varies with reference to particular groups or particular 'causes' within the same society. If one accepts the possibility that there would be variations within the same society in the recognition or non-recognition of different parts of the Declaration of Human Rights and even in the availability or non-availability of means to meet the obligations implied by the acceptance of these rights, one would also have to further accept the possibility that within the same society social work would face a variety of challenges and be required to take on a multiplicity of roles.

Neglect of One Facet of Social Worker Role

It has often happened that in societies which have generally recognised the values affirmed by the Declaration of Human Rights and have also the means to set up services to meet the obligations implied in their recognition, the efforts of social workers have naturally been devoted primarily to the operation and development of services in sectors where they come to be established. Not unusually, this has led to a preoccupation with certain types of problems and services to the neglect of others. In industrially advanced countries social workers have tended to concern themselves with the urban, industrial working class families. It may, in fact, be true to say that professional social work arose largely in response to the problems of a rapidly industrialising and urbanising society. The rural segments of the population did not receive the same measure of attention.

This was a consequence of the assumption that in the rural sections the traditional institutions of the community would continue to adequately meet the needs of the people and also of the assumption that somehow the problems of change were more important than the problems arising from lack of change. Partly, the lack of organised resources and employment opportunities in the rural areas and the social workers' unwillingness to be consigned to rural hinterlands might also have contributed to this situation. The consequence of all these factors might also have contributed to this situation. The consequence of all these factors has been that the awareness of the existence of poverty and unmet needs in rural pockets has come with a shock to countries which have otherwise accepted the obligation to provide for a minimum standard of life for their citizens and which have also the requisite material resources to meet this obligation.

Simultaneously, there has been another type of preoccupation and of a neglect. In some countries, the acceptance and acclamation of the value implied in the political and civil rights contained in the Declaration of Human Rights has led to the social worker's preoccupation with his healing and remedial functions and to a neglect of his duties to serve as a watchdog for basic human values. Often, therefore, when problems have arisen they have arisen with a violence and an unexpectedness that have thrown the whole society into convulsions.

It may be asked whether the movement for human rights generally—including the political and civil rights—is within the scope of social work activity. The answer could be conditional, but in societies which have consciously and articulately accepted representative, democratic governments and the equality of all their citizens, the protection of the rights of minorities and the ensuring of non-discrimination through constructive action form a part of social work. It is true that a measure of doubt, if not controversy, surrounds this area and I would therefore like to elaborate this point a little further. It has been suggested above that the stance of the social worker is likely to be gentler than the heroic stance of a rebel or a fighter but it need not, for that reason, be less effective, and his role need not be less important to society.

Social Action and Social Work

Despite the suggestion that social action may be considered to be a part of the three or four important types of activities engaged in by social workers, there has always been a lack of clear understanding of what exactly the scope of such activity would be. Specifically, the question remains unanswered whether the profession of social work can be actively involved in action which is likely to be (a) not acceptable to all segments of a society, and (b) likely to affect adversely the organised interests of some groups in society, though such action is in full conformity with the basic, well-articulated values of that society? What, for instance, is the role of the social work profession vis-à-vis the Negro problem in the United States, the Harijan problem in India and the problem of coloured immigrants in the United Kingdom? I think, in any examination of the human rights aspects of social work, this question becomes crucial. What is the role of the individual professional and of the profession of social work in situations where the value of the worth and dignity of the individual is denied in practice with reference to certain groups even when the society proclaims this value and generally accepts it in regard to the other segments of society?

One way of responding to this situation is to say that individually in their personal lives social workers should not act in ways which would be in transgression of this value. This mode of response evades the issue by converting a question which is addressed to the profession into one addressed to the individual as a citizen. Obviously, even this response is valuable and shows the individual's commitment to a particular value. But, it is not adequate.

Social Action and Political Action

Another response is to say that any organised action in this area is in the nature of political action and should be avoided because (a) it is outside the sphere of social work, and (b) is likely to be divisive of the profession as a collectivity. This response merits serious consideration, because it implies a certain definite concept of the nature of social work and of political action. Let me say at once that I do not look upon social work as the only instrument of solving all human problems and I concede that the social worker in his professional role should avoid getting entangled in the actions of political parties. But having said that let me say that it is difficult to identify any major programme of social action which is bereft of all political significance.

The question that is important to ask is whether a particular problem which is sought to be solved is of central interest to social workers in their professional capacity to require them to act in the interests of their clients. I would like to suggest that if a social worker is working in one of the villages of India, in the working class area of London,

Manchester or Birmingham, or in one of the racially torn neighbourhoods of an American metropolis, he cannot evade the responsibility of helping the deprived sections of the population in overcoming all obstacles to their exercise of the basic rights given to them by law. In accepting this responsibility he need not follow the methods of the political agitator. Every profession has its own choice of means and methods. But, from this perspective, the question is not whether this sphere of activity belongs to social work, but rather how a social worker would respond in a situation such as this.

Characteristics of Professional Practice

There are certain inherent limitations to the practice of a profession, especially a profession like social work. A social worker has to have an agency to sponsor his action and a known client to whom his action is oriented. The prerequisite of an agency means that the action of the social worker has to have sufficient legitimacy so that it will be supported openly at least by a section of the community. Also, the professional has to act with reference to, or on behalf of a client—whether the client is an individual or a group. As an individual practitioner he cannot argue a 'cause' in the abstract. Moreover, his methods must have the sanction of the profession. He cannot decide on the spur of the moment to pick up a poster and join a slogan shouting group in support of his cause. Fortunately, this is not one of the methods of social work yet.

But, where the conditions of the existence of a sponsoring agency and a client are fulfilled and where there are obstacles to the effective social functioning of his client, the social worker's responsibility for intervention is clear. This responsibility is not fulfilled by the response that as an individual he will not add to these obstacles and that he will not be prejudiced in his professional conduct. Minimally, he will be required to work effectively to enable his client to use fully all the available services in the community. In this pursuit he will use all his skills of persuasion and, if necessary, all the help that law can give to remove impediments in the legitimate exercise of his client's rights and in the normal fulfilment of his client's aspirations.

Limited Usefulness of Law in Value Change

However, not all obstacles to the exercise of human rights or to the functioning of an individual with dignity and freedom are tangible and such as can be legally removed. Also, there may be shortcomings in the available law itself which need to be removed. The individual social worker working in the local community cannot therefore lean heavily on law to serve the interests of his clients. Legal battles leave scars and if the worker is interested in furthering more harmonious relationships he cannot always brandish his legal stick.

The fact is that there are serious limitations to what an individual worker can achieve by way of change in community attitudes and values through his local action. On basic issues, like the treatment given to minorities, attitudes in the local community are influenced and supported by attitudes in the larger society. At this level, the individual social worker employed by a local agency cannot play an effective role. If social work is to serve as an effective instrument for giving reality to the formally accepted values and rights, it will have to enter upon an action addressed to the whole society. This role has usually been assigned to a 'social reformer'. In so far as the social reformer questions and even rejects some of the widely held values and proposes the adoption of new ones in their place, his role cannot be easily institutionalised and integrated into the activities of a profession.

The Profession and the Individual Professional

At this point the distinction between the scope of activities of the whole profession and the activities of an individual professional becomes significant. It is true that the work of bringing about a change in some of the values characteristic of a society, or a major segment of it, cannot easily be perceived as part of the activity of an individual professional, but, I suggest, that it can and should form a part of the activities of the profession as a whole. The professional organisation at various levels and professional leaders in their individual as well as representative capacity will have to address themselves to this task. This is an important role for the profession to play. It is a role that differs from that of a rebel as also that of a repair man. It retains the constructive orientation of professional action. Yet it compels the profession to see beyond the fashions and prejudices of the present so as to identify and promote instrumental values and practices necessary for the realisation of the goals of human dignity and equality which are at the core of the Declaration of Human Rights and which are basic to the practice of the social work profession.

The Human Rights Perspective

Even from this perspective social work will continue to be in the nature of an interventive action for the enhancement of the social functioning of individuals and groups. It will achieve this end through helping individuals and communities to grapple with problems of change at the social and psychological levels. But, this perspective will lead social work beyond its confines. It will additionally identify and promote values and practices necessary for the realisation of human rights through the use of means which are consistent with the rights of other individuals and groups. While this position is not unacceptable to social workers and will not appear new in its orientation, it has the advantage of clarifying what the moorings and long-term objectives of social work are. It will disturb the complaisance of the individual social worker who may be tempted to acquiesce in the values of the local community even when they conflict with the broader sympathies of the procession. It will require and compel the organised profession to take clear positions on social issues. As distances are reduced by the development of faster means of communication, we are going to be faced with the fact that the world is peopled by many races that speak many languages. In the midst of a plurality of cultures and values there will be need for the affirmation of one acceptable common denominator. The Declaration of Human Rights provides this necessary standard and direction to all constructive action.

Within the limitations imposed by the need for constructive action this perspective will give social work a role to play in societies which are economically advanced as well as those which are economically backward and societies which have generally accepted the values articulated in the Declaration of Human Rights and those which have not.

This exploration into the relationship between human rights and social work was begun in a tentative mood. Nothing has happened in the course of these last three quarters of an hour to make me feel more definite or dogmatic on the subject—however firm and definitive my tone may have appeared to be in the course of my presentation. I have tried to suggest that the relationship between human rights and social work can be understood better if we have an appreciation of the extent of value commitment to human rights which is characteristic of a society and its ability to transcribe this commitment into a programme of action. This commitment and ability to transcribe it into action may vary not only from society to society but even between groups in one society and with respect to different facets of the declaration of human rights. This varying equation between commitment and ability (or viability) provides one of the major determinants for the type of social work practice that will emerge or stabilise itself. And since this equation is a varying one our concept of the nature of social work will have to be broad enough to provide for the variations in practice.

Even as I conclude this essay in loud thinking I can sense the doubts that can be raised about the propositions that I have made. But, then, one of the few consolations available to modern man is that he is not always expected to answer all questions or settle all doubts. Even if he has raised additional questions or articulated better some of the older ones he is supposed to have fulfilled a useful purpose. I hope I have qualified myself by one of these latter considerations to gain the satisfaction of having been useful.

4

Social Development and a Strategy for Urbanisation

ABSENCE OF A POSITIVE APPROACH TO URBANISATION

In much that has been written about urbanisation, particularly in developing countries, there is a note of apprehension—apprehension of an approaching catastrophe. Some of the facts relating to conditions of urban life, which will be mentioned later, lend legitimacy to this feeling of apprehension. But, even in Europe and the United States, where the physical conditions of the city life are somewhat better than in Asia and Africa, life in the city is often depicted as a necessary evil rather than a positive value. The reasons again are not far to seek. The high rates of crime, the sense of physical insecurity in what is sometimes described as the 'asphalt jungle', and the strains and the tensions which result from an endless struggle to meet social, psychological and economic demands have tended to make the experience of the city life seem negative and something to be tolerated, adjusted to, or escaped from. There is an absence of a positive philosophy about the city life.

Paper presented for a seminar discussion under the auspices of the Departments of Social Work and of Extramural Studies, University of Hong Kong on February 21, 1973.

In India, Mahatma Gandhi would have nothing to do with cities. The India of his dreams was of self-sufficient, self-reliant villages which were linked to each other "in ever-widening, never-ascending" circles. He looked upon cities as economically exploitative and politically destructive of a true democracy. But Gandhi was at least consistent. If he was against cities, he was also against mass production of goods through modern industry and a life built on the individual's compelling drive for more and more material goods, the need for which is stimulated through high pressure sales drives and enticing advertisements. He believed in a simple life of relatively undifferentiated wants which could be satisfied locally through village production or through a system of marginal exchanges between villages. He believed in an economy where the tiller owned the land he tilled and the artisan owned his tools. He was against both the feudal and the capitalist forms of exploitation of the worker by the non-worker. A society based upon a greater degree of division of labour, a greater specialisation in skills and a production of goods for the market rather than for oneself or one's neighbour is a society that must reconcile individual greed and social interest through external means of social control. Or else, unbridled market processes will lead to wastage and to an exploitation of many by some. His answer to the problems of 19th century capitalism was a return to a peasant economy and a village polity.

Since all developing countries are actively seeking ways of achieving economic growth and since they seek to achieve it through a process of industrialisation, the solution that Gandhi offered for the problems of an urban and industrial society has no value for them. Historical experience indicates that large-scale industrialisation cannot be achieved without a simultaneous process of urbanisation. It is possible that modern technological development may at a future date make industrialisation possible without huge, multi-million agglomerates of population. Even so it will require the emergence of smaller cities and towns as an essential infrastructure for industrialisation.

GROWTH IN URBAN POPULATIONS

Even if we keep aside Gandhi's view of the city and its role, we find that there is very little available by way of a positive view on the growth of the urban population all over the world. On the one hand, as the *1970 UN Report on the World Social Situation*[1] (UN 1971) shows, in the developing as well as the developed regions of the world, there has been a substantial increase in urban population. In each of the two groups about 130 million people have been added between 1950 and 1960 to those already living in urban areas. This has meant a much more rapid increase in the developing countries since they had started with a smaller base of urban populations as compared with the developed ones. In India, the percentage growth of the urban population has been only about 2 per cent but even so the net increase has been of the order of 20 million. The present urban population of India is 109 million, which is roughly about a fifth of the total population of the country. The present population living in urban areas is small, but the absolute numbers are large by any comparison.

What is true of India is true of the Asian region as a whole. The regional level of urbanisation has risen only from 15 to 21 per cent between 1950 and 1970, but in a numerical sense Asia has more people living in urban areas (450 million) than the total population of Africa or Latin America or North America.[2]

NATURE OF URBANISATION

It has been suggested that the developing countries are probably overurbanised compared to the level of urbanisation achieved by European countries in the early stages of their industrialisation. What is certainly true is that many of the villagers who migrate to city do so not so much because they are certain of finding industrial employment in the city, but because they find no employment in the villages. Unlike countries in Europe, the Asian countries are witnessing a fall in their death rates and a consequent growth in the total population at a much earlier stage in their social development. The growing pressure upon land and the inability of the traditional modes of agriculture to support the growing population has tended to drive many villagers to the city in search of employment. When they move away from the village, they go not necessarily to the nearest town, but to the biggest town or city. It is these cities that can support a large proportion of people who are engaged in petty trades or casual work with no specific employment. This explains the rapid, selective growth of the larger cities rather than an even growth of most urban areas.

In India, about 56 per cent of the urban population lives in large cities of 1,00,000 and over, which constitute about 5 to 6 per cent of the total number of city-dwellers in the country. The smaller towns of less than 20,000 population, which make up about 60 per cent of the urban units in the country, accommodate only 17 per cent of the total urban population. What is more, even the total number of the smaller urban units has shown a decrease in the last two decades.

The preference of the rural migrants for large cities has meant that these cities, particularly the multi-million cities, are growing very rapidly. With the exception of Calcutta, all the major metropolitan complexes in India have shown a growth rate of 30 to 60 per cent over the decennium 1961-1971. This growth is accounted for only in a small measure by the locally born persons and is primarily a result of the large number of rural migrants who come to city in the hope of finding a job.

The process of urbanisation has been uneven between regions within the country. The three states which form the hinterlands of Bombay, Calcutta and Madras---the oldest of the modern cities in India---are the most urbanised with about 30 per cent of their population living in towns and cities. And even within each of these states urbanisation is unevenly distributed as most of the city-dwelling population being located in one or two clearly demarcated areas.

Indian cities, even the smaller ones, tend to be multilingual since their populations are drawn from more than one state. In the case of Bombay and Bangalore, the population speaking the local languages—Marathi and Kannada respectively—constitutes a minority of the total population of the cities, though they are the largest single linguistic groups. The multilingual character of the cities presents a major problem in the civic life of these cities and occasionally erupt, in combination with other factors, into riots based upon linguistic affiliations.

The large-scale migration to the major cities has also taxed the civic services of these cities. The migrant population consists of individuals who mostly enter the cities at the lowest levels of the economic hierarchy. They are not the groups that contribute to the cities' resources and they cannot buy the services or the facilities they need for themselves either in housing, water, power, medicine or education. The civic administrations are wholly unable to cope with the additional demands created by these groups and the result is a general shortage and a lowering of efficiency in all municipal services.

It is true that conditions of life in the rural areas are no better than in the urban slums to which a large proportion of the rural migrants shift. It may well be that consciously or unconsciously many of the villagers are recreating their rural environment even after they have moved to the city. The villages often have no water supply or drainage facilities and the dwellings of the poorer sections of the rural community are not very much better than the shanties which one notices in a city like Bombay. But there are two important differences. In the village context it is possible that a strongly motivated individual could provide himself with a neater house even if it is made only of mud walls and thatched roof. He can also maintain it better since the materials required for its upkeep are locally available. But, in the city, the individual experiences much less autonomy; he is dependent upon the landlord, the market mechanism and the availability of ready cash to be able to effect any improvements in his dwelling. The large numbers of people and the very high residential densities of the working class areas of most cities are not to be met with in the rural areas. When the villager attempts to use rural patterns of adjustment to the problems of housing, water supply and drainage in the urban areas, he creates an environment which has all the squalor but none of the advantages of a small community living in the midst of wide open farmlands. While urban conditions are no worse than the conditions of the rural poor, the problems they pose are much too large and serious to be tackled at the level of the individual or the small group. They have to be tackled at the level of the city as a whole and as we will see, at the level of the region and the country as well.

In Bombay and Calcutta, about a sixth of their populations live in makeshift dwellings constructed on unauthorised premises out of any material that comes to hand. Discarded sacks, flattened sheets of metal cans and paste-board boxes are used for roofing and walls. The occupants sometimes pay rents, but to unauthorised individuals who extort it from them.

Apart from those who live in such temporary shelters, there are several thousands who live on side-walks, in the porches and corridors of public buildings and on suburban railway stations. They include young children as well as adults and some aged persons.

About two-thirds of the total population of Bombay, consisting of those engaged in regular employment, lives in single-room accommodation with commonly shared facilities for water supply, toilets and bathrooms. The large cities chronically suffer from water and power shortages, the available water supply being less than a few gallons per head.

Their transportation systems are worked beyond their capacities. Trains and buses carry not only standing passengers, but carry them even sitting on top of the vehicles and hanging from the bars of the windows.

The net consequence of the absence of a positive attitude on the subject of urbanisation has been an unregulated, imbalanced growth in urban population without corresponding resource allocations for urban civic bodies and the essential physical and social infrastructure to meet the needs of the growing population. The deterioration in the quality of life described above is characteristic of nearly all cities which have crossed the one million mark and the problems become worse as the cities continue to grow beyond this size. In the smaller cities the conditions may not be as bad in so far as overcrowding is concerned, but even in cities of 1,00,000 and above—of which India has 147—we find that inadequacies of transport, water supply and power have already emerged as problems. Out of the 2,641 urban units in India, not even one per cent have a filtered water supply, very few of them—even among the smaller communities—can provide a 24-hour water supply, and only a minority of them have a system of distribution of water on taps. Most towns depend on systems of excreta and waste disposal that are not only wasteful and inefficient, but are also based on the traditional subjugation of one caste of people who must perform the dirty job.

NEED FOR A POLICY

If developing countries want to progress through a process of industrialisation, they will have to come to terms with a system of habitation which involves relatively large aggregates. There is not enough knowledge available to enable us to say what the optimum size of urban units should be and probably the sizes will have to vary depending upon the type of social, economic, political and other functions they will subserve. Even so, speaking for India, it seems reasonably certain that the net population living in urban units with populations larger than 20,000 will double in the next twenty years, even assuming that the proportion of the urban population to the total population does not increase very steeply. The chances are that with increase in industry and commerce the percentage of the urban population itself may show a substantial rise. Today, about 83 per cent of India's urban population, i.e., approximately 90 million people, live in habitats with a population of 20,000 or more. This number may double in the next twenty years, partly as a result of continued townward migration of sections of the rural population and partly as a result of the natural increase of the population already residing in urban areas. The likelihood is that as the proportion of increase due to urban fertility rates decreases, the proportion due to migration will increase. But, even if the urban population does not actually double, the net increase will still be substantial. If the Indian polity is not to totter under the strains generated by urban unrest, a more positive attitude to the process of urbanisation and its role in the developmental strategy is essential. This will have to be reflected in certain overall policy decisions relating to the goals, extent, distribution and social quality of the process of urbanisation.

This paper will seek to spell out some of the issues and alternatives that may need consideration in defining an urbanisation policy in the context of social development. The ruling overall objective at the social level will be the achievement of economic growth with social justice. Economic growth will introduce the criteria of efficiency and economy in the attainment of a higher GNP whereas social justice will raise questions about how widespread the benefits of growth are.

WHETHER OR NOT TO URBANISE

The first question to be answered by an urbanisation policy is whether the process of urbanisation, i.e., the process of an increasing proportion of the population living in large aggregates of, say, 20,000 and more, is something to be encouraged, regulated or actively discouraged. This, of course, depends upon an answer to a further question whether a higher outlay of industrialisation necessarily requires greater urbanisation? To this latter question there is no simple answer except for the fact that most societies which have a high GNP and are industrialised, are also characterised by a higher degree of urbanisation. In Europe (excluding the Soviet Union), the urban population is between 40-45 per cent of the total population. In the other more developed regions of North America, the Soviet Union, Japan, Australia and New Zealand, the urban population is between 50-55 per cent of the total population. In the less developed region of Asia and Africa the urban population accounts probably for only about 15-20 per cent. But, within the Asian region again, the more developed countries have higher levels of urbanisation. For example, Japan with a GNP per capita of $1,000+, has 83 per cent of its population in the urban areas. Iran, with a GNP per capita of $200-500, has a 39.3 per cent urban population, Philippines and Vietnam with about $100-200 GNP per capita have a 23 per cent urban population and India, Indonesia and Pakistan with less than a $100 GNP per capita have between 15 and 20 per cent urban population. It thus appears that there is a positive relationship between urbanisation and economic development.[3]

Independent of this relationship, it is known that medium and large-scale industry requires not only a population directly engaged in work in the industrial process but also commercial, ancillary, industrial, transportational, social infrastructural and petty trade facilities which cannot be provided except in urban communities. Urbanisation has, therefore, to be accepted and planned for.

Apart from the demands of the process of industrialisation, urbanisation may be desirable in that it might facilitate the process of modernisation, the spread of science and the attitude of economic rationality. Even from a purely social perspective urbanisation makes important contributions to national life. Large urban agglomerates are necessary for the support of art and literature. In India, the urban areas have served the important function of spreading the message of nationalism during the struggle for independence. Without the facilities that urban centres provide for verbal and spatial communication and for the development of special interest groups—whether religious, political, professional, cultural or any other—much of what one values in modern life would not be possible. It is true that the plurality, impersonality and pace of urban life pose serious problems, but these have to be tackled. The way of return to a primary rural society is probably closed; one may have to look for an appropriate and optimum size for urban communities from the economic as well as socio-psychological point of view. There is a need for research on the relationship, if any, between city sizes and the emergent social, cultural and economic services available to the population as well as the associated criminal and other anti-social activities. It may well be that size alone is not a determinant, but size of a community is an important factor in the kinds of civic and social problems it has to tackle, the kind of services it can support and the patterns of varied cultural activities it can give rise to.

SIZE OF CITIES

It was mentioned above that even without direct encouragement the urban population in India would probably double in the next twenty years assuming a moderate 4 per cent increase per year. If so, the question is whether this additional population will just be added to the existing urban units or whether it will be absorbed, at least partially, in new urban centres. The answer depends upon whether the central and state governments are willing to formulate and act upon an overall policy of urbanisation. We have as yet no clear understanding of the many processes by which particular habitats grow into large aggregates of cities and towns. But, a policy for urbanisation would, among other things, have to address itself to the location and size of future centres of urban growth. Should the towns be between 20-50,000, between 51-99,000, between 1,00,000 and 10,00,000 or above 10,00,000? While there is not enough data to answer the question from the point of view of economic criteria, some of those who have written on the subject suggest that probably existing cities of between 50,000 and 5,00,000 provide the best choice as potential nuclei of further urban development.[4] The argument is that townships of smaller sizes with no initial infrastructure or totally new townships are likely to prove too expensive in terms of the economic outlays that would be required and, at the same time, cities of over 10,00,000 are inefficient in terms of the civic amenities that they can provide for further growth. The social costs in terms of poor housing, inter-community tensions, crime rates, etc., also begin to mount up in cities of a million and above. The developing countries still have a choice and they need not follow a model of industrialisation and urbanisation which depends heavily upon a few points of centralised production and the growth of multi-million size cities.

However, if existing cities, particularly those larger than 1,00,000, are to be chosen as nuclei of further growth, they may be found to be located largely in the already industrialised regions of the country. This would raise questions of equity in regional distribution of economic resources since organised expansion of cities can only be achieved by greater industrial and other investments which would increase their employment potential. If, on the other hand, urban nuclei with 50,000+ populations are chosen, they are likely to ensure a better distribution of urban development between different regions or states. The final choice of particular locations, however, will also be governed by availability of raw materials, skilled labour, location in terms of the regional or national transportation networks, etc. William Bredo[5] suggests that the communities selected should preferably contain some enterprises already operating successfully. Their presence would indicate the existence of a tested market and also the availability of some local entrepreneurship. Additional factors to be looked for in the selection of urban locations are the existence of schools, colleges, vocational training centres, well-developed banking and credit facilities, etc. Based upon these considerations, he would suggest an economic strategy of "phased penetration of less developed areas".

One implication of adopting such a strategy may be that at least initially the better developed areas will benefit more than the less developed. A conscious attempt would, therefore, have to be made at modifying these criteria to ensure a more balanced growth. Some of this will result from the natural distribution of raw material resources. Heavy industries, which are based upon ready availability of various types of ores, should be located in or near the ore-sites so that savings on transportation may compensate partially for the extra investments on social overheads that will be necessary in these locations. In India, most of the ore-sites lie further away from the earlier established industrial, commercial and port-based activities.

NEED FOR COORDINATION

If a relatively even distribution of urban populations is considered desirable, it can only be achieved by a well-coordinated policy of industrialisation which takes note of regional, state and sub-regional needs and potentialities. It will also require the development of a properly articulated plan of road and rail-road transportation network for people and commodities. There are obvious difficulties in the way of integration of goals and coordination of planning activity in a large federal polity. Conflict of national, state and local goals often interferes with measures of coordination. Sometimes, even if the same political party is ruling at different levels of the political hierarchy, the leaders at these levels would be subject to different kinds of pressures. Yet, in spite of these difficulties, inter-agency and inter-strata coordination is necessary if effective planning and implementation of a country-wide programme of urbanisation is to be possible. Pitambar Pant[6] makes this point effectively when he says: "A positive approach is necessary to foster agriculture and industry, power and transport, and distribution and density of urban centres in a spatial pattern so as to achieve the optimum results in relation to the social and economic goals of the society."

Balanced urbanisation cannot be achieved unless it is made a matter of deliberate state policy. In the absence of such a policy, the tendency is for large cities to grow larger. They tend to attract capital and to create effective demands for social services of varied types. These facilities in turn attract more people. But all the time that the process of expansion goes on it is accompanied by an increase in land costs, costs of housing, costs of transportation and therefore costs of the variety of services that the community needs. Well-distributed urban growth is, therefore, beneficial not only for the less developed regions but also for the populations in existing metropolitan complexes since it helps limit the increase in their cost of living. There is however no way in which the migration of rural people to large urban areas could be stopped through recourse to law. This would be neither practicable nor constitutionally valid. The only strategy the governments can adopt is to provide wider options to the townward migrants. One has to assume in the case of a vast majority of unskilled workers, that they would prefer spatially and culturally 'nearer' cities to far-away centres for purposes of migration.

GRADED DEVELOPMENT

Much of the discussion above is based upon urbanisation as it subserves the function of industrial growth. But towns and cities---not necessarily of metropolitan dimension—also serve other important functions. For example, many of the district and tehsil towns have developed round governmental, administrative and judicial functions. They have been chosen either for their central location or for historical reasons of their already having served as seats of political authority, or for their being conveniently located along road networks. Some of the other cities have grown as university towns and education centres. These various functions must be identified and urban units of different sizes developed to serve these functions. Usually, the larger size cities meet a multiplicity of such social, economic and political functions. But, the concept of a graded development of towns and cities should form a part of the strategy of urbanisation. If such a concept is adopted, it can serve as a basis for a programme of developing new townships which can be so located that they criss-cross the major corridors of urban and industrial growth which link the large metropolitan communities.

At the other end, urban policy must also be linked with a policy of rural development. Employment opportunities in the rural areas must be improved through intensive agricultural development and development of cottage industries, animal husbandry, sheep rearing, etc. Some of these agricultural programmes—as for instance, the breeding of hybrid seed varieties—are highly labour-intensive and can help check the flow of workers to urban areas. Equally important are developmental programmes which improve social amenities available in rural areas. If vocational education, health and recreational facilities of a reasonably good quality become available in the villages, some of the lure of the city will be diminished. Making villages more productive and attractive should be part of a policy regulating urban migration. As the quality of services in the rural areas improves, even the migrant who moves to urban areas will be a more skilled person and he will not have to enter the urban employment market at the lowest rung of the occupational ladder. He is still better equipped to make the adjustment to urban life. A rural development policy will thus not only check urban migration but also help improve the quality of urban life itself.

LAND PRICES

A positive policy on urbanisation will have to find ways in which the price of land in urban areas can be checked. Land is by far the most important and also the least flexible of the basic resources needed for urbanisation. People who move to city have to live and work on land and as the population increases, there is a greater and greater demand for land in and near the business and commercial districts. This leads to speculation in land prices by individuals who can afford to purchase land while it is still cheap and wait until the demand for their land goes up simultaneously raising the price level. This affects the cost of building since the cost of land in urban areas is a very important part of the total cost of adding to existing housing or work space. This leads to a rise in house rents upto a point where a majority of the population is ill-housed in terms of space, structure as well as municipal amenities.

Various measures have been thought of to abolish land speculation and to control the price rise in urban land. The socialist countries have nationalised urban land in the same way as they nationalised agriculture by introducing collective farms. This has given the state and its planning agency complete freedom from speculative pressures, though even in their case there are still constraints imposed by the size of the population to be accommodated, since no country can allow unlimited areas of land to be diverted from other uses to urban settlement and also by the necessity to minimise distances between work places and places of residence.

However, outright nationalisation of land without compensation is not possible in non-socialist economies. The options available to them take various forms of control of land use patterns, direct control and limitation of land price, ceiling on urban land property, and, where possible, outright purchase of land at 'ruling prices'. The last of these gives the greatest freedom to the planner, but this option cannot be utilised to any advantage unless decisions on location of urban sites or on expansion of particular towns and cities are taken ahead of time and before agricultural land is allowed to be used for non-agricultural purposes. Pre-emptive action on the part of urban planning authorities is essential if through land acquisition the cost of constructing or expanding a city is to be minimised.

Another set of measures for controlling speculation in land prices would be to impose ceilings on ownership of urban property and simultaneously devise a city tax structure which serves as a disincentive against wasteful use of land and built up space in large apartments and independent bungalows for the use of the wealthy minority. Direct regulation of land prices and housing rents usually fails because of the operation of black market mechanisms. Even land and property ceilings or graded taxes on urban built up space can serve no useful purpose if the bureaucracy itself is corrupt.

HOUSING THE POOR

Apart from a land price regulation another important area of any national policy on urbanisation is the housing of the poor. To some extent control over land prices will help minimise costs on housing programmes. However, every planner learns fairly early in his exercises that there is a minimum income level for each country below which a household cannot be given any kind of built-up accommodation, unless this is done by resorting to heavy subsidies. It has been calculated for Bombay that if every household in the city were to be provided even a single room as housing accommodation, the costs involved would run into several hundred million rupees for initial construction and that since the residents would not be able to pay what would be considered economic rents, the annual subsidy for servicing loans and maintenance would have to be a few score million rupees.[7] Alfred P. Van Huyck[8] comes to the same conclusion based on his Calcutta experience when he says: "... there is a housing threshold: a point along the income distribution curve below which it is not possible to provide housing, either publicly or privately, on a massive scale commensurate with the needs at any reasonable set of 'minimum' standards."

A Policy of Moderated Standards

This realisation has led urban planners in India to accept the fact that probably the lowest 20 per cent of the metropolitan population that live in hutments, squatter's colonies or on pavements cannot in the immediate future be provided with any structure using brick, cement and steel, because at their income levels they cannot pay even highly subsidised rents. This has led to reconsideration of the appropriateness of accepting internationally specified or otherwise arbitrarily set 'minimum' standards. It is now argued that for the lowest one-fifth of the metropolitan income groups it may be necessary to accept a standard whereby each household is given a developed plot with a built plinth on which the occupant can build such a structure as he can afford—either in bamboo and mud, mud-brick, used corrugated sheet, processed paper or any other material that is available. The structure may be temporary but it can be improved as and when the householder can afford it. Such marked-out and developed sites will be provided with common water taps, streetlights and toilets on a community basis. The lanes will be paved and gutters will be built to provide draining of storm water as well as the waste water from the housesites.

Another answer to the problems of low-income housing may be the concept of "an *urban village,* a place with fixed boundaries, speaking one mother tongue and holding to the same general set of customs."[9] Though visualised primarily as an environment for the new inmigrants, it could also serve the more generalised purpose of housing the low income groups in metropolitan cities. Such villages would have to be subsidised in their services and the level of living of the population of these villages would be close to subsistence. The village would have one bazar, one clinic, one station on the transit, several primary schools and some common bath and wash facilities.

These seem eminently sensible solutions, for no society can provide services which it cannot pay for. But, if this is true, then it should be equally true that a society which is committed to egalitarian values and to social justice should not allow gross inequalities to emerge in housing facilities for different sections of the population. Available resources must be used economically as well as equitably. If the living space available to the lowest income groups in society cannot be larger than 180 sq. ft. of unbuilt space, there can be no justification for any section of society being provided with 2,000-4,000 sq. ft. of built-up space in the form of luxury apartments or individual bungalows located in their own separate plots. Planning authorities would have to impose a discipline in terms of residential areas as well as the types of construction permitted to higher income groups. This they cannot do except in so far as a national housing policy exists which is binding on all urban authorities in different parts of the country.

Conserving Housing Stock

Such a national policy should also provide for the conservation and improvement of existing housing stock in any town or city. This will mean regular annual repair and maintenance of buildings and improvement in the civic facilities in the poor neighbourhoods. As at present public authorities generally accept such responsibility only in the case of government or authority-owned housing projects. Even in such projects the work is not done regularly and well. However, it is necessary to adopt a policy whereby all buildings—whether public owned or owned privately—are regarded as a national asset and kept in good repair. For this purpose, the private owners may be charged a suitable cess on their properties. Usually, the private owner who chafes under the fact that he cannot raise his rents because of the Rent Control Act, is content to leave the house in a state of disrepair and hope that some day the building will become unusable and the tenants will leave of their own accord. In the large metropolitan areas the land on which the building is located is worth much more than the old structure itself. The owner would be happy to demolish the house and rebuild it for a higher rent-paying client or sell the property at considerable profit if he were able to find a purchaser. A purchaser, however, wishes to obtain vacant possession of the property if he is to develop it for profit.

It is becoming increasingly clear that a policy which expects private entrepreneurs to provide the housing stock and still operate within a system of regulated rents is unworkable and only succeeds in giving rise to a variety of malpractices both on the part of the owners of buildings and the administrators who wield the regulatory powers. In socialist countries land and buildings are regarded as national assets and the construction of housing is not left to private initiative. In non-socialist countries a policy of direct and indirect controls is sought to be operated allowing scope for the operation of private capital. The contradiction of this policy is that private investment and profit are inconsistent with the fact that a majority of the population are unable to afford rents for decent housing. The only possible answer to the situation seems to be that public authorities adopt more realistic standards of adequacy of housing, take on the responsibility of constructing and/or operating housing stock for the middle and lower income groups, and rigorously control the use of land and built-up space by the well-to-do.

Another implication is that the whole programme of housing will have to be based on a policy of progressive improvement in housing conditions, particularly in relation to square feet area specification. As more resources become available in the future, it should be possible to add and expand the area made available to the individual tenant.

Capital Mobilisation for Housing

The problem of housing in a mixed economy hinges upon whether housing is regarded as an essential service to be made available to the individual citizen or as a commodity for sale with profit. This is a question that goes beyond housing and affects the whole area of urban planning. What is the overall policy of capital mobilisation for urban planning? Will it be mobilised through direct and indirect taxation by government or through the operation of the market and price mechanisms? If the market mechanism and profitability of investment are to be used for capital mobilisation, it follows logically that planning will have to be done to suit the preference, convenience and need of the better-paying clients and it may even pre-empt the poorer sections in the community, who incidentally are in overwhelming majority, from benefiting by such planning. The market mechanism is the one least suited to achieve egalitarian objectives or to solve equitably the dilemma faced by governments of choosing between their politically necessary commitments to the poor and their need to fall back on the capacity of the well-to-do to finance their well intentioned projects.

Yet, this is exactly the mechanism that comes into operation when urban planning authorities are asked to undertake development on the basis of a fixed revolving fund where the authority concerned must inevitably expect to make profits on sale or lease of developed land to finance further developmental activities. A mixed economy functions on the premise of a 'fair' profit, but if developed land is to be offered by auction to the highest bidder, then this bidder in his turn must price his product for the highest paying customer. Where incomes are distributed within a small range of variation, this mechanism creates no major problems but in countries where the disparities are large and where the small well-to-do groups follow a life pattern based on wasteful, conspicuous consumption, the interests of the poor get sacrificed. This is reflected in differential qualities of housing, education, health and transportation services available to persons belonging to different income groups. It is reflected even in the quality of the surfacing of roads and the maintenance of civic services in the different parts of the city. Such a high degree of differentiation, under certain conditions, can give rise to social tensions which may express themselves, at the individual level, in varied forms of alienation, impotent resentment, and socially deviant behaviour and at the group level, in agitations, inter-group rioting and organised violence. It is difficult to calculate the exact costs of such phenomena but undoubtedly they must result in higher direct costs through arson and destruction of public property, in higher costs on police and internal security and in indirect costs of loss of social motivation and productivity. All these interfere with the overall progress in social development.

ENVIRONMENTAL PROTECTION

The fight against environmental pollution is another aspect of a policy on urbanisation where some decisions need to be taken at the national level. Local authorities cannot or may not wish to tackle pollution which arises from sources outside their jurisdiction or whose consequences do not have to be borne by the local population. The pollution of water streams, rivers and coastal waters belong to such a category where the local authority may either be a helpless victim or an indifferent culprit. It is necessary in such areas to have a national and state policy as well as enforcement authorities to make pollution control effective.

To the extent that industry is 'decentralised' the problem of controlling pollution within the limits of tolerance may be made less intractable, but industry is not the only source of pollution. It has been found that automobiles and city buses are an equally dangerous pollution source. This may imply on the one hand development of technologies which ensure more complete combustion of the fuels used in the engines but on the other it may also mean that cities would have to adopt patterns of habitation and systems of transport which reduce the number of vehicles on the road.

Apart from decentralisation or dispersed location of industrial units, it is equally necessary to develop the recycling and reuse technology to minimise the problem of pollution. Cities are now facing not only the problem of air and water pollutions, but also of pollution arising out of the problems of garbage and trash disposal, including the disposal of paper, plastics, glass and metal.

CITY TRANSPORT

Transportation in cities is another important area in which national decisions would have to be taken. It seems unjustifiable on economic as well as environmental consideration that developing countries should plan a road system based upon the use of the private car. The transportation system should be based on the use of buses or city railway network which can carry large number of passengers per vehicle, limit the hazards of environmental pollution and have the advantage of requiring much smaller initial capital outlays than any other system of public transport. Buses are not the cheapest mode of mass transport, but a subway or a suburban railway system involves huge initial outlays which cannot be justified except in the case of multi-million cities. Buses have also the disadvantage of being slower than railways, but if use of buses is combined with the adoption of a system of reserved tracks, the net time taken by the vehicle to cover distance between any two points can be considerably reduced. A decision to use buses and to discourage private cars would also reduce traffic congestion on the roads. A national decision on transport patterns is necessary because then it can be supported by a policy of partial transfer of the potential individual industrial units from the manufacture of private cars to the manufacture of various types of heavy and light chassis for buses.

The smaller cities of less than one million inhabitants would also permit the use of bicycles by a section of the working and school-going population. The design of the city should plan for such movement and provide special lanes along the roads and streets which connect housing areas and schools or workplaces.

URBAN FINANCE AND URBAN GOVERNMENT

A national policy on urbanisation would have to lay down the sources of revenue that urban local bodies can tap. Most municipal authorities have found it impossible to meet the increasing demand for municipal services resulting from increasing townward migration. The population that is added to the town or city every year is not the population that is likely to add to the municipal revenues, though their need for services is the same as that of the other sections of the population. They need increased financial assistance from government since the taxes on property, professions, vehicles, animals, drainage and fire protection are wholly inadequate and non-expanding sources of revenue under conditions of a growing influx of the poor.

While the urban poor make no addition to municipal revenues, they are fairly well organised to exercise political pressures to obtain at least some of the services that the city can give. The present form of municipal government is not suited to develop among the poor any sense of commitment to the city or responsibility for the proper maintenance of municipal facilities. A new structure of urban government, which involves the members of local communities in a more constructive relationship with the municipal authorities, is necessary. Such a structure would have to provide for mohalla and ward level representative bodies with defined functions. This might on the one hand enable the local residents to get better municipal services and also at the same time require the local residents to adopt more positive and participatory attitudes toward the solution of urban problems.

NEED FOR RESEARCH AND TRAINING

Urban planning will need several types of support at the national level. Research on roads, transportation, housing materials and designs, as well as on problems of pollution and technology for their control cannot be undertaken at the level of local authorities. National governments may have to promote and support such research and also indicate the options and norms that could be adopted by local planning authorities for their purpose. Equally important is the need for training and research in integrated urban planning in all its aspects---physical, economic, social, political, legal and administrative. Urban planning has often been looked at exclusively from the physical point of view. This is, in a way, natural since it seems to be concerned with allocation of space, housing and transportation. But, we now know that even if urban planning were only concerned with these areas (which is not the case), decisions on them involve basic questions of resource allocation, social values, political processes and administrative skills.

In underdeveloped countries where local authorities are poor, the national governments and financing institutions may also have to play an important role in providing loans and credits for making urban planning possible and effective. This is particularly necessary if the planning authorities are not to become completely dependent upon private investment and speculative market mechanisms for achieving their goals.

This chapter has attempted to discuss four or five of the issues of urban planning on which a national policy is necessary if urban planning is to serve the interests of social development. There are several other issues on which decisions have to be made at the level of the individual town or city and some of these will be discussed in the next chapter.

Notes

1. United Nations, 1971, "Housing, Building and Urban and Physical Planning", *1970 Report on the World Social Situation*, Ch. XII.
2. Ibid., p. 5.
3. Calculated from estimates contained in the *UN 1970 Report on the World Social Situation*, ibid., p. 151.
4. Britain Harris, "Urban Living Conditions, Overhead Costs and Development Patterns" in Roy Turner, ed., *India's Urban Future,* Bombay: Oxford University Press, 1962.
5. William Bredo, "Industrial Decentralisation in India" in Roy Turner, ed., ibid.
6. Pitambar Pant, "Urbanisation and a Long-Range Strategy" in Roy Turner, ed., *Urban Future*, ibid.
7. P. Ramchandran, *Social and Economic Rents*, Bombay: Tata Institute of Social Sciences, 1967.
8. Alfred P. Van Huyck, "The Housing Threshold for Lowest-Income Groups: The Case of India" in Herbert, I. D. and Van Huyck, A. P., eds., *Urban Planning in the Developing Countries*, New York: Frederick A. Praeger Inc., 1968.
9. Richard L. Meier, "The Design of Very Large Cities" in Roy Turner, ed., op. cit., pp. 299-323.

5

Urban Planning and Some Questions of Social Policy

SCOPE OF URBAN PLANNING

Urban planning has to be viewed in a local as well as a regional and a national context. There are some policy issues on which decisions need to be taken at the national or regional level and others which can be attended to by the local planning authority for a particular city. Questions relating to rural-urban migration, capital mobilisation for urban development, the laying down of the major social goals sought to be achieved through urbanisation and the need for close articulation between industrial location policies and urban development policies at the national, regional and local levels are areas in which the initiative rests primarily with the national and state governments. The local planning authorities have to work within the constraints imposed by the definition or lack of definition of these policies at the higher levels.

This chapter, which substantially incorporates an earlier paper under the same title[1] that I had written on the subject, will discuss some of the social policy issues that arise in urban development planning at the level of the planning authority of a large metropolitan city. Urban planning is concerned with such

---

Theme of a staff-student seminar held at the United College, Chinese University of Hong Kong on February 21, 1973.

physical activities as land development, road laying, laying out parks, developing systems of water and power supply, drainage, trash and garbage disposal and disposal of excreta; it is also concerned with developing policies for allocating land for different uses, with developing systems of control on housing densities and land coverage; and, in the planning of new towns and cities, it has also to define some policies in relation to school and health facilities. All these activities and policies involve choices between various options and these choices are governed partly by technological considerations and partly by certain explicit or implicit value premises. The very act of planning involves acceptance of the legitimacy of state or societal action in the pursuit of certain state approved goals in preference to action by individuals in pursuit of their individual interests and goals. Depending upon the political structure these state-defined goals may receive more or less acceptance and support from the citizenry. The urban planner should seek to provide a physical and social environment in which individuals and groups develop their own style of life depending upon their abilities, means and preferences. But, the physical and social plans, by their very nature, emphasise certain options rather than certain others and tend to define the opportunity structure for their inhabitants to develop infrastructures on which they can develop their own types of housing structures or live their own styles of life outside the home.

LAND ACQUISITION

Urban planning authorities face usually two different situations: one, wherein they are trying to solve or mitigate the problems of an existing metropolitan community which has already been ravaged by overcrowding, unplanned and unauthorised growth of housing and habitation in what were earlier fringe or suburban areas, and the overstretching of its power and water resources. Here, the options available to the planner are severely limited and he is often required to fall in line with the policy decisions that have already been made, and where a change of policy is required he may have to work patiently to bring about such a change over a period of time. Even if a change is effected it can only be useful in future physical planning since it takes much more effort, time and money to modify existing physical layouts. But, all programmes of urban renewal involve such changes in physical layouts and structures.

The other situation is where he is asked to plan a city in an entirely new location. His options are still open except in so far as he is subject to the same overall national policies and the greater or less availability of total natural resources.

In both the situations, the planner has to begin by finding or acquiring the land where the new urban community or extensions of the existing one will be located and in both cases the question of compensating the original occupants of that land arises. Land acquisition raises some important questions of policy. How should the occupants be compensated? Should they be compensated in money or by being provided with alternative sites? Should they be paid at the market price or at a price considered adequate by government? Should the purchase be effected gradually as and when the necessity arises and the funds for purchase become available or should the intent of purchase be notified at one point of time and the prices of land be frozen even though the actual purchase may still be done within a defined span of time? The answers to these questions will in each case tend to favour either the occupant-owners or the public authority. They cannot be given in isolation and must depend upon an overall approach to such questions in defining national policies. A gradual purchase of land in the open market at market prices will inevitably benefit the owner-occupant in a period of ascending prices and raise the costs of development of land for the planning authority. This, in turn, will adversely affect the people who will later be housed in the new tenements.

Often, in old cities, purchase of dilapidated structures for purposes of road widening, social housing or urban renewal involves the displacement of poor tenants. These tenants do not share in the appreciated land value that has been paid to the owner and yet they will be required to pay higher rents when they are shifted to alternative locations.

The tenants are, as a rule, unwilling to vacate their dwellings and this poses a problem to urban planning and civic authorities. Programmes of urban renewal may be required to accept the claims of local populations to compensation, subsidy, and alternative accommodation at rents not very much higher than those justified by the better amenities provided.

One way of checking the inflationary spiral set up by speculation in land prices may be to make available the land acquired from agriculturists by the planning authorities of new towns to private builders only on lease holds and not as outright purchases. If the lease-holder wishes to terminate his lease, the first option for reacquiring the land may be exercised by the planning authority. Even this will not completely check the rise in land prices so long as the planning authority is itself subject to the operation of market forces for raising its own capital resources for further development. This is likely to make it impossible for them to provide land for housing the poor on any basis of equity or consideration of their needs. Even cities planned by governmental authorities start with the premise that they can give no more than 180 to 200 sq. ft. of space per household of the low-income category.

The other alternative would be to treat land and housing as an essential commodity and make it available to the people on the basis of their needs. But, this is a major question of policy which affects not one city, but all cities and not only land and housing but also the operation of the national economy and policy as a whole.

REHABILITATIVE SERVICES

As mentioned earlier, when old properties are acquired by planning bodies in a city, the problem of rehabilitating the original residents arises. This problem arises in a somewhat different form even in the case of purchase of new land from agriculturists in the rural areas. When an existing city expands its borders or a new city is sought to be located in an erstwhile rural zone, the problem of rehabilitating displaced owners and tillers of the soil has to be tackled. The problem is particularly severe in the case of the non-landowning agricultural workers who receive no monetary compensation and who have none of the skills required for settling down as part of the urban work force. But, in both the cases, the problem is not of finding new homesites, so much as finding alternative vocations for the rural workers who may have been engaged in agriculture or in cottage industry. It is necessary that the planning body should adopt an active programme of vocational training, occupational and business loans, and compensatory payments in small portions of developed land to help the original village residents enter the urban economy with some assets instead of entering the labour force as unskilled workers.

HOUSING

Housing is the next major area of social policy as it affects urban planning. It has been indicated above that the problem of housing the poor in urban areas cannot be tackled with any hope of success unless a basic change in our approach to housing takes place. But, it should also be clear that even if government were to adopt a policy of rationing housing space on an equitable basis, it is unlikely that with the total resources currently available to the developing countries they can provide satisfactory housing conditions for all their population.

This has led planning bodies to adopt two types of solutions. On the one hand, the earlier emphasis on slum clearance as a major programme of housing improvement has been abandoned. In its place, the more modest programme of slum improvement is being adopted. This involves primarily housing repairs, strengthening of structures, and the provision of certain civic amenities and the laying down of roads and drainage facilities where these do not exist. At the same time, in the new cities that are being planned, an effort can be made to develop well-serviced, open housing sites which can be allotted to those who cannot afford regular housing. The allottees will then be allowed to build according to their needs and abilities, and add and improve their dwellings as their monetary conditions improve. As already stated, the sites so marked out are small and the housing built on these sites can hardly provide privacy to the individual dweller. On the other hand, the community facilities provided for such neighbourhoods can be considerably better. These can include not only water, lighting, roads and sanitation but also services such as school, community centre, etc.

Since about a sixth of the population of Indian cities can look forward to housing of no better standard than the one indicated above and since a majority of even the rest will probably live only in one-room accommodation for most of their lives, a question arises whether the cityward movement of people should be encouraged at all. The fact, however, is that even if no steps are taken to encourage cityward migration, it will continue to take place until better employment opportunities are available in the villages or at midway locations between the village and the city. While these opportunities develop, cities will have to accept and learn to cope with these problems. The alternative solution of 'fencing off' the cities and preventing the villagers from the migrating to cities is not available under law and would be difficult to administer.

There are one or two other questions of social policy in relation to housing the poor in urban areas. One of these relates to the location of poor housing. Should the sites for housing the poor be separated from the other groups or should they be intermixed with other sections of the population? Observation of the distribution of houses of poor persons in our cities suggests that they live intermingled with most other segments of the population. They need to live where they can find work to do. They work as load-bearers, cobblers, daily wage workers, small shopkeepers selling *bidis*, cigarettes and *paan*, vegetable sellers, vendors of sweets and other inexpensive eatables for children, and, occasionally, they earn their living by begging. They cannot spend on transportation and prefer to live near their work. Their work is spread throughout the city—at railway stations, vegetable markets, bus depots, new housing sites and even in high-income, exclusive residential areas where the domestic servants of the well-to-do are their clients. The presence of shanty towns in the midst of middle class and posh localities hurts the aesthetic sensibilities of some. But, the city depends upon them—upon their cheap labour. The road-makers and the building contractors would not be able to function if the readily available supply of unskilled, low-paid labour were not available to them.

The use of the phrase 'urban poor' as a distinct category is deceptive. The urban poor consist of several categories if one is to judge their poverty by their housing conditions. There are those who live in ill-maintained, ill-served, overcrowded permanent structures built by public authorities; there are others who live in hutments and shanty towns; and finally there are those who live on footpaths, under porches and awnings. Together they constitute well over half of the city populations in developing countries. So, the question, where their housesites should be located, is somewhat odd and displays a curious sense of proprietary rights over the city on the part of the white-collared minority.

COMMUNITY PATTERNS

In the allocation of sites a planning authority has to ensure that all sections of the population have easy access to open sites, beaches and promenades. It is also important that land uses should be so planned that work journeys do not take inordinate time or prove expensive for the majority. A city may be so planned that it can be divided into segments or relatively self-sufficient townships or communities and neighbourhood clusters. Schooling, primary health facilities, shopping centres, playgrounds and recreation facilities should be available within easy walking distance. These might provide for the development of neighbourly contacts and a sense of community to people using common facilities. If the communities are planned in units of, say, 50,000 and with smaller neighbourhood units of 7,000-8,000, it may be possible to accommodate within them even multilingual communities and still meet their diverse needs. For example, of the six or seven primary schools that such a community can support, one school or the other can provide instruction in the language desired by a particular segment of the population. The small neighbourhoods can be unilingual clusters, but the community will be multilingual. The city planner will not, of course, do anything to deliberately influence community composition, but in a metropolitan complex in India the existence of multilingual groups has to be taken into account.

While the communities should be relatively self-sufficient in meeting their health, education and shopping needs, they should not be isolated from other similar communities. The advantage of large urban aggregates is that they provide for a variety of choices in friends, occupational interests, educational facilities, types of entertainment and even choice in individualised forms of religious affiliation. Development of completely isolated communities would defeat this purpose.

Cheap and efficient communication and transport linking these communities is an essential condition for the emergence of the urban form. A rapid transit facility will enable a person living in one part of the city to go to another to visit a friend, see a movie, enjoy a picnic, study in a public library, attend a concert or a circus, and still return to the security and comfort of home the same evening. High densities, diversity of opportunities, a variety of choices in interpersonal relationships, the rapid pace of life, the feeling that you are close to events are unique aspects of metropolitan life. They depend upon the telephone, the mass media, the rapid transit system and other means of communication of persons and ideas.

Efforts must be made to ensure that the common man has a share in the experience of city life as much as do the elite. In its absence, the common man, particularly the poor and illiterate one, will remain alienated from the city. If he cannot reach these advantages and facilities of the city, the city must reach out to him through specially organised programmes and conscious efforts of planners in developing appropriate land allocation and land use policies.

The separation of the upper income from the middle income families takes two opposite forms as the city grows. In Bombay, the upper income households have adopted the high-rise, multi-storied structure in exclusive areas in the south of the city as their answer to shortage of land. The permitted floor-space index (FSI) in the most recently developed reclaimed land at Nariman Point is as high as 3.5. Luxury apartments are built in 16 to 25 storied buildings on land where, the annual lease value alone works out to as much as Rs. 800 per sq. metre. The middle and the lower middle class population is pushed out of the centre of the city further and further north into newly established and developed suburbs increasing their distance to work and depriving them of most cultural activities which are located in the central and southern portions of the city.

In New Delhi, the pattern adopted is one of a relatively low density development wherein upper income families live in ground and first floor bungalows located in spacious plots in the ever-extending new colonies to the south of the city. The overall pattern is diffuse. The middle income families also live in relatively low density colonies further away from the centre of the planned city which is occupied largely by government officers of the middle and higher levels of administration. The diffuse, low-density pattern of development without a good mass transit system has made inter-colony communication almost impossible except in the case of the car-owning upper income groups. Delhi and New Delhi, with a total urban population of approximately 36,47,000 occupies about 490 sq. kms of land as compared to Bombay with its 59,70,000 people accommodated in 480 sq. kms.

Segregation of housing areas in terms of income groups is also often accompanied by a differential standard of civic service maintenance in different areas. This involves a question of social policy. Those sections of the city where the affluent live are cleaner, have wider roads and may have better water and power facilities. The lower- and middle-income areas are inadequately served and receive less prompt attention. The usually high-density, poor class housing is the worst served in most cities because the inhabitants of those areas are unable to pay for municipal services. Many of these low-income habitations consist of an unplanned growth of hutments with no civic services to begin with. These services---drinking water supply, drainage and public toilets---come gradually as the community living in these areas turns into a vote-bank and can exercise some leverage on the municipal counsellors. A social policy which aims at distributive justice must ensure that basic civic amenities are related to needs and not only to the capacity to pay on the part of different segments of the population.

EDUCATION

In an urban industrial society, education is the major channel for upward mobility. In view of our emphasis on the value of equality we need to take all possible measures that would enable younger members in our society to take advantage of the facilities for education that the city is able to offer. This is true for rural areas as well. But, the problems of the urban areas impose certain special obligations and we may need to revise the minimum standards that we have set for ourselves in the propagation and spread of education in the country. Under the

Constitution of India, the government is committed to providing, as soon as possible, the facilities for compulsory, free, universal primary education. Primary education may be sufficient for the vast majority of the population in the rural areas and may meet their needs. In the urban areas, however, the completion of primary education does not equip a person to obtain a job which would assure him of a reasonable living and mobility in the occupational structure. We need to upgrade the minimal requirement from completion of primary education up to the age of 11 to compulsory free education up to the age of 14 or even the age of 16 in the urban areas.

Further, even the type of education provided for the age group between 14 and 18 years in the urban areas may have to be different. We may need to ensure that the young persons who do not plan to enter white-collared occupations have access to facilities of training in specific occupational and vocational skills suitable for urban areas. Vocational or technically-oriented education at the high school level is expensive and calls for major financial outlays. It is unlikely that private education societies, which today take the major responsibility for secondary education in urban areas, would be in a position to provide on their own, the needed facilities for technical education. The civic and state authorities would, therefore, have to undertake this responsibility either on their own or through an appropriate programme of financial assistance given to existing educational institutions.

Education for the Employed

Equally important in the area of education is the need to adopt a policy for providing continuing education to those who are already in jobs. Persons from lower income background are often under economic compulsion to discontinue schooling at an early stage and to take up jobs so that they can support themselves and their families. Some of those who are thus compelled to discontinue formal education at an early stage can benefit a great deal by opportunities to continue their education on a part-time basis, especially if they get the kind of education that is related to their work roles. Such continuing education would be useful in rural as well as urban areas, but it is particularly essential in urban areas because of the high rate of obsolescence in job skills in modern industry. Increasingly, as technological changes come faster and faster, we will need to provide an intensive programme of occupational training and of expanding the cognitive universe of a large body of our working population. The knowledge that they have gained in their schools, whether of a technical nature or a general character, will be found to be inadequate and would need refreshing if their efficiency as citizens as well as workers is to be maintained.

One of the major problems in devising an adequate educational policy relates to the goal of ensuring equality of opportunity. The provision of free education facilities at the school or even at the secondary and college levels is itself inadequate to equalise the opportunities between the children of the well-to-do and the children of the poor. Children from poor families are disadvantaged in many ways and are unable to derive benefit to any satisfactory degree from the facilities for education even when education is free. A major problem is the absence within the household of adult individuals who are educated and can serve as a model and a means of reinforcing the child's motivation to achieve in the area of education. Another problem is a lack of adequate room in their houses which they could use for study.

Civic authorities can do a great deal to overcome at least a few of the latter more obvious problems. It may be necessary to provide either in schools or residential areas separate study places where children can obtain both books and guidance in their school work. In some of the village secondary schools on the periphery of the city, the head masters have found it useful to encourage children in senior classes to return to school after their evening meals and spend the night there. This enables them to use the evening hours for study and also to gain guidance from teachers who take it upon themselves by turn to assist students in need of such assistance. In urban areas such facilities would be specially valuable. Many of the children of lower income groups come from homes where as many as six to eight persons, and sometimes even more, live and sleep in a single room. The opportunity to stay in the school and to use the school library would be a great help to them in their efforts to complete their education

Secondary vs. College Education

The provision of textbooks and an extension of the period of compulsory education from the primary to the middle or even to the secondary school would require the allocation of larger funds in urban areas. Educational authorities find it difficult to obtain these additional funds from governments in view of the fact that the constitutional obligation is limited at present to the primary education stage and even this minimal obligation has not been entirely fulfilled in most parts of the country. Against this background, the special problems of education of the urban poor may not appear very urgent. This may even raise a question of priority in educational planning. It is worth considering whether investments in strengthening secondary education will not bring better returns in comparison with the investment made on extending college education facilities for larger and larger numbers of students who do not seem to have a real interest in college education. One may find that in many cases those who complete their college education are not able to fully utilise the benefits of such an education. There may be a case for limiting the facilities for college and higher education only to those who are in a position to fully benefit by these opportunities. Increased expenditure on providing adequate facilities at the primary and secondary stages of education would justify itself in the greater skill and knowledge that workers would bring to their jobs. The policy of providing heavy subsidies to education at the college and university levels implies indirectly providing subsidies to higher income groups who are in a position to take care of their own needs more than members of the working class.

This does not mean that no public funds should be provided for university education, but it does imply that since such education cannot be undertaken except through large-scale state support, the government would be justified in ensuring that facilities for higher education are limited to those who are capable of fully benefitting from them and that these facilities are related to the nature and quantum of higher level employment likely to be created by the economy. If education at the secondary school level can be strengthened, it may be found that many of the employment positions that are at present occupied by college and university educated persons could be suitably filled by high school graduates or SSC passed individuals.

HEALTH

One of the first responsibilities of any civic authority in the area of health is the provision of pure water supply in adequate quantities for its population. In India, most of the municipalities are not able to guarantee a 24-hour supply of water and only very few of them provide filtered water. This imposes great hardships on all sections of the people, but again the worst affected are the poor. They are required to fetch their water from common taps and since the hours of supply are limited there are invariably quarrels about who will collect his water first. In any case they cannot get the necessary quantity of water supply required for washing, bathing and drinking purposes. For those sections of the poor who live in unauthorised hutments the problems are even greater. They may have no municipal water tap at all in the vicinity of where they live or even if a water connection has been provided, as often happens after an agitation and prior to a municipal election, the number of taps provided is even less adequate than in the case of the chawl or slum dwelling section of the poor.

The shortage of water inevitably implies the development of insanitary conditions. The toilets provided in the working class slums are of the flush type---the same as in other areas of the city---and they require several gallons of water for each cleaning operation. Since water is in short supply it results in clogged toilets which spread strong bad smell. There is a need for developing a type of toilet which does not require large quantities of water for use in urban areas.

Apart from supply of pure and protected water supply in adequate quantities, the two major problems faced by urban authorities in the area of health are of sanitation and the prevention of air and water pollutions. As a city grows in size and as the level of living of the common man rises, it is found that the sheer work of collecting trash and garbage and other wastes from the homes and disposing them of in a satisfactory manner presents a major challenge to urban administration. The problems of sewage collection and treatment, and of garbage collection and disposal call for a great deal of ingenuity and large financial outlays.

The danger of air and water pollutions in a rapidly industrialising society has only recently been appreciated. The liquid effluents and gaseous discharges of industry are major hazards to public health. Urban authorities are now required to take cognisance of them and to lay down procedures for their control to avoid a serious hazard to public health. Technology which has created these problems also offers solutions. It is now possible to treat most of the fluids in such a way that they are rendered harmless. However, there are many industries whose problems of pollution have not yet been successfully solved. In the planning of cities, it is, therefore, important to devise a policy about the location of such industries. The policy may lay down that the specified industries shall not be allowed to be located near major urban centres or even at points further away, where the liquid effluents are likely to pollute sources of water supply. It is equally important that public health authorities in major industrial centres set up a machinery to ensure that industries conform to such regulations.

It is usually the poorer income areas which are marked by insanitary environmental conditions rather than upper and middle class areas. The upper and middle class sections of the population can move away from highly polluted or otherwise insanitary areas and can travel down to their work. Their families and children are relatively protected from the ill-effects of pollution. But, the poorer sections of the population, who live near the work places, are exposed to the ill-effects of unregulated discharges and the inefficiency of sanitary services.

Medical care is another area of civic responsibility. Here, there is a great need for developing community-based preventive and promotive services, particularly for the children of the poor. They are usually brought to municipal dispensaries and hospitals for diseases which could easily have been prevented. An effective maternity and child health service and a coordinated school health service---at least in municipal schools where children of lower classes go---are essential for the prevention of disease as also for the promotion of positive health goals. If the school health service can include a programme of supplementary nutrition by way of snacks or school meals, it can help prevent the effects of undernutrition and malnutrition in the early years of life.

WELFARE SERVICES

Welfare services are devised specially to meet the needs of the more vulnerable sections of a community. By far the most obvious vulnerable group is the lower income group in every community. Poverty, in a country like India, is not the special characteristic of cities. It is common to rural as well as urban areas. But, the poverty of the cities takes on a special form and poses serious problems.

The urban poor live in the midst of affluence and the differences between the rich and the poor become glaringly visible in urban areas. The existence of shanty towns, hutment dwellings and dilapidated structures becomes a sharp contrast to the fashionable areas which are well served and where the affluent people of the city live. There is also a fact that the urban poor are much more conscious and articulate about the disadvantages they suffer from than are the rural poor. The working class movement and the role played by ideology and communication media make the urban poor conscious and resentful of their deprivations. While the urban individual, freed from extended kinship ties, enjoys a certain measure of autonomy and anonymity, he also experiences a greater sense of insecurity and a need to depend upon new group affiliations. The urban poor develop a culture of their own and may more consciously seek to organise themselves as an interest group which can bring pressure upon the civic authorities. The points of contact between the white-collar middle or the upper income groups and the lowest income groups in a city are limited to contacts at workplace. The social ties which link the poor and the well-to-do in rural areas are absent in cities. Because of the structural isolation of the poor from the well-to-do, the two view each other in terms of stereotypes and not in terms of their individual experiences of each other.

The city authorities which look upon the problem of housing merely in terms of certain set standards of minimal housing facilities forget that despite their insistence on minimum standards about one-sixth of the population of the city lives under conditions where they are not provided with water, electricity, lighting, roads or sanitary facilities. The conditions of life under which these people are forced to live constitute a danger to them as well as to the larger society from which they get alienated. The urban planner will have to devise a more intelligent social policy not only with reference to housing to which reference has already been made but also in relation to the problems of physical insecurity, juvenile delinquency, unguided childhood and the influence exercised by the anti-social elements in the community.

Community-based Services

Action to meet the needs of the poor usually takes two major forms in western countries: one is to provide economic assistance to raise or maintain their income levels at a certain accepted minimum and the other is to provide a set of direct services. In India, except for some initial steps toward the establishment of an insurance system for industrial workers, we have really no programmes which can be considered to be programmes of income maintenance for the low-income groups or the unemployed. Our approach has to meet some of the needs of the poor through provision of free services. The provision of free medical care through charitable dispensaries and hospitals and the provision of free education facilities at the primary and, now, the secondary levels are instances in point.

In the area of social welfare, there is no such commitment on the part of the government that most services are offered on an *ad hoc* basis. As it happens, these services exist, where they do, primarily in the urban areas. But, there is a need for the government and also for urban authorities to accept the provision of these services as a part of general policy.

Welfare services are organised in three ways. First, community-based services organised for the members of a residential community within the precincts of the community. These are largely services which have a preventive and promotional significance. Secondly, services offered by agencies which are available to persons irrespective of their residential location. And, thirdly, services organised in the form of residential institutions.

The community-based services face one problem. Should the community be identified purely in terms of residential location or should we take cognisance of different language and religious identities? It was noticed earlier that inevitably income groups do get separated by types of housing structures. This does not necessarily happen with reference to language and religious variations. In a formal sense, the answer is clear. A public finance service will have to be available commonly and equally to all groups. In practice, we may find that for a variety of reasons the services tend to get utilised more by one ethnic group rather than another. Also, at an informal level, the individual ethnic groups tend to develop their own systems of community linkages and services. What should be the relationship between the formal organisation based on universalistic principles and the smaller particularistic organisations? Should, and can, the latter be ignored? Should they be utilised? What are the implications of legitimising their status in the process of utilising them?

Coordinated Services

It is of great importance that the services offered by a civic authority in the areas of health, education and welfare are coordinated with each other. For the school-going population, the school is a convenient delivery point for child health services as well as recreational services. The school health service should liaise with community dispensaries and hospitals so that children with specific complaints are referred to them and receive prompt treatment. In the case of children found to be suffering from communicable diseases, the dispensary must contact the other members of the family and ensure that they are given a check up for the particular disease. Similarly, the school should be in touch with out-of-school programmes of recreation for children. Coordination between the various services offered in the community will ensure that the population is adequately covered. This is particularly essential in the case of the illiterate sections of the urban population, but it is useful even otherwise. A programme of coordinated, community-based services may help ensure adequate coverage and fuller utilisation of the services.

COMMUNITY PARTICIPATION

In organising community-based services considerable importance has to be attached to the principle of autonomy and self-reliance. The present civic structure, under which the participation of the local community is limited to the process of voting during a municipal election, is not suited to the management of local community problems. A modified structure which gives the opportunity to the local community for association with the operation of some of the services would help in making administration more responsible to popular opinion and would bring the decision-making process closer to the people. In devising this modified structure care will have to be taken to ensure that the overriding authority of the elected body at the city level is not impaired. But, within this limit, the local community should have a say in the manner of operation of particular services at the local level.

This modified structure may also be useful in developing additional social and welfare services which are not a part of the normal responsibilities of a municipality or corporation. Such additional services can be developed with some measure of local financial support—even if the support may be nominal in the very poor localities. Creches and pre-school activities for children, adult education, school support programmes of organised study, reading rooms and libraries are some examples of the kinds of services that can be developed at the local level with local support.

The creation of committees at the local level can give rise to some political pressures on local issues. This is not undesirable in itself, but the local committees should not be visualised as constituent units of the municipal structure. They should remain as consultative bodies so far as the normal municipal functions are concerned, but they should have organisational and supervisory responsibility for the extra-municipal services organised with local support.

Another aspect of welfare services which poses a problem of planning and policy is the fact that since many of these services---for example, services for the physically or mentally handicapped individuals—are not available outside metropolitan areas, the urban welfare services have to provide not only to serve the local population but also the population in the mofussil and rural areas. This is a strain on locally available resources. Since it would be undesirable and also impractical to restrict these services only to local residents, state and central governments must aid these institutions and equip them to meet the additional and sometimes specialised demands of a varied client population. The variation is not only in terms of the type of problem to be handled but also in the social background of the client population. Residential institutions for children, for example, would need to provide instruction in more than one language, since children in institutions come from different states. Hospitals which get rural patients must provide facilities for temporary residence for the relatives who accompany the patients to the city.

In this chapter, we have not attempted to list or describe all the services needed by the urban population. Its object was to consider some of the questions of social policy that face the urban planner in the provision of physical facilities and social services for the residents of the city. In this effort I have reviewed some of the problems of policy relating to land acquisition, housing, neighbourhood planning, and the development of social and welfare services.

Note

1. *Political and Economic Weekly*, Vol. VI, Nos. 30-32, July 1971, pp. 1619-26.

6

The State, the Police and the People

The police as an organisation were created to prevent and detect crime and to bring the criminal to book. Through this process it was thought the police would help to enforce the law and establish order in society. Even in this simple formulation it is assumed that there is law, a legal order, as different from the whim of the ruler whether such a ruler was a king or an oligarchy or a representative government. Obviously, the relationship between the police and the ruling authority would be different under each of these types of government but the common assumption would be that the police while they enforce the law are not a law unto themselves nor are they merely the tools of the ruler or the government of the day in enforcing their will or serving their particular interests. The police work under the supervision of the government of the day and they are a machinery to serve the interests of the state and not those of a particular government. This distinction between law of the land and the will of the ruler had come to be established, though tenuously, even under monarchies as can be seen from the fact that an important characteristic of a 'just' ruler was that the ruler accepted that he was as much subject to the authority of law as a common citizen. But, this distinction had not evolved fully and the line between law and the will of

---

Text of the Ninth IB Centenary Endowment Lecture, delivered on 23 December 1996.

the ruler was often thin. In the modern state which recognises the civil rights of the citizen, even the authority of the state to promulgate laws is limited by the concept that beyond a point the person and the property of the citizen remain inviolable and, except in times of a recognised or declared state of emergency the rights of the citizen shall not be infringed upon. Thus, the existence of law and conformity to the due process of law in the performance of their duties is expected of the police in a modern democratic state.

Yet, even in the democratic state, the role of the police as the agency for maintenance of order is a difficult one because order in society depends not so much on the use of force as on the existence of a measure of consensus in society on the objectives as well as the form of governance. The dictum that democracy is a government of the people, for the people and by the people, is in some ways rather simplistic. A democracy is not merely a rule by the majority. Democracy seems to assume that despite differences the people of a modern state are united in their interests and that such differences as exist can be resolved by a process of reason and discussion and, ultimately, by the principle of the rule of majority. In actual fact, however, the people of a country, though they may agree on the objectives and form of government, are rarely agreed on specific policies and programmes. And, if they are agreed on the programmes, they are not agreed on the manner of implementation. They are divided by their interests and by their identities as individuals and as members of sub-groups. The interests are often economic or political or those of group identity and may get organised on regional, linguistic, caste, or religion lines. While the objective of the state is to ensure the well-being of all its people, this well-being is not an undifferentiated common entity or an experience shared equally by all. The search for well-being often involves competition and conflict between people and pitches individuals and groups against one another. The nation-state is often united only against its enemies, but it is expected to be united in its broad objectives, the values and means of pursuing these objectives in an otherwise highly differentiated and in some ways divided society in the pursuit of individual or group interests of its members. These internal divisions and differences are reflected in their primary and secondary group affiliations. Political parties are one expression of these different affiliations and interest groups within society.

So long as the parties are willing to negotiate their different interests and objectives within the framework of the constitution and the laws, there are likely to be no major problems of order in society though there will always be problems of individual or group crime and of forces straining to subvert law to their individual ends. But such willingness to negotiate differences within a framework requires a firm commitment to political means and modalities. The question is whether a given nation shows evidence of such a commitment. In the absence of such commitment no amount of force can ensure order and the police will have an unenviable task confronting them.

In our own country the adoption of a democratic constitution guaranteeing fundamental rights to all citizens, irrespective of caste, creed or region, and stating the directive principles of state policy was a major achievement coming as it did after the holocaust of partition. There were differences and debates about the national language, the distribution of subjects between the centre and the states, the personal law that should apply to the citizens, the relationship between the union and the erstwhile princely states, the extent to which the right to private property should be protected, the rights of minorities, the type of protective discrimination that should be provided to the scheduled castes and scheduled tribes, the meaning of secularism, and a host of other subjects. But, under the leadership of Nehru and Patel and driven largely by the liberal ideology of the middle classes represented in the Constituent Assembly at that time, a constitution was adopted with a parliamentary form of government at the centre and in the states, conforming broadly to the British parliamentary procedures for transaction of business in the legislatures.

At the time of its adoption the Constitution of India seemed to enshrine above all a consensus on the creation of a new nation-state committed to usher in a democratic, secular social order characterised by equity and social justice. This consensus has, I believe, largely survived the happenings of the past 49 years but not without some challenges to it? We will consider the nature of these challenges and the role that they have thrust on the police from time to time.

The first challenge was to the integrity of India as a nation. First in the north-east in what was then called the NEFA region and later, much later, in Punjab separatist demands arose. (I am not mentioning here the problem of Kashmir because in many ways it is a problem in its own category.) After years of unrest and the creation of several states within the union in the north-eastern region the problem of the north-east has been largely met though not completely solved. During this entire period, the police organisation, including the BSF and the CRP, was under considerable stress. The BSF, of course, is a semi-military formation created to help guard the national border, but even the state police, the state reserve police and the CRP had to engage in operations which involved continuous confrontation with segments of the civil population and had to enforce law through the use of armed force. This task went much beyond the traditional concept of the police role as a law enforcement agency.

The second challenge was when, beginning with Andhra, the whole question of linguistic reorganisation of states arose and was sought to be tackled initially as a law and order problem rather than as a demand that could be tackled through democratic procedures or through consultations. Until the States Reorganisation Commission was appointed and again until after its recommendations were partially modified, there was considerable civil strife and the police had to be used as a repressive agency in many inter-state boundary areas.

The second challenge was in one sense more serious for the establishment and consolidation of democratic procedures because when the integrity of the nation was challenged as in the first case the sympathies of the civil society were with the government unlike in the second case where the sentiments of sections of the civil society were themselves questioned and the government failed to handle them through normal democratic procedures with only a marginal use of force.

The third and to my mind the most serious challenge to the consolidation of democracy within India has arisen in the unwillingness or inability of political parties to conform to democratic practice internally and even in the manner they function within the formal structures of legislatures. That many of our major political parties have had no elections to their decision-making bodies for years together is a well-known fact. What is worse those who are elected to legislatures do not often seem willing to accept the normal parliamentary procedures for the conduct of business. While it may be an effective way of expression of dissent by the minority in a legislature to walk out in protest against a majority view where basic issues are involved, it loses its moral force when it is used too often and members of an opposition refuse to stay and register their negative vote on important issues. Also, when members of legislatures -- sometimes even factions within a ruling party – exchange blows within the house, their behaviour cannot be said to contribute to the strengthening of democratic practice. Even the recent proceedings within the Lok Sabha during the passing of the vote of confidence in the successive governments were not particularly edifying though they may have been unwittingly educative for the common man.

But real problems of law and order were created in the political process when in their anxiety to gain plurality political parties had resorted to capturing of polling booths to prevent the casting of votes by the genuine voters and large-scale bogus voting took place. It is to the lasting credit of the Election Commission that during the last general election and state elections they were able not only to ensure a generally peaceful poll but also succeeded in enforcing a certain measure of discipline on the contesting parties in the matter of election expenses, election campaigns and the actual management of elections in the electoral booths. They have created a confidence in the mind of the electorate that law will be maintained come what may and have thus strengthened the prospects of consolidating democracy in the country.

If the promise of democracy has not been easy to fulfil that of secularism has proved even more elusive. Yet it is an essential component of our vision for our country. There is no other basis on which a multi-religious society such as ours can be consolidated into a nation. Communal conflicts have extracted a heavy price in life and property and the police have had to bear the brunt of the responsibility for keeping the damage restricted and for enabling the political forces to regain balance and initiative.

It was probably inevitable that the word 'secularism' should come to acquire a limited meaning in our polity because of the immediate past of communal strife through which India had passed. Communal violence and community-based division of the country had marked the birth of the country as an independent nation. The continuing strain in Indo-Pakistan relations and the contention over Kashmir has not helped to heal the wounds of division. The Khalistan-related happenings and the riots in Delhi after the assassination of Mrs. Indira Gandhi only served to widen the area of communal divisiveness, and the demolition of the Babri Masjid and the proposal to build a Ram Mandir on the site ensure that in the near future we will not be able to see an end to communal consciousness in our political life.

The value of secularism has got equated in the Indian mind with being equable on the Hindu-Muslim question or the Hindu-Sikh question or, for that matter, Hindu and any other religious minority. As a result, the progress of secular thinking in our society has suffered. To be secular should mean being willing to adopt reason and universalistic criteria in the conduct of day-to-day life. A secular government should not discriminate between its citizens on the ground of religion or race or caste. At a philosophic level secularism would also involve the rejection of a belief in the supernatural. But, when we say that the Indian state is secular, we only mean that it does not discriminate between its citizens or impose any disabilities on a class of citizens on the ground of their religious affiliation. Concurrently it should also mean that it would not sponsor or support activity which is initiated by and for particular religious groups.

The separation between the religious and the political cannot take place unless the current of reason is strengthened in our public life. Yet many a public figure, however, secular may be his secular protestations, seems to make it a point to assert the non-rational aspects of his being by being publicly seen to be associated with swamis, tantriks, astrologers and men claiming supernatural vision or powers and belonging to one religious hue or the other as his close associates if not as his advisors.

The fact is that though the Indian state is secular the Indian politician is not and he finds that in the short run it is advantageous to keep his secular convictions, if any, ambiguous. He does little to widen the universe of reason or science or rational discourse. He pleads for reason only when he finds that the consequences of his community-based politics land him or the government in an unsustainable position.

Yet, the premise of secularism is vital to our stability as a nation and if the present political scenario has made strange bedfellows of a number of political parties against one on the ground that the latter is non-secular, the blame lies at least as much with those that claim to be secular as with the other. A much greater depth and meaning need to be given to the concept of secularism. The secular parties must be able to state in what way their government will function better and make a difference to the common man. A negative platform of keeping a party out of government cannot be a basis for firm decisions and new developmental initiatives. The absence of such initiatives and early positive achievements will only weaken the polity and encourage further divisiveness. When the divisions will again show that the primordial groupings of caste and religion have proved the basis for drawing lines, the law and order situation will worsen and the police will again be called in to mop up the aftermath.

This brings me to the third premise and promise of our constitution, viz., the creation of an equitable, if not equal, society. It would seem strange that in a country as poor as ours the issue of poverty and deprivation of vast numbers of people has itself not become the major politically divisive issue or articulated into a major point of conflict between parties or between those that have vaguely been called the 'haves' and the 'have-nots' in our society. No political party in recent years has spelt out who the haves in Indian society are and who the have-nots or which have-nots they stand for. Ambiguity and equivocation are politically convenient tools but they cannot help in creating an awareness of what the real political or economic issues are. "Garibi Hatao" was a convenient slogan but too general to make any group or any socio-economic activity or process seem responsible for the *garibi* and to specify the programme by which to overcome it. It conveniently dispossessed the avowedly left or seemingly militant parties, the champions of the poor of their war cry. The slogan made poverty into an abstraction and at one stroke did away with the conflict model of explaining poverty.

Most of the Indian political parties seem to see poverty not as an economic fact but as a consequence of social status. So poverty is explained in terms of caste status and consequent deprivation, or a consequence of regional disparities which can be tackled by creation of new states, or as districts or sub-regions which need to be given special assistance for their condition to improve. Some explain poverty in terms of inter-communal differences and the consequent deprivation of opportunities for some. None of these diagnoses is entirely wrong but unwittingly, or, may be, wittingly, they serve to mask the problem of poverty as a problem of caste, or of religion or region. This makes political mobilisation easy in the short run though it may not help tackle the problem of poverty *per se*. Because, when new states are created, the poor continue to remain poor except that they are now poor in a new state; and when caste-related protection is provided, some of the better off low caste get into the lowest rung of the reserved jobs but the vast majority do not benefit -- not at least directly.

That social and economic problems get perceived and interpreted in terms of caste and region and community is probably justified by the real life interlinkages between these and the economic condition of the individual: but this is largely a consequence of the way the politician finds it convenient to mobilise his following by making it that much his special preserve as a member of the particular caste, region or religion. From the long-term point of view this does not help in bringing people of different castes or communities or regions on a common platform and in fact it only further strengthens particularistic loyalties and divisions in society. A secular, civil society cannot emerge with this pattern of mobilisation.

The only movement that brought people by economic categories together during the pre-independence days and even after independence was the labour movement in organised industry, particularly in the urban areas. To the extent that this movement exists it serves that purpose still, but the labour movement embraces a small population and is now no longer industry- or even-region based, except in the public sector or in government services. Unionism in industry tends increasingly to be individual unit-based, especially in the modern electronic, engineering and pharmaceutical industries. Further unionism is largely restricted to organised industry. Trade unions in this sense have ceased to be a major driving force to bring in workers consciousness or awareness of their secular, economic identity.

The problem of poverty, particularly the problem of poverty of workers in the urban unorganised sector and of the rural small peasants or landless agricultural workers, does not figure prominently in political debates nor are there specialist economic organisations which seem to pay any attention to them. The worker in the organised industry seems to have distanced himself from these groups and is caught up in the process of being absorbed in the lower middle class -- a process facilitated by the relatively better wages that this category can command.

The economic policy of successive governments seems to have been based on the assumption that if the GNP is increased the problem of poverty will get reduced. The facts seem to be otherwise. Despite the increase in agricultural and industrial production over the decades, the percentage of population below the poverty line now stands at 40 per cent of the total population as per the revised method of calculating poverty (*The Times of India* report quoting government sources, December 8, 1996). Even assuming that the increase in percentage is due to a change of definition, it still means an increase of several millions in the actual number of persons below the poverty line. For a nation which is committed to equity this is not a proud record. It means that the expansion of the economy and the increased production have only helped broaden the middle class and increased the disparity between the middle class and the organised workers on the one hand and the daily wage earners in the unorganised sector of the economy, on the other. The benefits of development such as they are, have not percolated to lower economic levels. The promise of equity remains far from fulfilled. The efforts of successive governments to tackle problems of poverty through different forms of rural employment schemes and to alleviate the misery of the poor through a weak public distribution system have proved inadequate.

This increases the sense of insecurity among the poor and leads to two types of consequences. On the one hand, particularly in rural areas, it leads to the problem of poverty being defined in the traditional terms of caste- and community-based deprivation and strengthens the demand for caste-based protective discrimination policies and the Mandalisation of political and economic arenas.

The other consequence is that dissatisfaction among the poor, particularly in urban areas, gets channelled into a variety of forms of deviance and to participation in organised criminal activity through membership of known gangs which undertake illicit and criminal activity at the behest of bosses with better economic resources at their command. Organised crime is visible in the urban areas. It also exists in the rural areas in the form of informal private armies used for suppressing protests of the landless poor. The individuals who mastermind crime and those who serve as their tools remain outside the normal political process and are available for use by whoever is willing to pay them. The police themselves are often seen by the public as a party to the crime and violence perpetrated by the gangs and as beneficiaries of the protection money system with which the criminal gangs harass the business community. The atmosphere of bribery, corruption and crime which has vitiated public life and has grown in dimension to an extent that it has invited pointed attention of the judiciary is one consequence of the failure of governments to actively pursue problems of poverty alleviation and of bridging the growing gap between the urban poor and the urban worker in the organised sector of the economy. The urban poor are fast losing their social moorings in metropolitan cities and stand in the danger of being lumpenised.

Police and the various investigating agencies try to tackle these problems as and when they arise. They are neither equipped nor expected to go beyond the immediate situation or an individual offense that comes to their notice. Nor can the wider problem of a general social malaise and of lack of probity in public life be left to be tackled only by judicial activism though the judiciary has helped bring it to the fore. The problem lies squarely in the area of political and administrative action and can only be tackled by political parties and bureaucrats being held accountable by an informed public. The use of police to down violence arising out of political differences or out of basic inequities in society politicises and brutalises the police force.

The police can at best enforce the law. They cannot create order in a society where there is no genuine consensus on the basic values to be pursued and the modalities to be adopted. Order in a plural society emerges in a context where individuals belonging to different sections of the plurality feel that their interests are better likely to be served within a larger whole than within the several small identities. The creation of such a consensus requires persons with a statesmanship of the highest order. Even when such a consensus is attained it cannot be taken for granted. It needs to be sustained by a continuing effort on the part of leaders in different fields of life but most particularly those in the political arena.

The present situation in our society is characterised by a general lack of faith of the citizen in all those who occupy high office, whether in politics, or in the bureaucracy, in business or even in the spheres of education and religion. It is held that any one who has achieved a high station in life or is conspicuously rich must have reached that position by some unfair means, by some misuse of authority, by corruption, or outright fraud. Such cynicism corrodes social life and makes difficult the restoration of any sense of values. Crime and normlessness in society are mutually supportive.

At present, we have plenty of politicians but hardly any statesmen – men of vision and rectitude. I am not thinking of men as tall as the Mahatma Gandhi or a Pandit Nehru. No country gets Mahatmas in successive generations. But I think we can do with honest men – men with a sense of public purpose – an awareness of the major problems facing the people and a sincere desire to tackle them. I am sure there are enough men of this calibre in the population. If they do not come to the fore it is because an illiterate electorate, shrewd as it is, still feels secure with individuals who exercise a charisma. Not all persons with a charisma are great persons – persons who have the interest of the people at heart. Their charisma has often come to them because of their lineal descent, or through their achievements in other fields like films or religion. They are often found wanting in ideas of social reconstruction or the acumen to see them realised. We should probably look for our leaders among politicians who are honest, show a sense of high purpose and have a capacity for leadership. Such middle-range statesmen, who are committed and who can act in the present with a steady vision of a future for their country, should serve us well and bring credibility to public life.

And I do not look for such leaders of change only among politicians. We need them among administrators and our police as well. I am sure we have them. Coming from the middle classes as I do I have friends among the governmental bureaucracy and the police as I have them among educationists. I feel that if the top of the judiciary and the Election Commission have made a difference and made us aware of the risks we run by flowing with the current and allowing things to go from bad to worse, a few such *path breakers* among the politicians themselves and among the administrators and the police can help carry the process further and ensure that we do not lose the momentum and help transfer what has been a traumatic experience for the country into a beginning of reconstruction. We do not need a big movement but just a certain number of individuals in decision-making and executive positions who will stand up to their own sense of values and refuse to become tools of subversion of our law and polity. They need to only insist that they will not consciously act against the law and public interest. They may at worst be denied promotions or suffer a few punitive transfers. But, if there are enough of them who will stand up, they cannot be wished away or pushed away. The price they will have paid will be much smaller than the price paid by the generation that fought for our freedom. Those individuals who paid the price then did not constitute the majority of the population nor do we need a majority of officers to bring about such a change. We need a committed minority. The others will follow. We just need enough of change makers to show that an alternative exists – an alternative at once more dignifying to the individual and wholesome for the society as a whole.

But, the possibility of such a group emerging whether in politics or administration or business and education will rest on the kind of lifestyle aspirations we set for ourselves and how realistic they are in terms of our incomes. As we need not look for Mahatmas in politics, we do not need our professionals to become *sanyasins.* But, as a class, we must be willing to recognise that given the state of development of the country we should not aspire to lifestyles which cannot be supported by our known incomes. Even if our middle class lives modestly it will still live a style which the poor can never afford. How much of conspicuous disparity in life standards can our society withstand in this age of instant communication and conspicuous consumption? How will we contain the potential disruption of civil life that this disparity threatens? Will we depend on the law and the police to maintain order? Or can we innovate other answers. From this perspective, the organisation of the polity in terms of caste and community is in fact hiding some real problems from coming to the fore in their true shape. Some think this is a blessing. But, in such a fuddled polity, there are seeds of unending civil strife. When it erupts, the police will not be able to handle it. Nor will the politicians be able to cope with it for long. We are at the crossroads and have to make a conscious choice.

7

The Social Scene in India at the End of the Century

I would like to speak today, somewhat impressionistically, about the social changes that have taken place and those that have not taken place though we intended them to happen over the past half century. The term 'social' is broad and it can cover everything relating to society and that could be economic and political changes as well. But, the previous two speakers in this series have covered the economic and political happenings of the last half a century. That helps to delimit the term 'social'. Even so it can refer either to changes that have taken place in relation to the basic institutional framework of society like marriage, family, education, religion, social stratification, i.e., caste and class, rural-urban patterns of habitation, and art and entertainment or it may refer to changes in social services in the various fields of health, education, rehabilitation, housing, environment and social welfare. This is obviously too long a list of areas and they cannot all be discussed in the course of one talk. So I will have to be selective about what I discuss and my reason for choosing these rather than certain other areas would be that I am somewhat more familiar with them than with others. In the time that I have I will limit myself to some broad

---

Text of the lecture delivered at Ramnarain Ruia College, Mumbai on February 1998.

social changes and not undertake a review of attainments or failures in the broad area of social and welfare services.

Our constitution has placed before us the goal of a society which would be equitable, secular and democratic. I will focus primarily on the promise of equity.

MARRIAGE AND THE SOCIAL STATUS OF WOMEN

I will begin with the institutions of marriage and family. In this area social reformers had planned and desired certain changes from the days before independence. The focus of these changes was equity toward women and, later, toward the other underprivileged groups in our society. Legislations regarding abolition of the *sati* system, abolition of child marriages and raising of the age of marriage were already on the statute book and the aim here was to mitigate the injustice and hardships that early marriage, widowhood and the *sati* system imposed on Indian women. There were other broad social objectives as well but improving the status of women was the primary objective. The promotion of remarriage of young widows, the promotion of education among girls, the acceptance, if not promotion, of various types of intermarriages, the enforcement of monogamy, and the prohibition of unequal marriages between old widowers and young child brides were some of the immediate targets that social reformers were pursuing at the stage of independence. Monogamy is now enforceable in the case of Hindus if the first wife makes a complaint against her husband's bigamous marriage and there are now no legal barriers to widow remarriage.

Most of these changes were part of a programme of improving the status of the Indian woman in the household that the middle class social reformers had been pursuing for almost half a century before independence. Some others were part of the Hindu Code Bill presented to the (legislature) Constituent Assembly but which could not be passed in its original form and was later passed in a modified form through several individual pieces of legislation. The women whose status the social reformers had been preoccupied with prior to independence were those of the middle class, or using a sociological term, women of the classes and castes that had been 'sanskritised'. Of course, many of the disabilities of women except the one regarding widow remarriage held true for women of the other classes as well. Girls of the lower castes married early and would already be mothers at least a couple of times before they had gained adulthood; women of these classes had even less opportunity for formal education, and they were more likely to suffer the consequences of their husbands entering into bigamous marriages than middle class women. But, with the exception of Jotiba Phule, the efforts of the other social reformers were oriented primarily toward the middle class women.

If the passage of the Hindu Code Bill faced opposition in the Constituent Assembly and had to be adopted largely through piecemeal legislation at a later stage, the issue of having a Common Civil Code is still hanging fire and the status of the Muslim woman in law is still vulnerable in respect of the mode of divorce and her right to property or maintenance. But, even among Muslims, I would imagine that the condition of the educated middle class woman is better than the women in the uneducated and economically lower class.

The Present Position

Today, among the middle classes and particularly in the urban areas, the age of marriage has steadily risen and child marriage is no longer common. Girls in this class are now getting the benefit of education and even have the opportunity of pursuing a career. More remarriages and intermarriages are taking place among this class than in others and more in the urban areas than in the villages. The reason for underlining this class/caste and regional basis of change is to point out that the success of a social reform depends not only on the facility made available by law or by the reformer but on the degree to which the objective situation supports it and the pressure that it exercises on the individual to change.

Two factors seem to have been responsible for middle class women taking to education and later to employment. The spread of education among middle class girls was first a consequence of the increase in the age of marriage in this class where the young man got his first job only after he had completed at least his school and in some cases college education. Delaying marriage until after the boy had secured a job was itself a change rooted in the changing occupational structure of the middle class in which the occupation and economic status of the eligible young man was no longer dependent upon his father's occupation and status and required that he gain and his social position based on his own appropriate qualification and subsequent employment promising him security and economic advancement.

The link between the family and its occupation had been broken for the urban middle class by the factors of urbanisation and industrialisation. This meant that young men of each generation had to find their own opportunities and achieve a social status based on their own equipment and skills. In this context, sending the girl to school until she could be married to an appropriately qualified young man seemed a better alternative than keeping her idle at home. Also, an educated young man, often living away from his parental home, preferred to marry a girl who had some education. Besides, with changing aspirations, the young family now needs two earners rather than one.

Effects of the Second World War and the Independence Movement

The other factor that accelerated the education of young girls in the urban areas was the demand for an educated female labour force created by the Second World War. The war generally facilitated the employment of educated young women, especially those of the lower middle class, in government offices, beginning with the newly established ration offices, and gradually extended to other government departments. Middle class men were being recruited on a large scale as short-term commission officers in the armed forces and, in a civil capacity, in military accounts.

There was also an expansion in the opportunity for employment for both men and women in the expanding industrial and commercial firms. These opportunities which arose with the war expanded after independence. But, until recently, middle class women favoured employment in government offices rather than in private firms. Such employment was considered secure both in the sense of personal security as well as from the point of the probability of continued employment. Until recently, government jobs were preferred to jobs in private firms even by men.

The spread of education and employment for middle class women mutually assisted each other during and after the war. Earlier, when education was considered only as an additional accomplishment desirable for a housewife, it remained restricted to a small number of upper middle class, urban families. The rising cost of living and the changing ideas of the kind of lifestyle the new lower middle class wanted to maintain was another factor leading to the spread of education and employment of women. The changing ideas of the preferred lifestyle for the lower middle class were themselves a consequence of greater exposure, through the films, popular, literature and the media, to the lifestyles of the upper middle class within the country and to ideas that had percolated from the West.

At the same time, the army opened up opportunities of employment for women as nurses and cadets in the Women's Auxiliary Corps. It was primarily young women from the lower middle class Christian families who opted for nursing as a career. Why Christian girls took to nursing more than girls from other communities needs examination. May be the Christian faith made the acceptance of individual care and service acceptable as a career for girls. May be there were more educated girls among the Christian poor than among the Hindu or Muslim poor. May be the high dowry requirements of marriage among the educated Kerala Christian families compelled the girls to look for employment. The alternative for such middle class educated girls unless they were already married was to join school teaching as a career. This phenomenon was noticeable among young Kerala Christian girls who opted for hospital nursing as a career. They probably constitute the largest single social group in the profession in India.

Employment among the lower middle class girls in other communities seemed to have remained largely confined to teaching until after the opportunities for employment in government offices opened during the war. Employment of women in commercial offices on any substantial scale was also a post-Second World War phenomenon and here again the lead was taken by Anglo-Indian, Parsee and Christian women at least in western India. The reason was probably to be found in the English language base of the education of these women but I suspect that their employment was also a consequence of the less restrictive attitudes in these communities to the idea of women mixing with men in social and formal work situations. Middle class Christian and Parsee homes have in some ways been less resistant to westernisation or Anglicisation of their social life and increased social communication between men and women is a part of this new orientation.

The considerable increase in the total number of educated, employed women has been one of the major social changes in the post-war, post-independent India. The participation of women in the nationalist movement, particularly in its Gandhian form, had been another major factor which helped the Indian woman to move out of the limits of the household into social and public life. Even the Hindu woman seemed to have experienced less opposition to her entering the freedom movement than to her entering the occupational world. Participation of women in extra-familial activities----social, economic, political----has been one of the major changes on the social scene in India and it has strengthened particularly since independence. Girls from middle class homes are now among the high achievers in school and college examinations as well as in competitive examinations. Women are to be found now in every field of economic and professional activity. One expects that this will have important consequences for social life generally and for family life in particular.

Changes in Family Life

The traditional form of marriage in most Indian communities required that marriages be arranged by the elders in the family, that they be within the caste, sub-caste or community and that they take place early. These considerations were important for the functioning and stability of the joint family. Marriages in the middle class are no longer early in the way they used to be. They are no longer marriages that take place before or soon after attainment of puberty. The girl who marries into her husband's family is now at least 16-18 years of age, has usually completed her high school if not college education and is not socially and psychologically as malleable a person as she might have been at the age of 10-15. The boy who marries is also not young and impressionable. He is educated, employed and is not a part of a joint family corporation whether in agriculture or in business. He has to function as a unit earner outside the household.

Marriages are still largely arranged if not through family contacts and the grapevine of communication within the caste and community then by use of the impersonal newspaper advertisement or through formal agencies which specialise in match-making and match-fixing. The opportunities for social communication between the young boys and girls are still limited in our society. Boys and girls do meet in colleges but not yet socially outside college. Also, the girls are expected to marry someone older, someone who is already settled in an occupation and whose economic standing and future can be assessed. Such a person will not normally be from among a young girl's cohorts at college unless she is prepared to wait. This happens often in the case of girls who are studying at the post-graduate level where there is a possibility of the boy and the girl settling down occupationally about the same time. In most other cases marriages are arranged.

But arranged marriages had earlier the functional implication of strengthening the joint family in a variety of ways. It tended to delay the point at which the conjugal tie between the young couple would gain priority over the filial tie between the boy and his parents or the fraternal tie between the boy and his brothers. The later age of marriage nullifies to some degree the effect of an arranged marriage in which the young girl remained away from her husband and functioned as a young girl under the tutelage of her mother-in-law. In a relatively short period of marriage the young son of the family and his wife become an identifiable, separate unit within the household with growing mutual bonds. This raises problems for the joint family and threatens the traditional authority structure of the family.

There are other factors as well which seem to affect the internal relations of the family. Probably, the most important of these is the occupational differentiation within the family. In the rural context where occupations were determined by caste, the middle class was typically the landowning class. Land was usually inherited and held in common by the males. Common occupation and common coparcenary rights on the land tended to reinforce joint living and an avoidance of family division and a division of the family land into smaller less economic units.

This happened even in the case of families where there was a common business inherited from an earlier generation. The coparcenary rights applied here as well. So common ownership of property and a common occupation became important reinforcing factors for the traditional joint family. The notion of inherited rights often extended even to the relationship of landlord and his dependent service giving families though here it might not exercise the same compelling influence that it did in the case of landed property or property in a common business.

The urban environment has completely changed this picture for most occupations other than hereditary individual family owned businesses. The other white-collar occupations are not hereditary in the urban areas. This opens up the scope for occupational diversification within the family between father and son or brother and brother and, as mentioned earlier, the gains of learning act has protected an individual's earnings from his non-hereditary occupation from being claimed by units of joint family.

Occupational differentiation also means the possibility of considerable differences in individual incomes of the earners within the same family and this adds to the difficulty of joint family living where the expectation is that one shares one's assets generally with all the other members of the family. In the short run this is offset by the sense of familial obligations that bind parent-child and brother-brother ties. But, over time, it becomes difficult to accommodate different standards and patterns of living within a common residential unit. Newer ideas of privacy, and the growing pattern of individualised styles of living and non-availability of private spaces in a common household unit where individual units could manage day-to-day living brings closer the breakdown of the joint family into sub-units.

This is facilitated by the fact that often the brothers in a family or even a father and a son who are now in different occupations are required to live in different towns or cities depending on the circumstances of their employment. This reduces the sense of guilt or awkwardness involved in family divisions. Separate residences for married brothers, even in the same town or city, have now come to be accepted as normal in the urban middle class though occasionally the point of separation may be postponed due to family exigencies or due to non-availability of housing accommodation in large metropolitan cities. There is also a trend whereby decisions regarding getting married get postponed and become contingent on the availability and affordability of separate housing.

What Happens to Familial Obligations?

Does this mean that the joint family has become extinct in the middle and higher income groups? Far from it. While the idea of separate residential units for married brothers and their families has generally come to be accepted in the urban areas the idea of familial obligations of each paternal unit for the others is still alive. This manifests itself in different ways.

Its influence is seen first in the acceptance of obligations for one's younger unmarried siblings who may not yet have completed their education. Educating one's younger male siblings and helping them settle in life is still accepted as a responsibility by elder males in the middle class. How far such help may extend depends on several factors including the degree of fraternal affection that particular families have developed. But, culturally, this is expected. In the case of younger sisters the earning brothers are minimally expected to help them get settled in matrimony. In the middle classes the education of younger sisters until they are married is also expected to be accepted as a responsibility by the brothers if the parents are not alive or are not in a position to take this responsibility.

The system of joint family obligations is seen to continue in the relatively willing support that sons give to their aged parents. The culturally preferred pattern is for the parents to live in the household of one of the sons---usually the eldest son. If this is not possible, then, the sons minimally are expected to support them financially to continue to live in their own home. If there is more than one son, the responsibility may be shared among them.

The family sentiment is still strong and in the absence of elder brothers sometimes elder sisters have taken on the responsibility of supporting the family. This often involves a special hardship because once married a woman is expected to give priority to the demands of her husband's family. If therefore she takes responsibility for her own siblings or parents it has to be by giving up or postponing the idea of her own marriage. But, this whole question of how far a woman who is educated and earning should accept responsibility for her parental family is still new and there are no defined and culturally accepted norms and practices.

In the case of aged parents it is not yet common in India for married daughters to take the financial responsibility of supporting their parents though many such cases are now in evidence. Earlier, accepting material support from a married daughter would have meant transgression of traditional norms for parents. This sentiment still continues but there are instances of widowed parents living singly with their daughters. As unitary households become common and married women increasingly have their own incomes, the possibility of a woman accepting responsibility for dependents from her parental family may increase.

In another aspect the family life of the middle class is undergoing an important change. The size of the family is decreasing fast. The educated professional family does not want to have many children and if the wife is earning they may decide to stop after the first child. There is still value attached to having a male child and sometimes a child of each sex. This may occasionally lead couples of this class to have more than two children. But, the attitude to having children has undergone a change. Children are not looked upon as assets for the future. Having children is now considered a value in itself—a type of fulfilment. At the same time, there is an increasing feeling that having children is a responsibility---financial as well as social and psychological. Parents of this class are beginning to be aware that having children involves sacrifices in their own lives and aspirations.

What is more this awareness and the attitudinal change are spreading to the lower middle classes as well at least in the large urban areas. Education of the woman is considered a key variable influencing the size of the family. To this must be added the factor of increasing employment among women of the middle classes. If the woman is educated and is also employed, she is less likely to have or to want more than one or two children.

Urbanisation, industrialisation and education have all contributed to these changes in the life pattern of the middle class. So have the efforts of social reformers and social legislators. Our middle class men and women are not yet as self-preoccupied or individualised as in some of the western countries but that is probably the direction in which they will move. If that happens, as is likely if we adopt a high consumer orientation, the life within the family will be affected not only in terms of the size of the family but also in terms of the interrelationships among its members.

CASTE AND CLASS IN THE YEARS SINCE INDEPENDENCE

I have been using the term 'middle classes' in the foregoing discussions regarding changes in the institutions of marriage and family over the recent past. I have done so to refer to that section of our society which is characterised by relatively higher achievements in education---at least high school and above---and generally by white-collar occupations such as clerical, managerial and professional. In recent years there has been a change. A section of the traditionally blue-collar employees have also joined this class. I refer to those who may be employed as skilled workers, operators, packers, time-keepers, etc., who are permanent employees in the organised industry and even those who are employed as peons in municipal and government offices and in government-aided institutions. Their wage levels have risen and they enjoy a measure of employment security which distinguishes them from casual workers in industry or workers in unorganised industry and, again, from agricultural workers in rural areas. Further, this is a group which has adopted middle class lifestyles in so far as their incomes will permit and middle-class aspirations of education for their children and goals of upward mobility. One may, if one chooses, label them as lower middle class but they are no longer the old workers in the textile mills of Bombay either in terms of their educational level or their earnings or their aspirations and lifestyle.

This middle class is more heterogeneous in its caste composition than it probably was at the time of independence, at least in the urban areas. At the point of independence or more generally prior to the Second World War, the urban middle class consisted primarily of the clerical, teaching, administrative and managerial employees, those who were members of the 'learned professions' of law, medicine and engineering, and those who were traders, merchants and moneylenders. To begin with, this class was recruited in Maharashtra largely from amongst Brahmins, CKPs, Pathare Prabhus, and, later, a section of the Maratha, Jain and Lingayat communities who had been influenced and had benefited by the Bramhanetar movement and the initiatives in education taken by Chhatrapati Shahu, and the merchants and traders who came very often from outside Maharashtra. This group depended upon education as a necessary equipment for entering into their occupations. The working class, including workers in the mills and peons in government offices and private establishments, was clearly separated from this middle class.

Since the Second World War the position has altered and a section of the urban working class has changed its self-image and its economic status—partly through labour organisation and partly through the requirements of education and training required by their work and consequently by the higher wages they command. The industrial working class is drawn from a wider caste, community and regional base than the traditional middle class and has thus widened the social base of the new middle class. This working class now also attracts some from the lower strata of the traditional middle castes in Maharashtra and the new beneficiaries of the constitutional provisions for reservations for the scheduled castes (SCs) and scheduled tribes (STs).

Caste Still Relevant

This does not mean that the economic opportunities have opened up altogether to all equally and that caste is no longer a relevant factor in upward mobility. Certainly, legally, that is the case but not in practice. Individual and family life is still lived very much within and through the caste. In small towns and in remote urban areas caste is still an important determinant of one's life chances in Indian society because social life is still largely governed by caste affiliation and that in turn determines chances of taking advantage of the opportunities that may exist for upward mobility whether through education and employment or through mobilisation of social contact and influence. Caste may not be an important influence in interpersonal communication in formal settings, particularly in the urban areas. But, it is generally important in the familial sphere and influences subtly the choice of intimates and friends even at work. This, in turn, vitiates the openness of channels of communication.

In the rural areas caste still governs economic life to an even larger degree and access to and utilisation of educational and occupational opportunities is determined by caste status. The higher the caste status, the greater the chances of one entering a school or college and remaining in it to complete one's studies. Caste is also the basis of the struggle for political power and upward mobility through political mobilisation in rural areas. In the case of Marathas in Maharashtra, and other comparable landowning groups in other states, politics combined with landownership has been an important channel of upward mobility—more important than the channel of education and white-collar employment.

In the last couple of decades this power elite has also taken advantage of the increasing opportunities for education. After the first few years of independence the plurality and the land base of these middle castes in various parts of the country helped their gaining control of the political machinery at least at the state level. This dominance of the traditional landed castes in state level politics continued well into the 70s. Recently, the dissatisfaction among the further lower strata has begun to manifest itself in an organised way. The Mandal Commission has led to political mobilisation among the further lower castes, the other backward castes (OBCs) and the SCs/STs. Such mobilisation is now proceeding apace. There are some efforts to use the somewhat undefined phrases like the dalits, the downtrodden and the deprived to build a common political platform for the OBCs and the SCs. How far it will succeed and whether such a combination will finally be led by the OBCs or by the SCs is not yet known.

But, the open democratic structure and the mechanism of reservations in jobs, if not in legislatures, has certainly proved an important channel to provide limited upward mobility to successively lower strata of the Indian society. First, the *savarna* intermediate castes—the non-Brahmins, then the SCs/STs as a result of the reservations provided in the Constitution of India and, more recently, under the Mandal dispensation, the OBCs have benefited by reservations in employment in government offices and offices of aided institutions.

To begin with, this upward mobility for the 'deprived' groups will very likely be political. The new politically upward mobile groups have yet to develop tools and mechanisms of converting their political base of access to power into more lasting social, occupational and economic strength. This cannot be achieved easily in the short run and not without a greater spread of education in these groups and without some access to capital resources. Even the intermediate and large landowning castes have only recently begun to consolidate their elitist position by entering in substantial numbers into education, the professions and the world of art, literature, science and philosophy. In Maharashtra, they have been helped largely by the cooperative movement and even in other states the landowning castes have benefited by the liberal subsidies offered by government for agriculture and agriculture-related industries.

The Strife around Class and Caste

The fact that the democratic polity makes it possible for different strata to stake their claims to political and economic opportunities does not however mean that the process of transfer is smooth and without conflict. The transfer of power from the Brahmins to the non-Brahmin middle castes in the southern parts of the country was comparatively smooth because the Brahmins in Maharashtra and in the southern states were generally a small minority and in electoral politics they could not present a serious challenge. This is not the case when we consider the challenge from the non-landowning OBCs to the landowning and currently powerful upper castes. This tussle is currently going on in Uttar Pradesh and Bihar. And, this is not merely being fought through the ballot box. It is manifesting itself through armed attacks and counter-attacks between the organised 'armies' of the upper caste peasantry and the relatively weak and unorganised untouchables. The government of the state has not been able to give adequate protection to the untouchables. The OBCs are being politically wooed both by the landed castes and the untouchables. In the meanwhile, the government in power is unable to control or turns a blind eye to the regime of repression and threats let loose by the big landlords.

Again, in the border districts between Maharashtra, Madhya Pradesh and Andhra Pradesh, the struggle between the landed and the landless has taken the form of a militant conflict between the government and the Naxalite-led landless communities including some nomadic tribal groups. The democratically elected government has to contain the militancy of the oppressed and yet not seem unresponsive to the woes of the landless. It would prefer to separate the problem of tackling militancy from the problem of the landless and disinherited poor. Such neat choices may not always be available to a ruling party. The failure of successive governments to get moving on the question of land reform and their inability or unwillingness to hurt the interests of the large peasant has lost them the confidence of the landless and poor. The prospect of illicit arms flowing into these pockets of unrest is what is making them sit up but it is unlikely that they will find in themselves the will to take prompt actions to redress the grievances of the affected groups.

The problem of the landless is at once a problem of class and caste because in most cases the two modes of social stratification converge and the lower castes are invariably also the poorer ones. In some ways this problem of the disaffection of the landless poor, whether in Andhra Pradesh or Bihar or Uttar Pradesh, is likely to pose a more difficult challenge than the ethnic-based problems of insurgency on the frontiers. These problems cannot be blamed on foreign elements seeking to weaken the Indian nation nor can they be treated merely as problems of accommodating the identities of groups lying at the physical periphery of the country. They are problems of and within our society, problems testing our economic and political professions of working for a free and at least relatively equal society.

These problems have meant repeated arson, looting and burning down of entire untouchable villages and the loss of lives of countless poor. They have also meant a gradual strengthening of forces which challenge the rule of law and order. In Andhra Pradesh, this situation has expressed itself in many instances of kidnapping of senior government officers and the murders of allegedly repressive landlords. The government may not be able to play for long the role of a tolerant bystander interested in but unable to address directly the grievances of the poor. They may have to actively enforce law and order and also act to remove the causes of unrest among the poor.

Caste in Urban Areas

One expects that caste has a very limited role to play in urban areas and that relationships are governed by class affiliations in individual social life and by objective criteria and contractual considerations in the formal sphere of economic and political activity. One needs to consider the extent to which these assumptions are valid.

In a small town one finds that neighbourhoods often crystallise with a broad caste category as its base---thus we may have a Brahmin alley or a Maratha alley, or lanes based on the occupation-specific caste groups such as baniyas, weavers, chamars, cane workers, etc. Even in the large metropolitan cities, the older portions of the city---for example, the middle class chawls in Dadar or Girgaum in Bombay---would tend to be caste-based. This is now more difficult in the larger cities because finding a house is no longer a matter of choice. One accepts whatever is available. But, where there is a choice, as for instance, in the formation of a cooperative housing society, one finds that the membership gets designedly limited to particular broad caste groups unless they are societies based on the members' affiliation to a place of employment as in the case of former government employees, or former port trust employees, etc. To the extent that a neighbourhood decides the choice of friends, the social interaction tends to be within the caste group if the basis of the formation of the neighbourhood is caste.

But, even if a neighbourhood is 'cosmopolitan', we find that intimate familial relationships tend to be limited first to the extended family and then to members of one's caste. There are of course exceptions and there is no doubt that the urban dweller is likely to be more exposed to inter-caste interactions at the social level than a village dweller. But, one may notice a tendency to limit invitations for family meals to persons of the same caste. While social occasions like celebrations of weddings and larger social functions will normally be attended by guests drawn from many castes close family contacts which would include communication with women in the family tend to be limited to one's caste.

When it comes to marriages all arranged marriages---and most marriages are still arranged—tend to be within the caste. The only change is that instead of being limited to particular sub-castes as they used to be they may now be a little broad based and may include socially close other castes. Even this is likely to happen only if the young boy or girl concerned has taken some part in the choice of the partner. To the extent that marriages of choice have become more acceptable in some of the social groups like upper class professionals, there may be a greater possibility of marriages across castes or linguistic groups or even religious groups taking place.

Class in Urban Areas

Social relationships at the workplace in urban areas are based on departmental proximity and rank in the hierarchy of an organisation and do not depend on caste affiliation. But, the likelihood of such relationships converting into family friendships is limited and where they occur they are more likely to be among members of the same or equal status caste groups.

In urban areas caste does not play any part in access to public places like restaurants, cinema halls or social clubs. Here, social and economic class plays a more decisive role. Affordability of access to a particular hotel, restaurant or club becomes a critical factor. Such class differentiation is also noticed in choice of residential area and more recent residential colonies are homogeneous in terms of class rather than caste.

Attainment of a particular economic class status may itself depend upon the caste or the regional group in which one is born. To the extent this is the case class differentiation also becomes an indirect way of caste- or region-based differentiation. Even class-based differentiation, in its negative implication, serves to keep out the lowest caste categories.

In the large cities, there is also often a regional or linguistic basis of differentiation in housing and choice of club membership. At times this may extend even to educational institutions. Thus, some colonies and clubs or schools are sponsored and predominantly patronised by particular linguistic groups than by others. There are usually no formal rules limiting memberships to particular language or caste groups in admission to these institutions but a process of self-selection based on lifestyles takes place and particular communities tend to predominate in particular institutions. Further, in the recruitment of staff, the minority status of particular communities may enable their institutions to ensure that senior staff positions are reserved for members of particular groups.

Thus, caste, class and regional background all play a part in differentiating social relationships in urban areas. Caste and regional background often go together because castes are most often region-specific and in that sense class and caste become the major differentiators in urban social interaction.

SOCIAL MOVEMENTS

I have said nothing so far about social movements of the period since independence. They constitute a subject by themselves and I will deal with them briefly in this presentation.

In some ways social reform and social movements share a common ground in that both are aimed at bringing about a change in the prevalent values and practices within a society with respect to a particular group. But, while social reform was often undertaken for a deprived group by one who did not belong to it, a social movement is usually initiated by and for the group by one who is also a member of the deprived group. In any case, even if a movement is initiated by an outsider, the deprived group has to be an active participant in the efforts to seek a change. Typically, in the 19th century, those who sought to bring about reform in the condition of women in our society were often men, and women did not figure prominently as leaders. Those reformers who sought the abolition of untouchability, including Gandhiji, were caste Hindus. Increasingly, now, those who are seeking to bring about a change are from among the group that suffers inequity. To that extent one finds an edge of militancy and impatience with the present leaders associated with social movements. They are led not by reformers but by 'activists'. They are protest movements and not reform movements.

One could say that as against the 'Harijan' movement initiated by Gandhiji which was largely reformist, the Ambedkar movement in the same cause was militant or activist. In the same sense, while Gandhiji's Harijan movement was reformist, his movement for freedom from the British was activist. There is an element of political mobilisation in most movements today and it has become easier to undertake such mobilisation in the post-independence period because the political institutions of post-independence India are more open. This is a major difference and a gain for those interested in promoting change.

There are as many movements as there are 'causes'—the women's cause, the environmental cause, the dalit cause, the cause of the agrarian labourer, the cause of displaced populations and so on. Often, there is more than one movement ostensibly for the same cause. This happens because 'causes' with a political potential tend to be utilised by more than one political party.

Activist social movements arise because there is inequity in many of our social institutional arrangements. Agitation through an organised movement is a part of the strategy for advancing a cause or advancing the interests of a particular group against whom an injustice is said to have been done by the prevalent dispensation.

The most deprived groups in our society are the SCs and the STs. Of the two, the SCs had a longer history of organised representation and agitation on their behalf since before independence. They were also the worse sufferers in the sense that apart from servitude and deprivation they also suffered the indignity of their very person being regarded as unclean and untouchable though they lived in a continuing interaction with the rest of society.

The movement for betterment of the lot of untouchables has now taken primarily the political route where the representatives of the SCs are expected to use their vote and influence to ensure betterment of the lot of their people. Free India has not yet been able to fulfil its promise to the SCs of providing the climate for their fullest development. They are caught in a network of unequal exchange and exploitation between the upper castes and the erstwhile untouchables. The worse case is probably that of Bihar where, as mentioned earlier, the economy of the landed gentry seems to depend on the subjugation and continued 'enslavement' of the untouchables and they have no qualms about using arms to suppress moves toward liberation. The political elite of the state has either sided with the landed gentry or has failed to bring them within the framework of law. Even, in other states, the problem of ensuring equal opportunity to the SCs is still very much with us.

The STs have also faced different kinds of problems depending on how close or far they lived from the main body of the Indian people. Those who lived away in distant hills in the northeast suffered isolation but they enjoyed relative freedom and maintained their cultural identity and dignity as a people. Free India, in its effort to ensure political integration, posed a threat to their sense of independence. They protested against being included in the Indian State and there was a long period of insurgency in the northeastern frontier region. The problem has only recently been tackled by dividing the area into separate culturally homogeneous states and ensuring that they have their own governments and also laws which protect them from being exploited by the plains people. The problem is not yet completely solved but has become more amenable to being handled within the political framework.

Those tribes which lived in the plains but occupied large contiguous geographical areas were also generally cut off from the main body of Indians and enjoyed relative freedom. But they began to suffer exploitation as Indian enterprise spread to these formerly tribal areas in search of metal ore and coal or found other reasons for encroaching on tribal land. The Santals in Bihar and the Warlis and Thakurs in Maharashtra are examples of tribal groups that had earlier lived in relative isolation though surrounded by settled agricultural villages. The Santals suffered loss of their relative freedom as the land where they lived turned out to be a major mining resource and collieries and iron ore mining spread to their villages. Their protest continues and the Jharkhand Mukti Morcha is its political manifestation. The Warlis and the Thakurs were a relatively small group. The cause of the Warlis received public notice because of Godavari Parulekar's efforts to organise their protest against virtual enslavement and economic exploitation.

Those who lived as nomads probably suffered the most deprivations in terms of finding the wherewithal for their daily life. They were partially dependent on the villagers with whom they interacted as roaming petty traders in forest produce or products of their own special handicraft. The bird catchers who are currently in the news either because there occupation is seen as cruel or as threatening the continuation of the diversity of species are an example of such nomadic group which has lived in a continuing economic exchange with the main society but is now facing a problem. These tribes which were divided into small groups have not been able to present any major organised protest.

Gradually, some individuals from among the STs who have benefited from the education opportunities first opened by Christian missionaries are now finding their way into the governmental administrative hierarchy through competitive examinations and the mechanism of reservations and a few tribals have also moved up the political channel and are important functionaries in the political arena either at the state or the national level. The tribals from the northeast have an advantage in that they have a higher percentage of literacy and education. The fact that in many cases their education is in English also helps them in their upward mobility and integration into the Indian elite. The problems of social and cultural adjustment however are still not resolved for the tribal communities as a whole. There is much mutual ignorance and suspicion between the tribals and the main body of the Indian society. The Indian government, while assuring tribal autonomy, also hopes that as they become involved in economic and political activities their isolationism will breakdown and there will be greater communication and exchange between these peoples living in the sensitive border area and the rest of the country at the social and cultural level as well.

It is neither possible nor necessary to cover all the social movements that are active in our midst today. I have touched only two of the most deprived sections in our society. It happens that movements relating to both these groups are today primarily political though the problems they face are both social and cultural. While protest movements against inequity are necessary, there is also an urgent need for strong movements for the promotion of education and internal reform among the SCs and STs. These are problems that would need to be addressed over a period of long years involving conscious social reorientation within the affected groups themselves.

CONCLUDING REMARKS

I began by saying that my presentation is in the nature of an impressionistic survey of the some of the important social changes that have taken place in India. I have restricted myself to the areas of marriage, family, caste, class and the situation regarding the SCs and STs. The promises that we made ourselves at the point of independence are still not fulfilled whether in terms of the main community or the minorities or the specially deprived groups. We have so far not been able to create an equitable social order. What we have is a generally secular and broadly open democratic polity. A democratic system should be a means to attaining a just society. It needs to be used for attaining our social goals. These goals will not be attained without conscious efforts on the part of those who are born to privilege as well as those who are deprived. It is such efforts that will give birth to a civil society.

8

Socio-Political Aspects of Development

THE WORLD CONTEXT

In recent years there has been considerable discussion on and analysis of the subject of social development. Most thinking on the subject tends to run along certain well-defined lines. It analyses the various strategies of development adopted by the countries which followed the 19th century capitalist model, or the 20th century welfare state model, or the Russian socialist model based on heavy industries and urban society, or the more recent one, rural-based Chinese socialist model. There is a certain internal consistency between the goals that were pursued, the means that were utilised and the larger political context within which these various models operated. There is also a consistency between the broader social ideologies and the ideas of appropriate personal behaviour that characterised life in these societies and where this consistency has been threatened major social problems have tended to arise. It may be useful to examine, even if briefly, the nature of the complex relationships between social philosophy, individual ethic and the broad politico-economic movements in some of these societies.

Capitalist society was clearly and firmly based on the concept of private property, the right of the individual to

---

Text of the Shastri Memorial Lecture delivered at Sambalpur University, 8-9 April, 1976.

maximise his profits and his wealth, the conviction that he who succeeded in achieving wealth was more capable, more intelligent and more skilled. Capitalist society did not accept equality in an economic sense as a value and it tended to regard inequalities as directly related to the industry or the indolence of the individual. The political economy of capitalism was based on free competition and a faith in the fundamental justice of 'free' market processes. The capitalist state was expected to protect the rights of private property but was otherwise not expected to intervene in the economic processes. It was expected that if each individual was free to pursue his own interests and did so apply himself, the interests of the larger social entity would be automatically taken care of. If in the process some individuals got thrown on to the scrapheap, it was only a vindication of the newly discovered biological doctrine of the survival of the fittest and the elimination of weaker strains in a species. The 19th century capitalism used religion as well as science to justify its procedures, explain its costs and boast of its achievements.

These achievements were manifested in a growing prosperity of the urban entrepreneur, the new middle classes and with the development of colonial markets of the working classes as well. The burden of the economic development of capitalist Europe was borne within each country by the working class and later by the Asian and African supplying territories which participated in the uneconomic exchange of supplying agricultural raw materials and receiving finished machine products.

There was an internal consistency in the economic doctrine of unbridled competition, the personal philosophy of rugged individualism, the doctrine of free international trade and finally, the white man's burden of civilising the colonies. They were all based on a sophisticated version of "success is its own justification" and on a denial of equality. The liberal humanism, associated with industrialisation, was a contribution of the newly emerging urban middle class which, in its own sense of social inferiority, was seeking an affirmation of its new economic well-being through concepts of civic and political equality, individual freedom, civic rights and finally, equal opportunity. Early capitalism had emphasised the moral virtues of hard work, enterprise, uprightness of character, fierce individualism and self-reliance. The idea that society had an obligation to provide opportunities to all its members was a later idea that was introduced by the liberals and it got further extended into the concept of the 'social rights' of individuals---the right to work, to education, to health, etc. 'Social' rights as different from the 'civil' rights came to be recognised when the working class had developed a certain amount of organisation and bargaining power. The intellectual impetus for it was provided by the liberal effort to meet the Marxist threat of class war; the material base for the recognition of these rights came from industrial prosperity and preferential trade with the poorer countries.

The concept of a welfare state grew gradually out of the idea of social rights. It was a response to the growing power of the working class and to the establishment of a socialist state in Russia at the end of World War I. It was an effort to combine the promise of a working class dominated socialist state with the individual freedom of the liberal-democratic state. The welfare state was very different from the state as conceived in the 19th century capitalism. It accepted the right of the worker to work and his right to compensation if he could not find work; it also recognised the right of the worker to organise and to fight for higher wages and for improved conditions of work. The social and personal philosophy had changed from rugged individualism and self-reliance to group dependence and social insurance. The state had to take active responsibility for ensuring the well-being of the citizen. While social and economic inequalities continued to remain evident in society, the disparities were greatly reduced. The value of equality was accepted and the responsibility of the state to ensure a certain equality of opportunities for all its citizens was emphasised. Educational expansion took place on an unprecedented scale and a network of health services became available to the citizen irrespective of his ability to pay for them. The welfare state bloomed into its fullness in Great Britain and in the Scandinavian countries. This state has allowed private ownership of capital and accumulation of private property to continue but it guarantees civil rights and provides a network of services to protect the social rights of citizens. If the capitalist state met the needs of the industrial entrepreneur and the aspirations of the rising middle class, the welfare state reflects the idealism of the established and enlarged middle class on the one hand and the aspirations of the powerful working class on the other. This working class has sought not so much an abolition of the class structure as an upward mobility within its framework. The workers gain this feeling of upward mobility through education, improved standards of living and through a subtle process of the professionalisation of skilled occupations. The extreme polarisation of class interests between the capitalist class and the workers, which was expected by Marxist thinkers, did not take place in the western capitalist democracies. The success of capitalist industrial enterprise and the expansion of the capitalist economy—based undoubtedly not only on technological superiority but also upon a long period of political domination of the developing countries and a further extended period of economic domination via multinational corporations—have minimised the possibility of workers in these countries engaging themselves in a bitter class war. In these societies liberal humanist values are still meaningful and all classes of society affirm them with a measure of conviction.

The socialist counter-argument against the capitalist path of development is that a capitalist society built on private property and the maximisation of individual profit is basically an unequal and exploitative society. The interests of those who control the means of production cannot be reconciled with the interests of workers. If the western capitalist societies seem to have escaped a major conflict of class interests it is because these countries were able to pass on the burden of development to their less developed colonies. The capitalist and the working classes of the industrialised nations jointly exploited the populations of the poorer underdeveloped societies. This is a temporary postponement of an inevitable struggle.

According to the socialists, the only way of overcoming the conflict is to abolish private property, remove the profit motive, bring all means of production under state ownership and regulate the economy to serve a common social purpose. Economic development should mean an increased well-being for the whole society and not for a small segment of property owners. In such a society all inequalities would stand abolished and the motivation for greater effort would be provided by satisfactions and rewards other than those associated with income differentials.

However, no country on earth has so far been able to establish such a completely egalitarian society. The Soviet society and all East European societies provide for income differentials commensurate with varying degrees of skill and responsibility involved in a job. The differences between the highest and the lowest incomes have certainly been reduced and stringent limits are placed upon the amount of property a person can accumulate and pass on to his children. Efforts are also made to provide free access to educational opportunity so that every individual who is talented will be able to get the education that he seeks.

The process of economic growth in socialist countries has depended upon their capacities to mobilise savings and capital resources within the country. This was achieved initially through expropriation of all private property and wealth and later through an imposition of rigorous limits on consumption. For the first time the state planned and developed the entire economy, controlled wages and incomes and imposed physical controls on production distribution and consumption of commodities. The expropriation of property affected not only the wealthy merchant and industrial entrepreneur but also the large and small landholder in the rural areas. The socialist states in East Europe as well as in China met with considerable resistance from these capitalist and feudal elements in their societies and found it necessary to develop an elaborate coercive mechanism to subdue these groups and their allies. These allies were drawn not only from amongst the old middle class, the bourgeoisie but also from the rural working class who were bound by considerations of loyalty.

There were thus important differences in the processes of development in capitalist and socialist countries. The former depended upon private property and the profit motive of the owner and mobiliser of capital to generate new wealth through adoption of new technology, minimisation of labour costs and a search and expansion of markets for their manufactured goods. The capital necessary for development was mobilised through personal savings (the importance of puritanism), an 'expropriation' of the surplus generated by workers working with new tools and later a regulation of the terms of trade with the colonies which supplied raw materials and purchased finished products. The subjective ethos of capitalist development was, however, one of 'freedom': freedom of enterprise for the entrepreneur, freedom of trade of the worker from feudal bonds, that is, the freedom to sell his labour for the highest price it would fetch. In actual practice, the freedom of the workers was notional since the workers competed against each other for work and the law did not recognise for a long time their right to organise themselves into unions to protect the terms and conditions of work. But, both philosophically and politically, the period of industrialisation in Great Britain, the USA and the North European countries was marked by a new sense of freedom: freedom in religion characterised by the protestant-puritanic sects, freedom of thought in the new-found rationalism supported by advances in science, freedom of the urban worker from feudal bondage and a gradual widening of the electoral base of representative political institutions. The new middle class was the backbone of this society; it generated a new life-view based upon individualism, rationalism and civil liberties. It spoke of such 'self-evident truths' as the dignity of the individual, his right to pursue happiness, to equal treatment in the eye of law and to be governed by his own chosen representatives. The concept of democracy applied not only to formal political institutions, but to various institutions in social life as well. Its faith in equality was based partly on the objective fact of the breakdown of the feudal social structure, partly on the experience of an expanding world of opportunity and partly on the great promise held out by education as a door to opportunity.

The socialist ethos was very different. East Europe was late and slow in its industrialisation. The middle classes did not experience the same expansion of opportunities that countries of Western Europe did. The landed, feudal aristocracy was still dominant even at the beginning of the 20th century. In countries of Western Europe the benefits of mercantile expansion, industrialisation and colonial occupation reached nearly all segments of the population though, may be, in different degrees. The working class, the middle class, the entrepreneurial class and the traditional landed aristocracy did not see their interests as necessarily conflicting. When industrialisation began in the countries of Western Europe, the Marxist ideology of class conflict and class war had not yet been born. When it was born and reached large segments of the people, the political economies of these countries had already progressed to such a point that in their economic prosperity they could absorb the challenge of the new ideology by making the adjustments implied in concepts of social rights, social security, the rights of workers to unionise and to bargain for protection and improvement of their working conditions. In

Eastern Europe, Marxist thought reached the intelligentsia and the middle classes long before they had become a part of the process of industrialisation under capitalist auspices. Further, the process of democratisation that had marked political developments in Great Britain and America had not touched Czarist Russia. It was still a land dominated by the court, the landed aristocracy and the peasantry. The young intellectuals who were influenced by Marx saw themselves as leaders of a revolution which, if successful, would bring about a change in the social, political and economic order. They wanted not only industrialisation and economic prosperity but also to establish a state which would be dominated by workers from the factories and the farms. They wanted to replace the rule of the aristocracy by the dictatorship of the proletariat. Marx and Engels had provided not only the economic argument and the philosophic base for the socialist state, but also the vision of the day-to-day life in a socialist state, and the strategy of establishing and consolidating such a state had to be worked out by the Bolshevik intellectuals. The strategy of a violent seizure of power and of a total revolution that the Bolsheviks adopted meant that it gave them the opportunity to cut themselves off from all old moorings and commitments and to start anew. The legal and philosophic base, the economic system and the political structure of the new Russian State that emerged from the revolution had nothing in common with the old Czarist State. The new state did not recognise the right to property or privilege; it expropriated land and other forms of wealth; it brought a whole new set of people---party leaders and party cadres---to power; it turned upside down the entire status structure of Russian society making the high-born to wish to pass off as commoners; it promulgated a new legal system, a new system of education and promoted the growth of new forms of art.

Though the new Russian State proclaimed itself to be the protector of the common man, the common man himself needed time and training to get used to new laws and modes of functioning. In the old Russian society the common man no less than the noble-born thought in terms of his possessions. His dream was to increase them, not to do away with them altogether. He envied the rich because they had more land and more wealth and his dream of a new order was to acquire them for himself. Particularly among the rural population the idea of being divested of all land was most unwelcome. The new Russian State, therefore, countered opposition not only from wealthy landowners but also from the poorer peasantry. The process of establishing the first socialist state was, therefore, a difficult one; it used physical force and coercion to subdue opposition from different quarters. The well-to-do, the middle class made up of shopkeepers, traders and professionals and even the small farmers in the rural areas found that the revolution affected them adversely and sought to oppose it to the extent they could. Some of these groups were won over, some were re-educated, some were sent away for long periods of hard labour and some were liquidated.

The use of brutal force generated an atmosphere of fear and uncertainty in which everyone except those who belonged to the party felt insecure. This was not only a short-term consequence; it has continued to the present. It is an irony of history that the western capitalist societies which were supposed to be economically exploitative and callous about the common man have in fact given him a greater sense of individual freedom than the socialist societies of Russia as well as China which speak of dictatorship of the proletariat. Allowing for the possibility that the days of intense surveillance, treachery and the fear of the midnight knock as depicted in *Darkness at Noon* are over, it is still true that the concepts of civil liberties and of individual freedom as they have developed in liberal democratic societies are not to be met with in the socialist societies. The mass media are controlled, the individual is not free to express himself freely on issues that are related to national politics and there is no freedom of association or protest in the sense in which these terms would be understood in a liberal polity. There are many reasons that have been given for this—the need to root out the internal enemy and to secure the freedom of the country against imperialist or fascist aggression being the commonest two. But, the fact remains that the socialist states of Russia and China have not been hospitable to ideas of individual freedom and have often abridged the concept of due legal process in judging individuals to have acted against the interest of the state.

This does not mean that these countries have not progressed. The achievements of the Soviet Union and now of China have by all accounts been impressive and it seems that in both these countries, though to varying degrees, the problem of abject poverty has been overcome and the great disparities of incomes have been substantially reduced. Their rates of economic growth have been among the best in the world at comparable stages of development. What is more, they have achieved this growth in the midst of general hostility which compelled them to set aside substantial parts of their national resources for defence.

The need to achieve rapid growth has been one of the factors that has led to the imposition of rigorous discipline on levels of individual consumption. While to some extent this discipline has been sought to be achieved through an emphasis on the individual's responsibility to the community, this effect has had all along to be reinforced by direct physical control on distribution of goods and services, development of an ideology of "simple is beautiful" and imposition of punitive sanctions against deviations from defined norms.

The socialist economy and the socialist state need to develop a philosophy of primacy of the community as different from primacy of the individual. If it can succeed in making community orientation an in-built part of the motivational pattern of the individual, it will have less occasion to use coercion to make the individual conform and it may well be that under these changed conditions the individual does not experience the deprivation that he would if he were socialised in a context where his individuality is itself a cherished value.

On this point of the establishment of community orientation as a dominant motivational pattern, the Chinese society has probably attained greater success than the Russian. The Russian population, which belonged primarily to the Judae-Christian faiths prior to the Bolshevik revolution, subscribed to the concept of the freedom and responsibility of the individual, whether for his own salvation or material well-being. This individualist emphasis has been a part of the occidental tradition and it would appear that neither the long and despotic Czarist rule nor the dominance of the orthodox church altered this basic individualist orientation. On the other hand, the Chinese tradition has been more favourable to thought conditioning and to integrating the individual into the community. Reading such material as is normally available on the Chinese revolution one gathers the impression that the Chinese have developed special techniques of bringing group pressures to bear on recalcitrant individuals in such a manner that he volunteers confessions and willingly participates in processes of re-education. This was noticed not only in the 1950's when the communists first began consolidation of their rule, but again during and after the cultural revolution of the late 1960's. The phenomenon of large numbers of persons in the army, professions and bureaucracy confessing to their shortcomings and seeking admission to the May Seven Schools for re-education is only comparable to the transgression-repentance-penance purification sequence in convents and monasteries, but then the number of individuals involved in the latter is small and select while those involved in the Chinese situation were literally thousands. It is of course likely that many of those who 'confess' do so out of fear of punishment than repentance, but it is difficult to avoid the impression that community pressure contributed greatly to the sense of shame associated with the so-called 'bourgeois', 'reactionary' or 'revisionist' sentiments and patterns of behaviour. At any rate, to the extent that such community pressure succeeded, it must have made it less necessary for the Chinese State to use direct physical coercion and custody. But this is at best a conjecture and it is unlikely that comparative facts will ever become available of the exact numbers of individuals who were liquidated, incarcerated or otherwise brutally punished during the Russian and the Chinese revolutions.

From the social developmental point of view the important point is whether there is any significant difference in the degree of community orientation achieved in the Russian and Chinese experiments. Since a socialist society must discourage individual profit and property as sources of motivation for its members, it would stand to gain if it can succeed in implanting community gain and community well-being as primary motivating factors in individual behaviour. Again, on this point, there is no knowledge as to whether the Chinese model has differed significantly from the Russian.

Independent of the success or failure in changing the motivational patterns of achievement, both the Russian and Chinese societies, after their respective revolutions, have had to find ways of mass mobilisation of children, youth and adults in nation building task. This is the socialist counterpart of the voluntarism which liberal democracies so greatly emphasise. Mass mobilisation, unlike liberal voluntarism, depends greatly on charismatic and authoritarian leadership. The mobilisation campaigns are important not only for the non-paid labour they make available, but also for the involvement and the immense commitment they generate among the people. The volunteer movements in liberal societies are largely based on individual motivation and to some extent, of course, on the desire to do what is currently fashionable. The mass mobilisation is often generated on the basis of political ideology and attains its results through systematic work done by trained party cadres. The process of mobilisation reinforces group identity, group activity and social-ideological commitment. Such mass movements characterised the early years of the Russian revolution, but in China the Maoist strategy seems to be to keep alive this populist base and also use it as a device to curtail the power of the party as well as governmental bureaucracy because in socialist societies the inevitable tendency appears to be for power to accumulate in the hands of the party, government and army officials as different from the western capitalist-liberal societies where it accumulates primarily in the hands of owners of capital and to a lesser degree in the hands of government and army officials.

Another point on which the Russian and Chinese models are often compared is the strategy of industrialisation. Any process of economic development involves a major programme of industrialisation. Both Russia and China had to begin by laying down the infrastructure for heavy and capital industry and the industry required for defence purposes. The resources required for this development were raised in both countries by stringent regulation of consumer expenditure and imposing heavy burdens and sacrifices on the peasantry. Despite these similarities there appears to be some difference in the Russian and Chinese patterns. From the beginning the Russians seem to have accepted the western capitalist model of a dominantly urban-based industrial society in which the proportion of the population engaged in agriculture would be systematically reduced. Of course, even today, there is a much larger proportion of the Russian population engaged in agriculture than is true of any major western countries, but the urbanward direction of change seems to be clearly set. In China, this does not look to be so clearly accepted as a goal. The population of China being what it is, it appears to have been realised by the Chinese planners that any attempt to convert this primarily rural-agrarian society into a primarily urban society in the foreseeable future is unrealistic. Perhaps, this is a policy dictated by current necessity, but there is a distinct impression that the Chinese political leadership is firmly aware of and rooted in its agrarian base. The Chinese achieved in a remarkably short period the task of organising the entire countryside into some 30,000 communes. They have been able to work out the problems of production, distribution and management of communistic agriculture with relative ease. They have also developed social services in the fields of health and education which would be consistent with their resources and availability of technical manpower. The Chinese have struggled to develop diverse innovations such as backyard steel plants, barefoot doctors, locally suited systems of sanitation and methods of agricultural cultivation in all of which the effort seems to have been to find solutions within the means available to the country and taking into account the plentiful supply of labour resources. The adoption of labour-intensive, rather than capital-intensive, methods of production, the development of education and health systems which would not depend wholly on highly qualified personnel and the use, wherever possible, of known technologies with suitable adoptions have been dictated by the particular circumstances of Chinese development.

The reason for undertaking this somewhat extensive discussion of the western capitalist, Russian and Chinese paths of development has been to show that though in all the three of them the effort had been to move toward an industrial society characterised by higher economic productivity, the historical antecedents and the social contexts within which these economic changes took place imposed their compulsions and each of the societies developed political instrumentalities, value structures and philosophies that met their own particular situations more or less adequately. This task of developing political structures and corresponding motivational and belief systems involves detailed thinking and working out of various strategies suited to the local social, demographic and cultural context. It may well be that the political leadership adopting a particular political-economic philosophy may seek to root out and transform the traditional structures rather than to accept them as limiting conditions. Even so, something approximating a total vision of the kind of life that is sought to be generated is necessary. Such a vision should outline the economic and political order that is desired, the type of education, health, housing and urban development that would be promoted and, above all, the motivational and attitudinal base of the new society. This total vision or an image of the kind of life and society that is sought to be created is essential for it to serve as a guide in detailed policy making in the various segments of life.

The need for such a comprehensive perspective of the type of society to be created is particularly necessary in those cases where the political authority undertakes to plan, regulate and direct various aspects of life as in socialist and communist societies. The early capitalist society had no blueprint of what it was developing into but in spite of that, capitalist society soon developed a philosophy—the laissez-faire, liberal, democratic philosophy—which guided and limited governmental as well as individual action in certain ways. Many aspects of social institutional life evolved over long periods of time and in their evolution philosophic generalisation and existentialist reality interacted and moulded each other. The politico-economic philosophy of western capitalist society can be seen to have evolved through a long chain of historical events and periods beginning with the Magna Carta, the Renaissance, the Age of Reason, the French Revolution, the enunciation of the American Constitution and the gradual widening of the electoral base of representative, political institutions. The specifically economic concept of personal property, the individual's right to acquire and hold, the role of the state in protecting the individual and his belongings, and the institution of family inheritance have in fact much earlier beginnings in history.

The ideas basic to capitalist society thus evolved over the ages; socialist society on the other hand is a recent artefact of human history. If one sets aside instances of primitive communism and instances of small groups living in closed communities at various points of history, socialism as a political philosophy can be said to have been born in the 19th century with the writings of Karl Marx and his contemporaries. The leaders of the socialist movement and of the socialist states have, therefore, had to think through the implications of their broad egalitarian philosophy in relation to the family, property, economic and political institutions, the role and place of the individual *vis-à-vis* society and have created an entirely new system of relationship to govern various aspects of individual and social life. Obviously, not all the facets of a socialist society could have been visualised and legislated upon at one time; each of the socialist countries has had to experiment and find its own answers and introduce variations. But, the total period for which socialist states have existed has been small—not even a hundred years—and the need within the period to create politically, economically, socially and psychologically viable social systems has compelled them to undertake a much more conscious and time-bound process of norm enunciation, socialisation and enforcement.

It is obvious that this whole process of creating a new society, or a new system of social relationships, is so complex that it could not have been all done at one point of time nor can it be said to have been done once for all. There was policy enunciation, experimentation, controversy and modification or change of policy in various aspects of life depending upon the social reality and response of people. In the socialist states such changes of policy have often been associated with party strife, scapegoating, purges and a re-establishment of a new political equilibrium. The socialist polities, because of an excessive centralisation of political power, despite widespread people's mobilisation at the field or implementation level, have so far shown an inability to provide for changes of policy without any attendant violence. They have also so far not found an easy institutional mechanism to ensure a smooth succession to high political office on the death of the leader.

However, despite these limitations, the socialist leadership and the socialist states have more or less adequately met the requirements of spelling out the programmatic implications of broad statements of social goals such as equality, abolition of private ownership in land and capital and the attainment of social and economic development within a comparatively short period of time.

To recapitulate our argument so far we have tried to argue that the capitalist, welfare capitalist, Russian socialist and Chinese socialist models of development differed from each other in some significant ways; each of them was inspired by social philosophies defining the relationship between the individual and society in somewhat different ways and each of them sought to create societies which were in some ways different. It is true that the capitalist and the welfare capitalist polities have some things in common; e.g., the acceptance of the role of private initiative, private property and private control over the means of production. Similarly, the Russian and Chinese models have certain characteristics in common; e.g., the concept of total state responsibility for economic initiative and planning, state ownership of the means of production and the near abolition of all forms of private property. But there are also important differences that separate each of these pairs. The early capitalist state began with the concept that each individual was responsible for his well-being and the state had only the role of ensuring free competition and providing protection of property. It was based on a fierce individualism where poverty was considered proof of individual failure. The worker was free to choose his employer, but he was not allowed the right to unionise since this interfered with the concept of free and open competition and bargaining. Welfare capitalism has given up this passive concept of the role of the state and argues that government has a positive responsibility for ensuring the minimum well-being of the individual citizen. While it allows private ownership and competition among entrepreneurs, it accepts the value of equalising opportunities for individuals at least to the extent of making education and health services available to all. Further, the welfare capitalist state finds itself under the compulsion to reduce gross inequalities of income because it is only by taxing the rich that they can provide services to the poor. Though welfare capitalism began as a movement in a few capitalist societies, it characterises today most of the industrially advanced capitalist societies and may, in a sense, be looked upon as a stage in the growth of capitalist society. However, there are important differences in the degree to which income inequalities have been reduced in different capitalist societies.

Similarly, we have seen that there are probably important differences between Russian and Chinese models of socialist development. From an economic point of view both societies are committed to rapid industrial growth through a state-owned and state-managed economy based on time-bound plans. In order to ensure this growth both the countries have found it necessary to mobilise savings by imposing sacrifices on the agricultural sector. Yet it appears that in a social and political sense the Chinese are reconciled to continuing as an agrarian society for many years to come and that the rural communes are a much more important political power in China than probably they are in Russia. From a socio-philosophical point of view it seems that the Chinese pattern of mobilisation had tended to emphasise more successfully than the Russian the need for a basic change in motivation. In that sense Chinese society is more completely contra-positioned to the pure capitalist society than the Russian. It has sought not only to abolish private property, but also de-emphasise if not root out self-orientation as the basis for economic activity. It has sought consciously to reduce variations in clothing and other items of consumption as a part of the strategy to reduce diversionary demands on limited productive resources but this is also likely to have helped in subordinating individualism to a consciousness of the communal entity. Another important difference between the Russian and Chinese patterns, emerging from the latter's acceptance of a rural agrarian base, is the active search by the Chinese for an intermediate technology and for models of social service delivery more specifically suited to a large, far-flung agrarian society.

It would be an interesting exercise in social analysis to try and ascertain how far these variations in patterns of socio-economic development are due to variations in the objective factors of class relationships and how far due to variations in the influence of ideas in these different societies. That however is not the purpose of the paper. Our emphasis rather is in underlining the fact of diversities and in arguing that despite broad similarities different societies seem to find it necessary to define their particular paths to achieve these goals to suit their own conditions. These conditions are made up of the objective reality of social relationships as also of the values and belief systems in terms of which this reality is perceived. If this perspective is valid, then the important question before the countries which are currently facing the challenge of social development is not "which model of development shall we follow?", but rather "what development strategy or strategies shall we evolve to suit the social relational and cognitive compulsions of our society?" The path that we will finally follow will be seen in retrospect to have had some similarities with the paths followed by other societies but it will not have been the same as any other. Our solutions may have to be our own.

This does not mean that a study of the developmental experience of other societies has no use for countries launching on the process of development now. They have a value in suggesting probabilities of success or failure of particular paths in given contexts but they have an even greater value in suggesting that in social phenomena there is a strain toward consistency and societies which have adopted one path of development have to ensure that the necessary social and psychological supportive structures also exist or are created. There is a need for a unity of perspective in the type of society sought to be created. We have seen that the capitalist and socialist political economies create their own compulsions and have to be supported by appropriate social philosophies, motivational systems and social institutional mechanisms. Therefore, if our society aims to build a democratic socialist state, it would be necessary to understand the implications of this goal for all the major institutional frameworks of our society. This is of course a task too forbidding for any single person to undertake. What is attempted in the next section is something more modest. It seeks to show what contradictions emerge in the absence of a consistency between the social vision and the social reality and what might be some of the implications of our accepting the goal of democratic socialism for our society.

THE INDIAN CONTEXT

The people of India gave themselves a Constitution in 1950 which declared India to be a Sovereign Democratic Republic. The Fundamental Rights defined in the Constitution of India guarantee the civil rights of the citizens. It clearly depicts India to be a secular state with a federal structure based upon universal adult franchise and representative, parliamentary form of government both at the Centre and in the constituent states. The Preamble to the Constitution, the Directive Principles and the Fundamental Rights also speak of equality of status and opportunity for all the citizens of India. This equality is primarily equality before law, freedom from discrimination on grounds of religion, race, caste, sex or place of birth and equality of opportunity in matters of public employment. This is not equality in an economic sense or income equality. The Directive Principles of State Policy also lay down principles which under Article 39(b) require that the ownership and control of the material resources of the community are so distributed as best to subserve the common good, and under Article 39(c) which requires the state to direct its policy towards ensuring that the operation of the economic system does not result in the concentration of wealth and means of production to the common detriment, and under Article 41 to guarantee within limits of its economic capacity and development the right to work, to education and to public assistance in certain needs. Thus, Articles (39)(b) and (c) are the only indication of what might be regarded as the socialist orientation of the Constitution makers and Articles 38 and 41 are the closest they come to declaring the 'welfare' goals of the state. But Articles 38, 39 and 41 are all parts of the Directive Principles of State Policy which are not enforceable by any court, though these principles are regarded as fundamental and as directing the state to use them as a basis in the formulation of laws. On the other hand, the right to property is a fundamental right under Article 19(1)(f), though this right is abridged by Article 31 which provides for compulsory acquisition of property by the state and by Article 31(c), a later amendment, which gives precedence to the egalitarian goals contained in clauses (b) and (c) of Article 39 of the Constitution.

Certain facts emerge clearly from this discussion. In 1949, when the Constituent Assembly adopted the Constitution, what it gave the country was a liberal democratic Constitution which accepted fully the concepts of civil rights, secularism, equality before law and equality in matters of public employment. It also laid down principles, which were not enforceable in courts of law, directing the state to provide work, education, social security and public assistance. The principles also laid down that the state policy must ensure that community resources serve the common weal and do not get concentrated in the hands of a few people or a section of the community. But, the welfare goals as well as what may be called the socialist orientation of the Constitution are limited by being only 'directives' given to the state.

It would seem that in the Constituent Assembly there was unanimity on providing a parliamentary democratic form of government for the country. There was also agreement on the broad liberal thrust of the values enunciated in the Preamble but the egalitarian objectives were only acceptable in their humanitarian sense, not in the sense of an egalitarian economic order. Even the humanitarian concept of 'social rights', represented by the right to work, education, health and public assistance, is conditionally accepted as a goal subject to the economic capacity of the state. The only way in which socialist goals have gained an entry is through clauses (b) and (c) of Article 39. The word 'socialism' finds no mention in the Constitution.

But, the functioning of a democracy in a poor country develops its own political compulsions and it is a testimony to the democratic nature of our polity that over the past 25 years political parties and government have been under continual pressure to adopt policy goals which are people-oriented. It is under this compulsion that the nation's major political party has moved from 'welfare' to 'a socialist pattern' to 'socialism' as its goal. It is in the context of this shift that one hears declarations by political leaders that India has adopted socialism as its political goal. But what exactly does this 'socialism' mean?

In the classical sense socialism has stood for a form of economic organisation in which the means of production—land as well as industry---are owned by the state. It is possible that all the 'leftist' and 'left-of-centre' parties have this as their goal, but this has not been reflected so far in government's policies either in relation to land or industry. The Industrial Policy Resolution passed by the Indian Parliament speaks of a division of industries wherein some would be wholly or dominantly in the public sector and some in the private sector. And so far as agriculture is concerned, though there have occasionally been schemes and programmes for encouraging cooperative farming and joint farming, there has never been a move to completely nationalise agriculture. The term appropriately used for describing this form of economy is a 'mixed economy'—one in which private and public owned enterprises will coexist in the industrial field and wherein imposition of ceilings on land will be legislated in the agricultural sector. One may go further and say that this is an economy in which government will retain the initiative to interfere through legislative, administrative and fiscal measures, the justification for such intervention being the interests of the poor who constitute nearly half the Indian population.

The Indian economy is thus not a socialist one. Politically, socialist societies have not had a representative democratic base; in Russia, China and Cuba there are single-party governments which allow for participation of the common man at the local level, but the elections to party office are limited to the party cadre. This is not true of India. India has a parliamentary form of representative government and the most drastic constitutional change so far suggested by some is that the parliamentary form be replaced by the presidential form of government. So, even in a political sense, the socialist society visualised in India is not the same as that in the currently socialist countries.

The dominant reason for the use of the word 'socialism' in the Indian political context seems to be that it stands for a less unequal society, a society where everyone will have the right to a livelihood and the provision of the basic necessities of life, a society characterised by greater equality of opportunity, and a society where private interest will not be allowed to conflict with public interest nor to impede the effort to ensure the well-being of the majority. It is this kind of a vision that seems to have motivated the socialist within the Indian National Congress prior to independence and many of the middle-class socialists of the left-of-centre variety have still a commitment to the concept of a democratic polity but they are hoping that this democracy will give rise to an egalitarian society.

The crucial question is whether in conditions of gross national poverty and in the context of a highly stratified society India can succeed in developing an economically strong, self-reliant, egalitarian society through democratic political processes and a 'mixed' economy. From a Marxist or socialist point of view the answer would seem to be that the Indian experiment cannot succeed. A mixed economy, despite state regulation, is not a socialist economy. It may at best be a non-capitalist economy, but it is subject to the same internal contradictions as a capitalist economy. The contradictions would arise from at least two sources---the unresolved conflict of class interest and the inevitable paradox between social good as seen from the point of view of the individual in pursuit of his own interest and social good as seen from the community's point of view. The basic capitalist institutions of property and private ownership of means of production are not attacked and so long as they are allowed to continue they will dominate the political and economic decision-making processes in the interests of the well-to-do minority and against the interests of the mass of poor people. The socialist critique points out how under a mixed economy the rich have tended to grow richer and the poor poorer in terms of real incomes; how the political system which should in principle be responsive to the needs of the poor who are in a majority has in fact become dependent upon the small industrialist and the urban trading class for financial support to enable the parties to meet organisational and electioneering expenses; how the caste structure has on the one hand prevented the polarisation of class interests in a political sense and has on the other ensured the continuance of the hegemony of upper caste groups in rural life; how the efforts to mobilise developmental resources through taxation are impeded by large-scale tax evasion; how the attempts at regulating investment in different sectors of the economy are hindered by a corrupt bureaucracy; how the redistributive and price regulatory measures of government are countered by the inflationary pressures created by black money; how the developmental expenditure on education, health, housing and other services gets channeled in such ways that public subsidies seem in fact to lighten the burdens of the middle and upper income groups rather than of the poor; and how in short every well-intentioned move even to reduce iniquities let alone inequalities gets defeated by the contradictions of a mixed economy however welfare-oriented and well-intentioned it might be.

The western capitalist welfare societies with their network of social and social security services arose at a late stage of economic development when they could mobilise the resources to support on the one hand the need for additional capital investments and on the other the demand to raise the general levels of consumption for the entire society. Even at this stage of development it is argued the high standards of life in these countries cannot be supported except on the basis of an international system of stratification in which the developed countries seek to maintain control over the raw material resources of the underdeveloped world. The implication is that in the absence of such stratification and the exploitative nature of the terms of trade between developed and underdeveloped countries the welfare orientation of many of the developed countries cannot be sustained except by a major internal redistribution of incomes and the capitalist nature of their economies may prove an obstacle to such redistribution.

The possibility, therefore, of a poor, underdeveloped society being able to meet the dual challenge of finding the necessary resources for capital investments so essential for development and of meeting the needs of the mass of their poor must, therefore, seem remote, except under conditions of socialist mobilisation. The two major characteristics of this mobilisation are a violent change to complete the initial process of expropriation and a subjugation of the individual to the party and state bureaucracy.

The concept of democratic socialism is born in this context where the effort is to achieve both individual freedom and social equality. The essence of the Indian experiment---not as enunciated in the Constitution, but as elaborated by national leadership over the years---has been this effort to see whether the democratic process of open discussion and adjustment of conflicting interests can succeed in developing in all segments of the population a social commitment which can keep in check the rapacity of individuals and help fulfil the liberal promise of freedom as also the socialist promise of equality. It is obvious from the above summary of the socialist critique, and much of it is valid, that the Indian polity has not succeeded so far in fulfilling its promises to the poor. This awareness has made the liberals more and more receptive to the need for a statutory limitation on the right to property and on private control over major segments of industry. But how far can such statutory regulation help? Can the conflict between private and public interest be minimised; can measures for reduction, if not removal, of inequality be legislated; and can such legislation be enforced in a society which is formally democratic but where gross inequalities stifle the process of open discussion, organisation of interest groups and election of true representatives?

The answer to these questions would depend a great deal on the meaning given to the term 'democratic socialism' and the steps taken to operationalise it in specific policies. In India, the term 'democratic socialism' is used confusedly and interchangeably with the concept of a welfare state. However, as we have seen, there are essential differences between the western liberal model of the welfare state and the concept of socialism. The welfare state is typically an industrially advanced, democratic capitalist state. In place of economic equality the welfare state introduces the idea of 'equal opportunity' and this equal opportunity is sought to be provided through open access to social services and particularly to education. If the term 'democratic socialism' is used ambiguously in place of the term 'welfare state', certain consequences are likely to follow and certain questions will arise. In a poor country characterised by gross inequalities a greater emphasis on the concept of individual freedom in comparison with the concept of equality is likely to prove self-defeating. Usually, freedom has also been interpreted to mean free enterprise. In the short run it will lead to a worsening of the social and economic disabilities of the poor since they are not organised to protect their own interests and in the long run it will affect the political stability of the country. The concept of democracy in the western world gained strength in a period of economic expansion where first the middle classes and later the working class experienced a perceptible rise in their standards of life. This was also accompanied by the expansion of education and the growth of a strong workers' movement which enabled the latter to fight for their rights through collective bargaining and through legislative action. The attempt to reduce inequalities of income directly and through provision of social services did not directly threaten the principle nor the profitability of private enterprise. In the developing countries the operation of a democracy will depend on the extent to which the goal of equality is accommodated and reflected in the legislative and economic policies of government. In a long-term perspective it is possible that the various disadvantaged and weaker sections of the community will have gained sufficient consciousness and organisational strength to assert their claims to a share in national wealth, but in the immediate perspective the responsibility of ensuring that these claims are recognised will lie with the government. This may seem a somewhat paternalistic view of the role of government, but there is always an element of altruism, if not paternalism, in any social arrangement which begins by rejecting the principle that might is right.

The acceptance of the claims of the poor will have wide ranging implications for state policy. The state will have to begin by defining poverty and stating the basic minimum needs that it will seek to fulfil in the case of the poor. Since the poor, by any definition, will constitute almost half the populations of most developing countries, any commitment to meet their needs even at the minimal level will involve relatively large financial allocations. This will compel the state to adopt policies of reduction of consumer expenditure on the part of the somewhat better-off and very well-off sections of the population. This will also raise questions about the appropriate technology that a developing country should adopt; should it continue to use labour-intensive methods (which incidentally are often also less efficient in terms of time and worker productivity) or should it adopt highly mechanised capital-intensive technologies with high productivity ratios but low employment potential? Or, are there any intermediate technologies available? The attempt to reduce consumer expenditure among the middle and upper middle classes will also raise questions of the modus operandi. Does one allow high profits to be made and high income to be earned and then seek to regulate consumption by high taxation and direct physical controls, or are there ways of effectively limiting the accrual of high incomes in the hands of individuals? What are the implications of the economic necessity of checking consumer expenditure on the style of life that is generally adopted by the rich and the one that should be encouraged in formal and informal ways?

The socialist state seeks to solve all these problems by abolishing the role of private initiative and decision-making in the economy. Simultaneously, it uses direct sanctions and the pressure of public opinion generated by ideological indoctrination in checking overt deviance and inculcating appropriate attitudes and lifestyles. In many ways the policies and actions of the socialist states are anti-individualist in their implications, but they succeed at the level of giving the state the necessary initiative and control. The democratic socialist state in India has been experimenting with the device of gaining a controlling interest over the economy without really displacing private enterprise. However great the control it may gain, the premise of a mixed economy is that private initiative, private enterprise and profit making are necessary and legitimate activities. These ideas seem to be a part of the traditional liberal ethic and seem inseparable from the concept of individual freedom which is at the core of much liberal thought. The economic policy of the state, therefore, tends to be to first allow high incomes to be made whether at the corporate or individual level, and then to try to mop them up through a system of direct and indirect taxes. This in its turn raises the familiar problems of bureaucratic corruption, fringe benefits and black money. Will the democratic-socialist state give up its experiment of a mixed economy and accept the socialist alternative of abolishing private enterprise and of directly controlling and managing the economy, or will it be able to develop other effective ways of generating savings, minimising wasteful expenditure and reducing economic disparities? Can we devise a system of production which does not give rise to gross inequalities, does not create pressure towards conspicuous and wasteful consumption and yet ensure high productivity? The state-managed socialist economies provide one pattern. It has been suggested that the Gandhian concept of a village-based economy provides another pattern. But, the concept of Gandhian economy in its relationship to the modern world has yet to be developed, though the Gandhian emphasis on village industry may have great relevance as a socially protective policy during a period of transition.

The acceptance of the claims of the poor also raises questions of priority in the types of consumer goods that will be allowed to be produced. Should scarce capital and raw material resources be utilised to produce cars and refrigerators or should they be allocated to develop mass transit systems? There are also questions about the relative priorities and investments in agriculture and industry. They in turn will influence policies on land legislation and the maximum units of land that a family can own. There is no aspect of social, economic and political life which will not be influenced by this basic decision to accept the claims of the poor.

The democratic socialist state also faces another set of problems in the areas of education, health, housing and other services. In all these spheres the existence of gross inequalities has meant a different quality and set of services being available to those who can pay and those who cannot. This in turn has also meant that a greater proportion of the nation's resources are in fact being utilised to provide trained and professional personnel in the form of teachers, doctors, engineers, etc., who will selectively serve the higher income groups rather than the lower income ones. In the field of education, we spend several times more per student on higher education then we spend on primary and secondary education. The enrolment in institutions of higher education is still predominantly from urban, higher income and high caste groups. Government is continually under pressure to expand higher education facilities even when a substantial proportion of the graduates remain unemployed or underemployed.

In the field of health, the services of qualified doctors do not reach the rural areas and an increasing proportion of those who undergo post-graduate education in medicine opt to go abroad and serve in the USA, Canada, the UK or Australia. In effect, our scarce national resources are subsidising the health delivery systems of developed countries.

In the education of engineers, again, the experience is similar with considerable numbers of post-graduate trained persons from the Indian Institute of Technology migrating to other countries.

Thus, the inequalities in incomes lead to the creation of educational facilities which meet the desired income goals of the well-to-do and since the country cannot afford to engage their services, they migrate to other countries. Further, the inequalities in income also lead to unequal services becoming available to different income segments of the population.

In housing and municipal services in the urban areas, again, we see the emergence of gross disparities in the facilities and services that are available to the well-to-do minority on the one hand and the middle and low income majority on the other. Three-fourths of the population of Indian metropolitan cities is made up of those who live either in one-room accommodation, shanties or on footpaths.

In all these areas of economic and social planning, the democratic socialist polity faces major dilemmas. Its efforts to reconcile individual freedom and equality in its polity have usually proceeded with a somewhat greater emphasis on the concept of freedom (including free enterprise) but they have fallen short of their own limited goals in ensuring equality, or even equal opportunity. Can this situation change? Can democratic socialist politics find answers to these dilemmas? Will they be able to develop strategies which while retaining the democratic structure also meet the socialist egalitarian goals? Is an orderly change from elitist to egalitarian socio-economic policies and social structures possible?

It was suggested at an earlier point that the answer to the question, "Is a democratic socialist polity possible in conditions of underdevelopment" depended on the meaning given to that term and the capacity of governments to devise and enforce strategies which give at least as much emphasis to egalitarian goals as to the goals of individual freedom and free enterprise. It may now be said that part of the answer lies in the kind and degree of value commitment among those who would lead such a society. The important role played by ideas is recognised both by the liberals and Marxists. In the case of one it takes the form of idealism and in the case of the other of ideology. Based upon his idealism a liberal would like to believe that this kind of orderly change is possible. He would like to admit that the record of achievement so far is not impressive, but instead of giving up he would like to examine what has gone wrong with the experiment and seek to introduce correctives and alternative strategies within the framework of an open society. The Marxist would say that an orderly or democratic change from a mixed to a socialist economy is not possible since all those whose interests are threatened will put a last ditch fight before they surrender their interests, i.e., civil strife and expropriation of private property are essential conditions for the birth of a new order.

However, neither orderly change nor revolution would come about by themselves. There is a need for some group in society to provide the leadership and to undertake the task of bringing about change. The urban middle class which had been in the forefront of the freedom struggle has, along with the large farmer, industrialist and trader, benefited by the large volume of expansion that has taken place in employment in government, industrial middle management and professions. It is true that in comparison with the wealthy farmers, industrialists and traders, the middle class, particularly the salaried segment, has always felt overburdened by rise in prices and tax rates; on the other hand, in comparison with the rural poor made up of the small owner-cultivators, tenants, landless agricultural workers and artisans as also in comparison with the unorganised worker in the urban areas, the middle class has benefited a great deal from the programmes of development.

While the real incomes in middle class occupations may not have gone up equally at all different levels, the members of this class have had a feeling of upward mobility---perhaps only a movement from rural to urban occupations in some cases---and a sense of share in power as it is exercised by the bureaucracy and the professional groups in society.

The middle class still continues to be politically active and provides the leadership not only in the ruling party but also in parties of rightist and various shades of leftist ideologies. However, on the whole, the middle class has lulled itself into a feeling that with the achievement of freedom its various social, economic and political goals have been achieved and what remains to be done can now be done through the normal legislative processes. Liberalism, which even in the developing countries has been the philosophy of the middle classes, has been blunted by a false sense of achievement. While the political goal of liberalism has achieved, though only in a formal sense, its economic goals as reflected in the concept of a welfare state or in the later neo-liberal concept of a democratic socialist state are far from being achieved. It has now become clear that the legislative process by itself cannot achieve results; in a primarily illiterate and politically non-conscious society the benefits of legislation get diverted to groups for whom they were not intended. There is, therefore, an unfinished task still left for the middle-class liberals to perform in ensuring that the actions of the democratic polity are supported, guided and channelled to serve the interests of the poor through education, organisation and democratic social action. In this task, the mild-mannered reformer, the ascetic self-sacrificing worker and the aggressively militant organiser have all a contribution to make.

Some will say that the middle class which has aligned itself with the industrialist, trader and large farmer can hardly be expected to promote or participate in activities which are likely to be frowned upon by its masters. There is some truth in this remark. Yet it is the same middle class that leftist and revolutionary parties look at for new recruits to undertake organisational work. In the underdeveloped countries there is often no other class which can provide the initial leaven for any change whether of the reformist or the revolutionary variety. At times some aggrieved and discontented individuals of the middle class may make a convenience of the sufferings of the poor and use their cause in an effort to achieve their own social or individual objectives. At other times it may be that some of the socially conscious individuals who have taken the altruistic values of their culture more seriously than others feel strongly motivated to register protest at the flagrant violation of these values. It may also be that a part of the middle class also shares in some of the economic and social deprivations of the poor to a greater extent than any other group and see the opportunity of their own interests being served by espousing the cause of the working class and of the poor. Whatever the reasons, history has shown repeatedly that the middle classes have played an important role in initiating movements of social change-----at least until the less advantaged groups have gathered the courage and the strength to fight their own battles.

In the Indian situation it would seem that in the first 25 years of independence the middle class had lost its moorings in idealism (or even ideology) and had been preoccupied in getting its share of the benefits of a very unequal process of development. This is not to deny the fact that even today the leadership of some of the poor and working class-oriented movements comes from the middle class but rather to underline the fact with a few exceptions the vast numbers of those who participated in the struggles of the 1930's and the 1940's did not stay with the movements of protest but chose to become a part of the establishment. Even the variety of socially conscious moderates who had stayed out of active politics but gave dedicated service in the fields of education and social service seems to have thinned out in numbers. Also, during the first twenty-five years of freedom, the people's attention and hopes had been focussed almost exclusively on the central and state governments and their doings; the Gandhian constructive worker, social reformer and the leaders of left protest movements had not caught the imagination of the people. The constitutional promises, the party manifestoes and the personal charisma of national political leaders had pre-empted their arguments and made their exercises superfluous.

Yet, no democratic society can function effectively and expect to maintain its dynamism if the citizenry expects that its problems will be solved for them by governmental action alone. A modern democratic society takes cognisance of the existence of varied interest groups in society and looks upon the legislature as a place where, through discussion, exercise of political leverage and open lobbying, decisions are made which allow for more or less 'adjustments of rival interests'. The decisions are very often compromises and the several groups must maintain pressures and seek to gain decisions more acceptable to them.

If such a democratic process is to become a reality, then, there is a major task of education and organisation to be undertaken on a continuing basis. In a large country the responsibility for undertaking this task must be shouldered by the small minority of educated, white-collared, middle-class individuals. Whether they will do so will depend partly on the objective situation in which they find themselves—on whether, for example, they see their own chances of upward mobility increasing or decreasing—and partly on the value system to which they are committed. If they have a commitment to a democratic society they will seek to use and expand the opportunities provided by the system of openly elected representatives to organise and press the claims of the disadvantaged. If they have a commitment to theories of interest conflict rather than to interest reconciliation, they will seek to mobilise the disadvantaged for a constitutional but militant struggle. Even these value commitments may not be wholly discrete or entirely unrelated to objective experience.

Cross-sectionally, at a given point of time, they may appear distributed randomly among individuals and the result of their own individual choice, but over a historical period of time there will be a tendency for certain values to gain greater acceptance than certain others.

Speaking for the present, it is possible that the influence of the liberal tradition on the middle class is still strong, but the idealist urge has weakened so that one sees in many places a kind of negative goodness and an absence of active social concern. If this situation continues the middle class will not be able to play any significant role in channelling the developmental processes within the country along the democratic socialist lines.

On the other hand, if this situation can be changed and if idealist influences can prevail, the liberal leadership can still help to find a way to achieve an egalitarian society along a democratic path. In order to be able to do this, the liberal leaders will have to undertake a vigorous and wide-flung campaign of education and organisation.

The education campaign will have to reach both the well-to-do as well as the poor. The well-to-do will have to be persuaded of the need to change their life view and adjust to a new way of life in which the claims of the poor will have to be recognised not only through symbolic, philanthropic gestures but centrally as the major thrust of state policy. Among the poor this education will have to bring a new awareness of socio-economic reality and of the need to give up traditional attitudes of helplessness or impotent rage. The poor are as used to a hierarchical organisation of life as the rich; this makes them look down upon and distinguish themselves from those who are even more unfortunate. The industrial worker looks down upon the unorganised worker who in his turn looks down upon the itinerant artisan, who looks down upon the roadside vendor and all of them, probably, consider themselves superior to the helpless agricultural labourer. Equally, the dreams of the poor are only those of becoming rich though their concept of riches may be very limited in its sweep. The concept of a society with narrower margins of income differentiation is as unfamiliar to the poor as to the rich.

While education is important, it is not enough. The faith of the 19th century liberal in education was based upon its being considered the door to opportunity. That, in a limited sense, it may still be but education is not the key to social change especially a change involving a major adjustment of material interests of different groups in society. For that purpose organisation is important. In the early 20th century some of the liberal leaders undertook the task of organising industrial workers; they now need to carry on this task to the other unorganised workers in the urban areas and more particularly the agricultural workers and artisans in rural areas. Without organised strength no occupational group can protect itself in the modern contractual society, whether this society is capitalist or socialist. The task of organising rural workers is likely to be even more difficult and politically explosive than organising industrial workers, but unless this task is successfully undertaken the interests of the poor can never be safeguarded in a primarily agrarian society.

Whether this task of carrying education and organisational strength to the poorer segments of society will be shouldered and successfully carried out by the liberal, democratic-socialist leaders is yet to be seen, but without it the hope of creating a socialist society through democratic means is not likely to be fulfilled. What is worse, in the absence of people's education and organisation—that is in the absence of an effective base for popular participation---socialism as well as democracy may both stand in the danger of turning into some variation of 'national socialism' or 'fascism'. It is, therefore, urgent that both old and new liberals devote themselves to these tasks.

9

Social Policy and the Sociologist

Today, I wish to speak on a subject which, while it may seem to lack theoretical sophistication, is still of great practical import for the Indian sociological profession. The subject is the 'Role of the Sociologist in Formulating Social Policy' in a country like India. The reason for my choosing this theme for discussion is not that it is new but that the need for the sociologist's involvement in social policy formulation is still largely unmet. After three decades of planning and after early two decades of the realisation that there is a need to give a 'social' dimension to the planning of development, the actual involvement of the sociologist in planning is still marginal. I do not blame the government for not involving the sociologists in the planning process nor am I going to make a plea here for this hereafter. My plea, if any, is for the profession of sociology to take the area of social policy formulation as one of its direct professional concerns.

The sociologist has largely left the field of developmental planning and social policy formulation outside his area of study. While there are some areas like industrial sociology, sociology of education and sociology of medicine that are being slowly developed as courses of study in applied sociology at

---

Presidential address delivered at the 16th All India Sociological Conference, Annamalainagar (Tamil Nadu) in December 1982.

some of the Indian universities, there is to my knowledge no university department where any systematic effort is being undertaken to study the processes of social policy formulation and to develop skills which would equip sociologists to participate in the process. A few research institutions and some schools of social work have however started taking interest in this area but the sociologist seems to have generally kept himself out of it either on the assumption that his generic skills of social analysis are not adequate to meet the needs of the situation if he is called upon to play a policy making role or because of the feeling that this applied area is not strictly his professional concern.

I would like to submit that neither of these two positions is sustainable. While, undoubtedly, the basic analytical skills of the sociologist are useful---in fact, essential—for a proper understanding of the problems in social policy formulation, they by themselves are not adequate to meet the needs of social policy formulation. Policy formulation involves not merely analysis but also an ability to formulate intermediary, viable goals towards which sustained social action---on the part of the state as well as the wider community---would be required. These goals cannot be stated at the level of global generality but have to be operationalised as measureable targets which can be attained through a set of action programmes. There is nothing in the equipment of the sociologist as presently trained which enables him to think in these terms. This is a set of skills that needs to be systematically developed through research, training and practice.

On the other hand, I would not concede the position that these are tasks outside the domain of sociology. If the sociologist is concerned with questions like---Do we have an open system of education in the country? Does it succeed in equalising opportunity to different segments of the population? Is our system of elections truly democratic? Does our political system allow people of different strata to participate effectively in it? Whom does our legal system benefit? Are your hospitals serving the poor? and other questions of this type---the sociologist must also necessarily take interest in policy formulation, policy assessment and policy implementation. Our professional interest need not be restricted solely and arbitrarily to the development of analytical skills. These skills have to be fortified by the ability to participate in various processes of policy formulation to the extent that opportunities become available to different individuals. A sociologist cannot merely be a detached observer of social reality; he has also to interpret the implications of what he has observed for the individual citizen and for the larger community in terms of certain stated or implied values and goals. If he is a good and conscientious interpreter, he may even feel the need to be an advocate of a cause or a group. A person interested in social policy has to be much more explicit about his values and goals than a sociologist generally tends to be.

SCOPE OF SOCIAL POLICY

A policy statement is an indication of the direction proposed to be taken by an authority in a given field of activity. A social policy is a policy concerning the social aspects of community's life. Even in a narrow perspective, social policy can be said to be concerned with programmes and services in the areas of health, education, housing, rehabilitation, social welfare, and welfare of the backward classes, or the weaker sections. But, from another perspective, there is hardly any area of governmental activity in which some social issue is not involved. Decisions relating to location of industry, overseas trade, nuclear research or a choice between investments on the infrastructure for the building of buses or the making of small cars—all involve social questions, such as regional development balance, national self-sufficiency, commitment to goals of peace and the relative primacy given to the needs for the many rather the demands of a well-to-do minority. Areas as removed as those of civil and criminal justice systems also involve issues of social policy because on their functioning depends a possibility or otherwise of the proverbial common man receiving justice in a reasonable time and with minimum costs.

The social policy pursued by a country expresses itself in many ways even if the government has not consciously identified specific areas as areas of social policy. The presence or absence of measures for an equitable distribution of national income, measures of social insurance and social assistance, governmental pronouncements on industrial location and industrial ownership, legislation on industrial relations, legislation on marriage and divorce, the very nature of legislation and jurisprudence, of the acceptance or otherwise, of the concept of *habeas corpus* express the nature of social policy adopted by a government.

To my mind, social policy is primarily concerned with the following sets of issues: (i) human freedom and the rights of the individual citizen, (ii) equality and equal opportunity and, finally (iii) human welfare. They arise because the modern state has accepted the idea of the responsibility of the state for the well-being of the individual citizen. In a *laissez-faire* state, there are no social rights, just as in a non-democratic state there may not be many political and civic rights. Social policy involves both these sets of rights and the guiding value considerations in both these areas are those of individual freedom, social equality and humanity. The concept of 'welfare' is variable and somewhat residual depending upon how passive or active a state is in recognising different human needs. But, whether in a capitalist or a socialist state and irrespective of whether the state is passive or active, there will always be the general, unspelt expectation that the state will ensure the well-being of the citizen. This expectation is linked to the basic assumption on which an organised community comes into being. Thus, issues relating to human welfare arise in all different polities, though the specific human needs that would be covered by 'welfare' consideration will vary considerably depending upon the initiative taken by the state in anticipating and providing for potentially problematic situations in the life of its citizens, as a part of its regular package of service. This does not mean that welfare programmes are of a residual category but the extent of state response to welfare needs and even the identification of certain situations as constituting 'need' is still largely dependent upon individual governments.

SOCIAL POLICY AND SOCIAL STRUCTURES

In the literature on social development the issues of human freedom and social equality have come to be looked upon as constituting a dichotomy. There is a suggestion that a state will tend to emphasise either one or the other and not both. The common stereotype is that democratic states, which follow the parliamentary forms of government based on adult franchise and a secret ballot, tend to emphasise individual freedom, but because they also protect private property and freedom of private economic enterprise they tend to be characterised by gross inequalities of income distribution and thus fall short on the value dimension of equality or even equal opportunity. Correspondingly, the 'socialist' state imposes limitations on private enterprise, regulates the distribution of national income and probably achieves a greater measure of equality but such a state carries its restrictions from the economic to the social and political areas and denies the individual citizen his freedom of association and expression.

These stereotypes, like all other stereotypes, are overly simple and in the history of the last thirty years, particularly in Western Europe, where there have been many efforts to see whether the virtues attributed to the two polities cannot be combined. The Scandinavian countries, in particular, have undertaken several experiments to combine free economic enterprise with greatly reduced social inequalities. It is claimed on behalf of these countries that speaking in terms of averages the difference between the highest and the lowest levels of income in these countries has been reduced considerably and it is now of the ratio of 1: 5 or 1: 7. This has been achieved largely by increasing the pay packets of individual employees (a result of the strongly organised workers' movement in these countries) and by an increase in the social insurance and social assistance coverage available to the different segments of the population. These countries are still 'capitalist' though most of them have had varying periods of socialist and social democratic governments which came to power through the normal electoral process. All these countries are also democratic and ensure to their citizens the maximum degree of individual freedom as visualised in western political philosophy.

It may be conceded that in no society can the goals of freedom and equality be achieved in any absolute sense. The achievements are relative, even so there is a distinct difference in the quality of life in different societies depending upon whether and to what extent the societies allow these values to be realised. Using the two values dichotomously one obtains four types of societies: (i) those in which citizens experience the maximum degree of equality and freedom; (ii) those in which economic inequalities have been reduced considerably but which allow less freedom to their citizens; (iii) those in which considerable freedom is experienced by the individual citizen but which are otherwise characterised by gross inequalities; and (iv) those in which the citizen enjoys neither equality nor individual freedom.

Countries of Western Europe generally may be said to be characterised by a considerable degree of freedom for the individual citizen, but despite their prosperity and general economic well-being, they are also characterised by the existence of considerable economic inequalities. Countries of eastern Europe---the socialist countries---are said to be characterised by a considerable reduction in economic disparities but deny the basic freedoms of expression and association to their citizens. As mentioned earlier, the Scandinavian countries are supposed to have approximated better the twin goals of freedom of the citizen and reduction in social and economic inequalities. Finally, one may identify many sheikhdoms and rightist dictatorships of the world as representing societies in which their is neither freedom nor equality.

The Indian Constitution speaks of a democratic, secular and socialist republic being established. Our record on individual freedom is on the whole good, though it has been blemished by the emergency, the many 'encounters' between police and anti-social elements and the recent draconian measures in one of the states aimed against the freedom of the press. Our record on social and economic equality has been very unsatisfactory. Not only have we not attained a semblance of economic equality, but also our society has failed so far to remove gross poverty and has not been able to assure even a reasonable opportunity for the poor to rise above the condition in which they are born. The only remedial steps that have been taken so far are in the direction of a policy of positive discrimination in favour of those born in the backward castes or in tribal communities.

The failure of the Indian experiment so far in removing gross poverty despite considerable technological development and a satisfactory food production situation has raised a basic question in the developing world as to whether the experiment of combining freedom and equality in the process of development can at all succeed in a poor and traditionally inegalitarian society. Within the country itself, there are protagonists of the right and left paths who would like the country to opt clearly for their particular solution. The sociologist who is interested in social policy would have to study this relationship between social structure, level of technological development and the social policy alternatives that have been experimented with by different countries with a greater or lesser measure of success. One of the questions that is crucial in this discussion is whether a poor country can retain an open policy and yet develop a 'hard' state, in the sense in which Myrdal uses the term, to achieve better income distribution.

SOCIAL POLICY IN THE AREA OF SOCIAL WELFARE

Apart from questions of freedom and equality, there is the third value dimension of human well-being in the simple physical, material sense. At one end, this implies the minimisation of human suffering through provision of at least the basic human necessities of food, clothing and shelter. At the other end, this is a continuing effort to provide a structure of opportunities in which individual human beings can achieve the maximum possible growth they are capable of. At this end, the concerns of social welfare and those of social development generally overlap because among the structure of opportunities which would enable human beings to grow the conditions of freedom and equality would also find a place. However, social welfare tends to focus on the more obviously handicapped or underprivileged sections of society and while freedom and equality would have an important place even in their context, primacy tends to be given in their case more often to providing necessities and accessories of life which would enable disadvantaged individuals or groups to overcome the limitations to which they are subject and rise above them to the experience of a richer life.

In an analysis that has by now become a classic in social welfare literature, Richard M. Titmus has sketched out the three different models that seem to have been adopted by different societies in meeting basic human needs. He called them the Residual Model, the Achievement-Performance Model, and the Institutional-Redistributive Model.

Under the Residual Model the state took only marginal responsibility for providing food and shelter to cases of extreme need arising out of physical handicap such as old age or joblessness over an extended period. The dominant idea was to make the service so unattractive that no one except persons in barest need would want to suffer the humiliation of accepting them. Individuals in need of such services would be put in institutions where they test both their initiative and freedom. Those institutions were often supported by the church and the local nobility as a part of their charitable work. These arrangements came into existence during the later middle ages and continued through the 19th century in Europe. The individual's immediate or extended family had the first responsibility to help him in his need. Those who could not muster such support and were not aided by kind neighbours or individual philanthropists became the responsibility of the church or state-supported institutions. The state accepted very limited residual responsibility for the care and well-being of its citizens.

The second model obtained in West European societies of the early and mid-20th century. In some of the western capitalist societies it is even now the prevailing model. The state provides primary education and public health services but for the most part the philosophy is that the individual should obtain these and other services by paying for them, by deserving them. This idea developed through mutual benefit and cooperative societies into different types of insurance and pension schemes in which the benefit drawn is proportional to the amount of contribution by the beneficiary during his active life. The puritanic ideals of achievement and performance dominate the welfare scene and those who do not merit assistance by reason of their contribution to the common fund are aided as cases of charity and public dependence. This model is still the most dominant one, with some variations, in most capitalist countries. In this model, a clear distinction is made between social insurance and public assistance cases.

The third model that Titmus has identified is the Institutional-Redistributive Model in which the state provides the citizens with all the services, such as health, education and housing as well as the services of welfare for the specially needy, as a charge on the exchequer and as normal expenditure. This is based on the principle that each will be given according to his needs, independent of what his contribution may work out to be. This is the socialist model of providing social and welfare services. Of course, even in the operation of the model, there are limits to the benefits derived by individual citizens. The principles of merit or achievement necessarily centre at certain points. For example, while education is free in this model, not everyone will be able to have as much of it as he wants. He will have to maintain a certain level of achievement if he is to proceed beyond the stage of compulsory education. There is bound to be a relative scarcity in terms of demand in the provision of health education and housing facilities. The state only guarantees a certain minimum to all.

In the sphere of social welfare services, again, the sociologist focuses on the linkage between social structure and the pattern of services made available in that society. Under what conditions can a country mobilise resources to support a system of full distributive justice? Can a poor, developing country maintain an open polity and still find ways of mobilising people and resources for supporting such a system? What organisational forms and motivational impulses need to be generated to achieve this?

DATA NEEDS FOR SOCIAL POLICY

The goals of social policy analysis are to facilitate an improvement in the quality of life of people in terms of certain value criteria and material objectives. This requires on the one hand an unambiguous statement of the values cherished and sought to be achieved by a society. We have discussed so far some of the value dimensions of social policy that can be identified from a study of our national constitution as also the pronouncements of government from time to time. A social policy also involves the attainment of marked objectives or the delivery of specific services. A study of social policy, therefore, also necessitates an assessment—a quantitative assessment—of the material needs of the people in terms of specific services like those of health, housing, education and social welfare.

Such an assessment of needs can be undertaken on the basis of data which may either be readily available or may have to be collected specifically for the purpose. In many countries, the general population census provides the most important single source of assessment of what some of the needs of the population might be. The census data give the total population as also the breakdown of the population by age, sex, civil status, religion, occupation, education, rural-urban location, etc. Preliminary census data analysis also reveals certain trends on population structure, population mobility and migration, the rate and extent of urbanisation, etc. Usually, however, census data give no information on health status, housing status or on attitudes and practices of the people in areas relevant to social policy. Even so, the census data are extremely useful as they provide the basic information on which one can base estimates of how many units of particular types of service structure are likely to be required to meet the needs of different segments of the population.

The National Sample Surveys (NSS) provide additional qualitative as well as quantitative information on aspects which are not covered either by the census or in the same detail or with the same frequency. So far, the NSS studies have focussed largely on economic and demographic aspects. Social services, their coverage and effectiveness have not been commonly covered by these surveys. For this purpose, special studies have to be undertaken. The data for these special studies may be collected either through the existing service units at the field level or afresh through specially organised studies.

Data about social and social welfare services have to be of three types: (i) those that indicate the extent of service needs based on some yardstick, (ii) those that indicate the adequacy in number of the present services available in the field, and (iii) those that evaluate the adequacy and effectiveness of the services in terms of the quality of service rendered. Effectiveness again may be judged in terms of meeting some set administrative targets or in terms of achieving the further goals of improving the quality of life.

There is a great deal to be said for a fuller utilisation of available census and NSS data. In general, sociologists have tended not to use these twin valuable sources of information. In the area of social policy these two constitute the most vital data with which one must begin. Additionally, there are results of studies undertaken by the individual departments or the Programme Evaluation Organisation in the Planning Commission. All these must be used fully for undertaking an analysis of social policy issues.

After the data from those sources have been fully utilised, we may still find the need for special epidemiological studies for assessing the prevalence of particular problems or small diagnostic studies for establishing the relationship between particular sets of factors which may be suspected to be 'causally' related to the occurrence of particular problems. There may also be experimental studies undertaken to judge the efficacy of newly devised remedial measures in the context of particular problems.

The sociologist must develop the skills necessary for the effective use of available data in analysing social policy and in planning as well as executing special studies wherever they might be necessary. In both these aspects of data use and analysis, the sociologist will need to develop appropriate indices for enabling him to monitor a situation over time to say whether the various services are helping us to move closer to the goals of individual freedom, social equality and human welfare through distributive justice. These indices may be positive or negative.

Positive indices might be in the nature of measures of spread of education and literacy, the existence of a free press with a wide and responsive readership, the existence of a system of representative government and the regularity with which periodic elections to various bodies are held, the degree of participation by members of the legislature in the discussions, the degree of contact between the selected representatives, and their constituents, the existence of an open access to education, the extent to which this access is in fact utilised by the relevant population, the existence of positive enabling measures to help the disadvantaged sections to benefit by services in the areas of health, education and housing, the type and variety of programmes for fostering distributive justice in the community, and the like.

The negative indices for social policy could be derived from many types of data, viz., (i) data on infringement of individual freedom, cases of detention of individuals without trials, the frequency with which the Maintenance of Internal Security Act is used, the number of deaths that take place in police encounters with suspects, the number of deaths in police or in judicial custody, etc.; (ii) data on denial of equal opportunity in jobs or admissions to educational institutions based on considerations of sex, race, religion, caste or region, and on prevalence of bonded labour; (iii) data on extent of income and wealth inequalities in the community; (iv) data on extent of unemployment or underemployment; (v) data on number of orphaned children, run-away children with special handicaps who are not cared for by any system of familial or institutional care; and (vi) data on handicapped, aged or needy who are not covered by any programme of social security.

A new infrastructure will have to be developed or existing agencies may have to be strengthened to facilitate the collection and dissemination of data on issues of social policy. As pointed out earlier, some of the data should be routinely available on a periodic basis to the concerned departments of government to enable them to plan services. May be they are available in raw, unaggregated form in some of the departments, but they are not publicised or utilised because most social planning in India tends to be symbolic in nature. There is so far no commitment to provide services to all the needy groups and individuals in the country in any given period of time. In this context, the publication of data on 'needs' may sometimes be actively discouraged by administration. This would make it all the more necessary for sociologists who have an interest in social policy to raise the issues time and again until government takes note of them and commits itself to plan social services on the basis of universal coverage and not symbolically, experimentally or on a pilot basis as at present.

SOCIAL POLICY AND THE ROLE OF THE SOCIOLOGIST

The sociologist can play many different roles in the promotion of a social policy which will help achieve a humane, egalitarian and democratic society. He can be an analyst and help identify problem areas as well as inadequacies in the policies and programmes devised by government. He can be a teacher of social policy and help in inculcating the skills of research and analysis in his students. He can be an interpreter and an advocate on behalf of disadvantaged groups to bring home their difficulties to the planners and policy makers and finally, he can himself participate in policy formulation directly as a social planner. If he has to perform these various roles, he must first take an active interest in issues of social policy and be more articulate on them.

I believe, the time has arrived when one no longer needs to make out a case for involving sociologists and other behavioural science specialists in the process of social planning. The limitations of planning with purely economic parameters have been generally realised, but the necessary expertise to provide the social component has not yet developed. It is not likely to be developed except by a process of participation at various levels of the planning process. This is what the sociologist must do. For this he must first become better informed about and more involved in activities associated with planning at different levels.

If sociologists wish to take their social policy formulation role seriously, they must develop seminar and lecture courses, undertake more research and write more on social policy issues. As mentioned earlier, there are a few research institutions that have taken a lead in this and some have even sought to familiarise themselves with various social action groups in the community. University departments must now pick up this trend and carry the interest in this subject to the classroom both for purposes of teaching and for discussions with senior students. This will give rise to more doctoral and other research as well as to more insightful writing on the subject.

An important point for the sociologist to bear in mind in the area of social policy and social planning is that he is not the only specialist required in this field. Social planning is a team exercise. Economists, political scientists, psychologists and social workers among others would also have significant contributions to make in this field. He has, therefore, to be prepared to work with persons from other disciplinary orientations as members of the team. If he loses sight of this fact, he will commit the same mistake for which he has frequently blamed the economist so far.

10

Defining Basic Social Needs for a Programme of Social Development

The concept of needs is a relative one. Human needs vary with time and place, from society to society and within a society from individual to individual. They vary with education, economic standing and in response to individual idiosyncracies. The concept of a need involves a judgement, first, that the denial of a particular object---a commodity, a service, a position, even a particular attitudinal orientation on the part of others---is likely to lead to undesirable consequences for the individual concerned. Except for the very basic, organic needs of hunger, sex and physical protection against the environment, most other needs have a strong social base. Even the physical needs mentioned above are culturally conditioned. There are approved ways of expressing and fulfilling needs—even the most basic and simple need for food. Certain times of the day are appropriate for eating and certain types of food are appropriate to eat. In fact, most societies seem also to dictate directly and indirectly who shall eat what kind of food. In this sense, all human needs are social, i.e., they are socially conditioned.

The effort in this paper will be to identify needs---physical as well as social---which are likely to be most pressing in a developing society, and whose non-fulfilment will impede the process of development. Such needs are by definition basic to the survival of human beings as well as to the achievement of relatively long-term developmental goals for society. The word 'basic' recognises a certain primacy and immediacy of certain needs; it presumes a certain distinction between the short-range and the long-range perspectives in the fulfilment of various needs. It assumes that the developmental process is gradual and one that widens in scope and gains in tempo at later stages in the time sequence. In terms of this perspective, there are certain needs which must be met here and now and others which can be met later when greater resources have been generated.

The availability of resources is one factor in determining which needs, or rather how broad a range of needs, is likely to be recognised as 'basic', but equally the social values and the developmental goals of that society are an important determinant in such recognition. Plans of development invariably call for sacrifice of consumption in the present so that proportionately much more may become available in the future, but how this sacrifice is distributed between different segments of the population will depend upon the politico-economic values, the political realities and the developmental goals pursued by a society.

Early industrial development in Western Europe called for heavier sacrifices by the poor and the working class whose life in the urban areas was characterised by pauperisation, long hours of work, low wages and a denial of the right to organise themselves for protection of their employment. Even the municipal services of health, protected water supply, sanitation and primary education became available to them only in the last quarter of the 19th century. Industrialisation and agricultural development in Russia followed a war, a revolution, an expropriation of private property and the denial of all traditional privileges to the erstwhile aristocracy and middle classes. The condition of the poor was not very much better than their condition at the beginning of industrialisation in West Europe and the USA, but efforts were made to ensure supply of the necessities of life—food, clothing and shelter—to all segments of population. For a long time, the condition of the agricultural workers in Russia was worse than the urban working class. The political economy was characterised by nationalisation of all means of production, a state regulated economy, the development of a strong party machine and a stern, ruthless pursuit of economic development and political consolidation. In case of Western Europe, the right of the poor to work, regulated conditions of service and a minimum supply of food and clothing were not accepted as a responsibility by the state. The poor were provided for through charity and later they benefited as the total economy of these countries prospered through industrialisation and colonialism. Gradually, through the 19th century, their material conditions improved and by the end of the century they benefited by the expansion of social services undertaken by the state but it was only in the 20th century that the right of the workers to unionise was recognised in these countries and the workers gained social protection against unemployment, ill-health, etc. In the Russian pattern, the actual conditions of life of the poor were not necessarily better, but their deprivations were shared by the white-collared groups as well and they were sought to be provided with the necessities of life as a part of the responsibilities of the state. But, while the concept of economic equality in a relative sense was accepted and formed the basis of the political economy of communism, the idea of individual freedom—in the sense of freedom of speech and association—was not accepted by this society.

When we attempt to define basic needs in a developing society in this last quarter of the 20th century, we have to take into account not only the available resources but also the ideological influences that are operative in the developing and the developed world today. The developing countries of the world are all characterised by mass poverty, large and growing populations, bad housing, illiteracy, high mortality rates, unproductive agriculture, gross inequalities of social and economic status and a very thin industrial infrastructure. Most developing countries of today were colonies of European nations and suffered, what Marxist economists call, a long process of 'systematic underdevelopment'. They are newly independent and in most cases are still caught in a system of international economic exchanges which breed dependence. The development goals of all these countries include, first, economic growth---a growth in the total resources available to the country at the societal level as well as the individual level. But, apart from economic growth, they have made ideological commitments variously to equality or freedom or both. Not unusually, even where two societies use the same words, such as freedom or democracy, they imply entirely different political structures by it.

We have to identify basic social needs against this background of the socio-economic reality and the social values of the developing societies. Given this background it is not surprising that all developing countries are agreed that the highest priority should be given to the removal of poverty. There is, however, no unanimity on the strategy to be adopted for removing poverty. Is poverty something to be tackled now, or is it something that will wait until after the process of development has been completed? Besides, what does poverty mean? What type and level of deprivation is to be regarded as characteristic of poverty?

Speaking for India, one may say that poverty implies malnutrition---inadequacy of food intake in terms of total caloric requirements of the human body and, of course, in terms of the different types of nutrients required by the body. I need only refer to the well-known study of V. M. Dandekar and N. Rath to make the point that even by this minimal criterion nearly half the population of India is poor. The removal of this poverty---the poverty of starvation---is, therefore, the first basic social need for development. This needs to be done now and cannot await a future stage of relative growth.

But starvation is only one face of poverty, though the one most easily recognised. Such poverty is necessarily accompanied by the deprivation of the other necessities for physical survival such as clothing and shelter. The generally warm climate makes scanty clothing and shelter somewhat tolerable, but at least for a quarter of the year in the northern states of the country, the climate is so severe that persons who are ill-clad and poorly housed die of exposure to the weather. Such deaths are reported every winter and though they may be few in number, they represent only the most extremely affected segment of the population. There must be large numbers of people who suffer because of inadequate clothing and cover against the cold but whose suffering is not reported since in a poor country sustained suffering is a common occurrence. The need for shelter takes a particularly acute form in the larger metropolitan areas where the solutions offered by the modern technology of housing, sanitation and water supply seem to be particularly ill fitted to the resources available to poor countries. The problems of accommodating large populations in small areas with high residential densities seem to call for an expensive technology of house building and servicing. Since the poor countries cannot mobilise the order of resources required, they witness the growth of blighted areas, slums and shanty towns where the individual shelter is inadequate as a protection against the elements and the colony as a whole is likely to face a problem of environmental sanitation.

One way of looking at the problem of poverty is to look at it as a problem of gainful employment. Certainly, at the level of the individual, paid employment seems like a solution to the problem of poverty and the creation of employment opportunities is thus a basic social need. But, payment of wages for work is only a way of distributing access to the totality of goods in the community. Where the essential goods are in short supply, as in developing countries, the poorer segments of the population are likely to be outbid in their efforts to exchange their wages for these goods. In the last analysis, of course, there is no solution to national poverty except through increased production in every sector of the economy. In the immediate context of scarcity, however, there is a need not only to create more jobs, but also to ensure proper distribution of essential commodities through systems of physical control.

Thus, gainful employment, coupled with an assured supply of essential commodities, is the first basic need in developing countries. The generation of such additional employment may result from the adoption of normal development plans aimed at an increase in the gross national product (GNP). But employment should be regarded not as a possible by-product of economic growth, but as an instrument of achieving it. The provision of employment is the best form of social security and if new jobs are not created in sufficiently large numbers in the normal course of development, special efforts may have to be made to achieve this goal through reordering priorities as between the agricultural, industrial and tertiary sectors either through the adoption of an intermediate technology or specially designed programmes of employment generation such as guaranteed employment schemes, rural works programmes, etc. The creation of conditions of full employment must be a developmental goal in poor countries and a means of development as well.

It is likely that in the short run the provision of full employment through the adoption of labour-intensive technology and schemes of guaranteed employment may appear to be uneconomic and a drain on the scarce resources which are needed for industrial growth. On the other hand, sustenance of human life must be accepted as a minimal precondition to any planning and if any sacrifice has to be made for mobilising capital, it must be called forth from groups who live above the poverty line and its incidence should be proportional to the level of well-being of the citizen. This is one aspect of the concept of social development—reducing the iniquitous burden of development from the shoulders of the poor.

Beyond the immediate goal of removing poverty through employment creation and guaranteed supply of essentials, the most important need in a developing society is to ensure individual freedom and equal access to opportunity. Freedom and equality are interdependent values; there can be no equality except in the context of freedom; any constraints, whether social, economic or political, which limit the freedom of the individual also limit his access to opportunity. Needless to say, freedom is not a licence and he who would be free must also learn to accept the responsibility for his actions. But freedom to think and speak within the limits set by the rules of civilised existence is a necessary condition of individual growth and social participation. Freedom cannot be held back and then given to a people as a gift after economic development has been achieved. Similarly, equality is a condition of freedom in society; one is not free in the social context except in so far as he is equal or has equal access with others to opportunity. An inegalitarian society cannot be a free society; equally, an authoritarian society, or a society where individual freedom is curbed, cannot ensure equality of opportunity. Freedom and equality are both essential conditions for human development whether in an individual or a social sense. The fact that neither of them are fully realised in any society is countered by the fact that throughout history human beings have searched for it in every society and in the face of all adversities. Freedom and equality are essential for the achievement of human dignity.

The next basic need is health, not only in the sense of freedom from disease, but also in a positive sense. Such a concept of health requires not only, or in fact, not so much the provision of clinical and hospital facilities, but rather the provision of preventive and promotive health care through adequate and nutritious diet, supply of pure drinking water, environmental sanitation, freedom from pollution, provision for active recreation and prophylactic care. Good health is necessary for all the hard work and increased productivity that social development calls for, and it is equally necessary for enjoyment of the fruits of development. Experience of the poorer countries has shown that preventive and public health measures had a greater share in reducing mortality rates in the underdeveloped world than dispensary and hospital services had. Preventive health measures are less expensive and make less demands in terms of technical manpower and equipment than the clinical and hospitalisation services do. Countries at the beginning of the process of development may find it wiser even in an economic sense to give greater attention to preventive measures of health protection and health promotion. From this perspective, the basic health needs would have to be spelt out in terms of diet, personal hygiene, environmental sanitation, prevention of all types of pollutions, protected water supply and prophylactic measures. Such a programme requires a much higher level of public awareness and participation than a clinical-curative health programme does. Health education must, therefore, receive high priority in the health programmes of developing countries.

Another aspect of health programmes in developing countries would be that since the emphasis has to be on prevention rather than cure, the services should be specially geared to the needs of children. A great deal can be done for laying down a sound basis for health while a person is still young. The first few years in a child's life are crucial for his physical as well as mental health throughout his life. Developing good health habits among children and giving them adequate food are an important aspect of health measures in any community, particularly in the poorer countries.

Of as much importance as the health need is the need for education. Education is, of course, a need from the point of view of the individual and his life aspirations but it is equally important from the societal point of view. The large degree of unemployment among the educated in developing countries has currently led to a certain disenchantment with education in some of these countries, but while the exclusively upper class orientation of education in these countries may have to be modified, there can be no doubt that education is both a political and technological necessity for modernising society. Even in the early stages of development, education---at least education in the sense of an ability to read, write and count---is a minimal necessity for communication and political mobilisation. Government in a modern society, of whatever political hue, must communicate with the people and must continually transmit messages about what it is doing for the citizen. An exclusive reliance on the spoken word is far too limiting; written communication in the form of regulations, job instructions, extension advice and just plain information has to be utilised as between the individual citizen, his family, his work-setting and the several governmental agencies he daily comes into contact. It has been seen that without education a citizen cannot protect his interests, he cannot grow in the job or in his occupation, he cannot fully benefit from the services, viz., health, education, welfare, etc., that a government offers and to which he is entitled as a citizen. A citizen who is not educated, cannot keep himself informed, and maintain a level of awareness which would enable him to participate effectively in the life around him and even less to contribute to the society. Further, a developing society requires the creation of a sense of common identity between many ethnic groups that comprise it. A minimum level of education is necessary to make the individual accessible to messages which in their subtlety or complexity would otherwise go beyond the daily experience and the routinised pattern of his life. An ability to change, or to look at things in new perspectives, is more easy to promote among those who are informed and educated. Education in this sense involves developing the ability to comprehend and communicate ideas and experiences beyond the level of direct sense experience, though such an ability is not directly proportional to the number of years spent in school or college, but formal education is useful in developing it.

Further, despite the general disparagement of much of higher education in India, no one can deny that higher education is necessary for technological development and self-sufficiency. The pattern of education may have to be modified but it cannot be done away with. The need for education in this sense, i.e., general, basic education and higher education, is a basic need that must be met. It has the potentiality for enriching the life of the individual in a literal and figurative sense; it also provides the kind of citizenry and economic manpower that a developing country needs.

Another important social need in developing countries is the need to lower the fertility rate and reduce population growth. Some recent thinking on problems of development has tended to emphasise that large populations need not be looked upon as liabilities but rather as assets. There is also an increasing emphasis on adopting appropriate technologies which are suited to the situation of manpower surpluses, especially at the level of low skills, than manpower shortages. But, both these are basically adaptive responses to the demographic facts in developing countries. No one has seriously suggested that developing countries should be encouraged to enlarge their population because large populations are an asset. In the short run developing countries have no option but to accept the fact of populations which are rather large for the resources that they can generate, but in a long-term perspective limiting the size of their population is seen as a developmental need if the levels of living for the general run of people are to improve. Today, in many countries, the rate of economic growth is counter-balanced by the rate of population growth so that the added resources are being utilised to meet the additional demand of the population that has been added over the same period. Given the increasing inequality in the distribution of the national income in many developing countries, a growing population means that despite an increase in GNP the levels of living of the poorer segments of the population will in fact be adversely affected.

Since, however, population increase at the national level is a consequence of very personal attitudes and behaviour at the individual level, any success in attaining the objective of lower fertility rate will depend not only on the regulative or promotional strategies that government will adopt at the macro level, but also on the socio-economic and cultural factors that affect the motivations of individuals in their own family groups. So far, all over the world, the motivation to restrict the family has followed a rise in the material standards of life; the developing countries are faced with the challenge of using the technology of family limitation as a means to attaining higher standards of life. We do not know whether the efforts will succeed, but we do know how important this need to limit population growth at the national level is.

Employment with assured supply of essential commodities, freedom, equality, health protection, education and fertility control have so far been identified as important basic needs for developing societies. Nothing has been said about the needs of the specially handicapped or vulnerable segments of the populations of developing countries because the needs of these groups have been the chief concern of welfare services and social workers and so do not necessitate to be identified specifically. On the other hand, social work has tended to neglect, or be itself neglected, where the basic needs of the larger population are concerned. Even in the case of the underprivileged groups where large numbers and whole communities are involved, as in the case of the scheduled castes and scheduled tribes, they have failed to identify and gain acceptance for the specialised contribution of professional social work. It is from this point of view that an attempt has been made in this paper to list the basic needs of the general people and of society as a whole. It would be important to briefly indicate what the role of social work may be in relation to these broad need areas.

The employment programmes in rural areas should be seen both as programmes of production and social security in a primarily rural society. In an important way social security programmes based on employment are superior to those which adopt income maintenance through direct financial aid as a strategy. Income maintenance through employment generation protects the self-respect of the recipient and maintains his motivation for self-reliance. The khadi and village industries programmes should also be viewed as a part of this strategy of maintaining family income through productive activity even if such activity has to be protected by regulative measures and subsidised through cash grants or tax exemptions at the stage of marketing their products. Social work graduates should be encouraged to associate themselves with the implementation of these programmes. Welfare agencies working in rural areas would also have to see that they cannot artificially separate welfare problems from those of social and economic development. If this change of perspective takes place, these agencies will also involve themselves in the total development programme, their important contribution being to see that governmental and other efforts at development reach out even to the most disadvantaged sections of the community. It is here that their welfare contribution will be seen to be distinctive. They would have to work with and for the landless and the small landowning families.

In the area of health services social workers will have to develop a role in promoting community health services, in addition to their current preoccupation with hospitalised medical and psychiatric cases. Here, again, one of their concerns may be to see how the most backward groups and regions can be helped derive benefit from the services that governmental and other agencies offer. They may also have a special contribution in bringing the social aspects of health and disease to the notice of the health team, in planning strategies or in overcoming the difficulties that arise as a result of cultural factors.

In the field of education, one important need is to widen the social base of education in terms of the enrolment and retention of backward class individuals in schools. What steps can social workers take at the community level---as different from the individual family level----to ensure better participation by the poorer and backward groups in the villages? Another goal to be pursued is to carry education to those who are not in schools. This may mean literacy for the illiterate, continuing education for those who have already had some schooling but wish to benefit by skill-improvement programmes, or education related to workers' organisations or to their citizenship role, or education for recreation, or education for the sake of wider awareness as an end in itself.

In all these areas social workers may have direct service-giving roles, educational roles by way of orienting other workers to social work skills and methods, or the role of mobilising volunteers for community development functions. The role of social work in developing and implementing the national service programme, for instance, is partially the role of mobilising student youth for development.

In none of these areas are social workers going to be in sole charge; they are largely secondary settings in the sense that social workers will have to work along with other professionals---sometimes under them, sometimes leading them and sometimes simply as colleagues. But this is true of the total field of development and also in relation to all professions. Whether social work will succeed in identifying a set of specific work roles which are exclusively its own is difficult to say. What is essential at present is to accept the challenge and participate in the developmental tasks.

11

Formulating a Social Welfare Policy: Role of the Social Work Profession

A policy statement is a statement of intent----the intent to act in a particular direction and towards a particular goal. It is not an end in itself. It is an indication of the direction proposed to be taken by an authority in a specified field of activity. It is expected to serve as a guide to planners, executives and administrators in the process of overall planning as well as in the day-to-day decisions that they may be called upon to take in that area of activity. A policy statement provides, by implication, positive as well as negative guidelines for action; it may indicate what may be considered desirable activities as well as those which are necessary to be undertaken. A policy statement, to be complete, must state the goal to be pursued, the choice of overall strategy to be adopted, the major programmes or activities planned, the manner of mobilising material, organisational and manpower resources, and at least give a broad indication of the time perspective over which the policy is expected to achieve the goal.

A policy statement is based on the assumption that the authority concerned has the jurisdiction, the necessary

---

Key-note address delivered at the Asian Regional Seminar on Processes and Approaches to Social Policy Formulation and Planning with Special Emphasis on the Role of Social Workers, October 11 , 1977.

capability (political and administrative) and the resources to take action in the direction and in the measure that is considered desirable. In the absence of these a policy statement is at best a pious expression of wish and will not be treated seriously by the policy makers, the administrators or the potential beneficiaries for whom the statement has been made.

The significance of a policy statement is derived from several sources: (i) the authority making the statement, (ii) the importance attached to the field of activity to which the statement refers, and (iii) the substantive content of the statement and how far-reaching it is in that field.

Since in all modern societies power and resources tend to be concentrated in the hands of government, a statement of governmental policy in any field arouses considerable interest and comment. Within the sphere of governmental action, again, political and economic policies receive greater attention than policies in the area of social services and these latter policies may arouse greater interest than policies in field of social welfare.

However, in no field can a policy statement be enunciated or followed by itself as though it were a completely independent sphere of activity without interchange with other policies in other areas of life. For example, a meaningful policy statement in the sphere of education or health cannot be made except in the context of the economic, political or other policies that are being pursued. This applies to welfare policies as well. A policy statement has to be a part of a larger, integrated system of propositions covering various related segments of life. In the absence of such an integration a policy statement will encounter or generate many contradictions which will stultify action and lead to a failure of policy. It is difficult, for instance, to pursue egalitarian goals in the field of education, health or welfare if the economic policies encourage an unequal distribution of national resources or again if the political institutions discriminate between citizens for reasons of race, caste, religion or region. Social welfare in an inegalitarian society will tend to become philanthropy or remain a kindly sentiment or bold rhetoric.

SCOPE OF SOCIAL POLICY

Since the policy pursued by government in one sector of national life has implications for its policies in other sectors, it is difficult to delimit the scope of a social policy statement. A social policy issue may be involved in every decision that a government takes, whether the decision relates to the location of industry, overseas trade, nuclear research or a choice between building buses or manufacturing small cars. Each of these issues involves social questions such as those of regional developmental balance, national self-sufficiency, commitment to peace, and the relative priority to be given to the need of mass transport and the demands of a well-to-do minority. In this sense, all government decisions, in whichever field they are taken, have social implications and persons interested in social issues must keep these decisions under continuous scrutiny.

At the same time, there is need to pay somewhat special attention to a narrower range of programmes and services which may be said to be the core of special policy; this is the policy in respect of social services including social welfare services. This core area of social policy concern is made of health, education, housing and social welfare.

From the social worker's point of view, however, the area of concern may often be further narrowed down to social welfare services. For him, the term 'social policy' may primarily mean policy in respect of the poor, the handicapped, the unadjusted or otherwise deprived groups in society. Additionally, it may also mean a policy in respect of prevention of handicap or disability and a policy of promoting enhancement of the quality.

THE INDIAN CONTEXT

In this paper I will limit myself to some of the problems that arise or some of the issues that need to be borne in mind in developing a social welfare policy in the Indian context and the role that the social work profession can play in this process. However, to the extent that most countries surrounding us are poor and developing ones, I hope, my observations about some aspects of the Indian situation will have relevance for other countries of the region as well.

It was mentioned above that a statement of policy must begin with a statement of the goal the policy sets out to achieve. The social goals of the Indian polity have been clearly and unequivocably stated in our Constitution though our progress towards them may at best seem halting. The overall goal is the creation of a democratic, secular and egalitarian society where everyone will have work, security, access to cultural opportunity and a decent standard of living. The Directive Principles even mention the right to public assistance in the event of unemployment, old age, sickness and disablement or other cases of undeserved want, but the state is expected to pursue these latter goals within the limits of its economic capacity and development.

Right to Work

The goals of a welfare policy are thus already contained in a general way in the Directive Principles of the Indian Constitution. These principles specifically mention security and public assistance in cases of undeserved want, but the state is expected to pursue these goals within the limits of its economic capacity and development. Since no one can lay down norms for assessing economic capacity, the first task of the profession of social work will be to work hard to gain acceptance for an interpretation of economic capacity which can be reconciled with the goal of equality. The idea that the right of the citizen to work and to security can be guaranteed only after the economic capacity of the state has been developed is a sterile idea by itself and it can be turned into a dynamic concept only by insisting that the right to work and security be guaranteed now at whatever level of economic development we are. The right to work must become the basis and the instrument for achieving economic development rather than making it contingent upon the achievement of an unspecified level of economic development in the future. There is a good body of expert opinion within and outside government which subscribes to this view and social workers must help to bring out the extreme significance of this view and must equip themselves for this role. Until the problem of employment is tackled, many of the other problems of 'undeserved want' will remain invisible and unattended.

Apart from the right to work, the Directive Principles also mention the right to education, but the right to health and the right of the individual to seek full growth of his potential are not specified. However, since India is a signatory to the Charter of Human Rights where these and other social rights are specified, we may assume that the state in India is committed to these goals as well. The broad goals of social policy therefore do not need further enlistment though the specific content of these goals will go on changing from time to time as the needs of the people undergo change. A policy statement in the area of social welfare will have to identify the varied groups and the particular needs towards which the welfare programmes and services are oriented. This task is not attempted here. I would, however, like to state that new needs may arise out of more factors than just 'undeserved want' or economic factors. The needs may be of a social and psychological character and may not necessarily be due to poverty or want, whether deserved or undeserved, and as mentioned earlier, these needs may change with time and place.

THREE MODELS FOR STATE ACTION

Having identified the goals that will guide the development and operation of a welfare policy, an equally important task---and somewhat more challenging—is the choice of an overall strategy or model for the development of social welfare programmes and services. Richard Titmus, in his address to the delegates at the International Conference on Social Welfare at the Hague (1972), identified three different models for state action in the area of social welfare. These are what he called the residual model, the achievement performance model and the institutional-redistribution model. Since these models have already been discussed in an earlier chapter, I will not elaborate them here. Briefly, the first one corresponds to the situation where the state accepts no direct responsibility for ensuring the well-being of its poor beyond what is achieved through private or public acts of charity and philanthropy. The second model corresponds to a situation where the responsibility of the state in the area of social welfare is limited to providing certain limited facilities programmes intended to equalise opportunity for the poor and handicapped. The third model is the one where access to various services is open to all universally on the basis of need, and the state recognising its responsibility for ensuring the citizen's well-being and for redistribution of social resources makes specific provision through financial and institutional services.

Every modern government, consciously or unconsciously, adopts one of these three models depending upon its resources, level of technological development and the pressure exercised by organised political opinion in one or the other direction. It is a part of the responsibility of the social work profession to create a public opinion in favour of a model of social and welfare services consistent with egalitarian goals. The residual and achievement models are iniquitous and unresponsive to the aspirations of the people who are mobilised on promises of equality and prosperity. At the end of more than thirty years of independence we have not made much progress in the direction of equality and the operative social policy in our country may still be described as one based on a residual welfare services model. If a change is to be effected, we must begin minimally with a commitment to abolish destitution and create universal employment. The creation of additional employment must be regarded not as a desirable goal to be achieved indirectly and as a consequence of general economic growth but as a first charge on national resources and as a means to achieving this growth. This would be the first broad programmatic priority in the statement of social policy in a poor country.

While the social work profession may not be able to create new jobs, it can play a role in creating a public opinion in favour of this strategy in enabling and motivating the poor to take the jobs where they are created and may be, in providing an organisational base in the rural areas through which schemes of employment generation can be implemented. In the Indian context social workers may have to help overcome traditional prejudices against certain kinds of work which may be considered unsuitable for reasons of family or caste tradition. If the profession is to attend to these tasks, it must bring about a major change in its orientation----a change of orientation from a primarily urban to a primarily rural focus and a change of orientation from an individualised clinical and therapeutic perspective to an organisational developmental perspective. While it may not be possible for all schools of social work to shift their emphasis in a short period, there are at least three or four programmes of specialisation at graduate and undergraduate levels currently oriented to rural work which would find this reorientation somewhat easier to initiate. The profession can help by establishing a link between government planning agencies and these latter institutions of social work education.

Implications of the Redistributive Model

The adoption of the redistributive model for a social policy would thus tend to focus at one end on the major programme of poverty removal, but at the other end it would have important implications for social and welfare services as well. The social work profession would have to pay special attention to some areas of social and welfare services in addition to programmes of poverty removal. In social services, the overall policy orientation would be to extend these services to the farthest and poorest segments of society, both in urban and rural areas. The role of the social work profession would be to ensure that the poor segments utilise these services wherever they are available and that the barriers of ignorance, prejudice or mere social distance between those who man the services and those who need them, do not prevent their utilisation. This may require a reorientation of the programmes and the personnel and a modification of some of the rules governing the delivery of services. These rules, at times, sacrifice the norms of utility and/of utilisation of a service to the norms of financial and administrative accountability. In the sphere of school education, the social work profession may try to see how the dropout rates can be reduced and a fuller enrolment achieved and how the opportunities for better education can become increasingly available to all children on the basis of merit rather than the ability to pay. In the area of health services, the social policy goal may be to strengthen and extend public health and prophylactic services so as to reduce the cost of medical advice and medication to the poor. The social worker may be able to help in increasing the receptiveness of the community to these services and its observance of the norms of health through programmes of community health education, removal of prejudice or misinformation and the strengthening of indigeneous beneficial health practices among rural and tribal communities.

The profession of social work would have a more extensive role in defining social policy with reference to welfare needs and problems. The profession would be expected to participate in formulating goals, working out broad strategies, developing programmes and implementing them and provide a feedback to planning on the basis of research in implementation of programmes. The broad policy objective in the area of social welfare is to meet the special needs of handicapped, disadvantaged or unadjusted individuals and groups with a view to enable them utilise the services provided to them and become self-reliant, contributing and participating members of society. The specific services that develop would be dependent upon the availability of resources and the perception of needs in a particular society.

RELEVANCE OF SOCIAL FACTORS

A situation of generalised poverty and limited resources has the consequence of leading to a simplistic emphasis on economic needs as well as to a comparative loss of sight where social and emotional needs are concerned. The social work profession has a dual responsibility here. On the one hand, since economic needs are important, the profession must equip itself to help the handicapped as well as the normal population in meeting these needs. On the other hand, the profession has also the responsibility of pointing out that even economic problems of physical survival cannot be tackled without taking cognisance of the social and psychological aspects of these problems. Social groups, which are economically backward, cannot be helped merely by offering them monetary aid very often as their capacity to use this aid is impeded by their social disabilities or inability to perceive opportunities. Identifying and drawing attention of policy makers to these socio-psychological factors that impede utilisation of inputs by the poor is an important function of the social work profession at the policy making level. Later, at the stage of implementation, social welfare may have to devise and operate services which overcome the disabilities or remove the gaps in communication and perception.

RESPONDING TO RESOURCE LIMITATIONS

The constraint of resources has other consequences for social policy. One of these is the need to develop services which are less capital-intensive, both in terms of expense on buildings and equipment and costs of employing very highly trained personnel. Social policy in developing countries may necessarily have to devise several ways of meeting this situation. Maximising the services which can be organised for the community as a whole, rather than for special needy groups in specialised institutions, organising preventive services along with rehabilitative services, utilising volunteer help and extending the role of voluntary agencies, and strengthening the capacity of lay workers in the community to spot problems and meet them locally are some ways in which the situation of paucity of resources can be met. The profession must help in this process of meeting the challenge of limited resources by organising appropriate programmes of service and training. A new strategy of matching programmes to needs, of matching training to programmes and of matching both to available resources may have to be developed.

However, all discussions of the size of available resources for social and welfare services get confusing because there are no absolute criteria by which a particular allocation can be judged to be legitimately the maximum possible for a particular area, sector or stage of development. The problems of the legitimacy of relative sectoral allocations and the total size of the resources to be mobilised for all the sectors become crucial in a society which is committed to an egalitarian social order. The organised interest groups in a modern democracy seek to protect their own interests by seeking increased allocation of resources for services they need and in a wide variety of other ways. The unorganised groups suffer in comparison. The needy and handicapped segments of the population belong to the latter category and it is the responsibility of social workers—lay as well as professional—to ensure that the interests of these segments receive due attention. The profession plays the role of an advocate and helps the groups themselves to become articulate.

Whenever one talks of resources he thinks first of financial resources. These are, of course, important. But well-equipped manpower and an organisational base for services are two other types of important resources. While finances are required even to build these latter resources, they cannot by themselves create trained manpower or an organisational base. This calls for a carefully worked out manpower policy and an equally careful and sustained effort to build the structure necessary for delivering services.

Manpower Resources

The problem of manpower development is complex. One of the core problems in developing countries is the choice of the level of preparation of the functionary. The professions in each field invariably strain towards a higher level of training and excellence but as stated earlier this tends to raise the cost of training and subsequent employment of these trained persons. It is, therefore, necessary to match training to the level at which needs can be met. Or else, the profession will get increasingly isolated from the needs of the services and the agencies meant for the poor and will become restrictively oriented to the needs of a well-to-do paying clientele. The fact that much of our higher education is in English and most of the poor have little education, accentuates the problem of isolation—isolation from para-professionals as also from the clients. New strategies in training at different levels of job specificity and theoretical sophistication may have to be worked out. The profession again has a role to play in actively associating itself with the many programmes of orientation, short-term training, part-time training and training at different levels of the educational hierarchy that would be needed to meet the complex differentiated needs of a heterogeneous and segmented society.

Manpower resources require time to be built up and different short-term as well as long-term strategies will require to be formulated. In developing these manpower strategies a definite place will have to be found for voluntary workers at different levels----as board or managing committee members and field personnel, and drawn from among educated women of leisure as well as from amongst students and youth.

Organisational Resources

If the building up of manpower resources is a long-term process, even more long-term is the task of planning and building up organisations. Building organisations means building up people with experience and leadership qualities; this is a part of the problem of identifying and developing manpower resources. But building organisations also means building up healthy organisational traditions. This is not just a question of framing appropriate rules and regulations though these are important. For example, both in governmental and business sectors, organisations are built round the wholly-paid functionaries who are trained in business rules and whose motivation is strengthened by chances of promotion or increased profits of business, whereas the social and welfare services organisations, built wholly on bureaucratic procedures or considerations of private profit, do not succeed in reaching out to the people. They call for a measure of commitment to the profession as well as to the people which cannot be developed overnight nor purchased easily with money. Besides, as we saw earlier, the financial resources may not always be available in the quantum required. Community leaders have, therefore, an important role in setting up organisations, nurturing them and expanding them. A statement of social policy will have to visualise a strategy for building these intangible resources in organisations and leadership. In the last analysis, the acceptance and the extent of change will depend upon what the community considers important.

So far, the search for appropriate leadership has remained limited to the urban, educated groups and particularly to educated women. A break with this tradition was achieved only in case of Project Implementation Committees of Welfare Extension Projects, the Welfare Committees of Panchayat Raj Institutions and Mahila Mandals. Even in these latter organisations the rural community is represented somewhat marginally and the initiative rests largely with the district-level educated middle class women and government officials. We have not succeeded in involving the farmer's wife as an articulate participant. So long as this situation remains welfare services, like most other services, will remain confined to the urban areas and to urban outposts in the countryside. The policy formulation and activity planning will remain largely external to the village population. Is there any way of making social welfare an area in which the non-middle class, non-urban, non-college educated can participate? It is possible that when this happens our concepts of what the village women and children need will undergo a change. New priorities and programmes may take the place of those that we think are good for them.

The transfer of effective leadership from the white-collar minority to the cultivator and the artisan class will not, of course, take place in isolation in the field of social and welfare services alone but it will come as part of a larger process of social transformation. An important issue, therefore, is the orientation of the social work profession and its role in this larger process of social transformation.

SOCIAL RESEARCH

Finally, I would like to touch briefly on the role of the social work profession in the application of social research to welfare planning and policy formulation. This should not need to be argued seriously since one would expect that any profession as a knowledge-based activity would be already familiar with it. It is true that a certain measure of verbal familiarity exists among social workers about the role of research in planning and implementation of welfare services. But this awareness is not transferred to practice. Part of the reason for this situation is that our total resources are so woefully inadequate and the major problems appear so self-evident that most welfare services are initiated on an ad hoc basis without waiting for any prior research. It is said that one does not need to count the number of mosquitoes that bite us before putting up a mosquito net. But, research has many applications besides the assessment of the size of a social problem. Research can be used in understanding the nature of a problem, in ascertaining the suitability and effectiveness of various services, in determining the reasons why particular programmes do or do not find acceptance from the potential consumers and in obtaining routine administrative intelligence about the operation of a service. Social welfare research has still remained a very marginal activity and it does not form an integral part of the process of policy formulation or an evaluation of its effectiveness. The social work profession must pay greater attention to the contribution that research can make.

CONCLUSION

In this paper I have tried to identify different stages and facets of policy formulation in the area of social welfare services and indicated the nature of the contribution that members of the social work profession—both educators and practitioners—can make to these various stages or facets. The profession should participate and help in specifying the implications of larger societal goals to the narrower area of its practice and competence. It should also participate in the process of choosing a suitable model and in the development of appropriate strategies for the organisation of welfare services. It should help identify suitable manpower policies, promote the growth of relevant welfare research and play its role in bringing about a social transformation. When one speaks of the role of social workers, particularly in these tasks, he is not necessarily thinking of social workers sitting as experts on various policy making and planning bodies from the Centre to the Block Panchayat. The profession can help as much by research and communication, discussions of problems and issues, educating public opinion, canvassing for legislative action, and above all, by showing in action the feasibility of its proposals through operation of programmes on the ground. Though one speaks of the profession in the singular and suggests that there is one united perspective and one agreed-upon line of advice, this cannot in reality be so. Any profession worth its name will have its areas of agreement and also its areas of contention and disagreement. This is true of social work as well. When social workers move from the present stage of seeking a role for themselves to the stage of fulfilling this role, there will emerge several approaches and prescriptions. They will have to decide upon which ones are relevant and in which situations. The search for relevance is at the core of most policy decisions.

12

Mobilising Youth for Social Development

Young people have probably always been active in movements of change in any society. Yet, the concept of 'mobilising' youth belongs to the 20th century and more particularly to the post-World War I period. In a narrow sense, 'mobilisation' as different from enlisting the involvement of a group reflects a certain instrumental attitude to the person(s) mobilised. It involves use of authority. As explained shall be later, this social authority in the last analysis is never totally absent in any society whether it is democratic or totalitarian but the styles and procedures evident in the exercise of this authority may be different. On the other hand, no mobilisation can ever succeed if it relies wholly on the use of authority for achieving its goal. It will have to depend on exciting the imagination of the young and tapping their own inner urges, especially if such mobilisation is going to call upon youth to make significant sacrifices.

The term 'mobilisation' also suggests a conscious process different from the spontaneous involvement of youth in an activity or a movement. Not all people who 'participate' in a movement may have been consciously 'mobilised' by the leader(s) of that movement. On the other hand, in the concept

---

Talk delivered at the Commonwealth Asia-Pacific Regional Centre for Advanced Studies in Youth Work, Chandigarh in 1976.

of mobilisation, there is always a mobiliser—an individual or an organisation---and a mobilisee. A discussion of the process of mobilisation must, therefore, take both the mobiliser and the mobilisee into account and see their mutual relationship. This relationship depends upon the mobiliser's goal, the extent to which this goal is shared by the mobilisee, the type of cooperation and the extent of sacrifice, if any sought by the mobiliser from the mobilisee, the rewards that the mobiliser can offer or the sanctions that he may use to elicit such cooperation, the mobilisee's assessment of the mobiliser as a person, leader, organiser, etc., and his assessment of the total situation in terms of the chances of success or failure of the movement in attaining the goal.

If the mobiliser and the mobilisee share a common goal, it should be obvious that the first condition for cooperation is set. If they do not share the goal, then the mobiliser would have to depend either upon some extrinsic reward system or sanction system to obtain the cooperation of the mobilisee. If, on the other hand, the two share the goal, the former may depend at least partly on the intrinsic value of the goal for the mobilisee to get his cooperation. The degree to which the mobilisee regards the goal as important from his own point of view would depend upon what the goal is and the extent to which the mobiliser has been able to interpret and communicate the goal to the mobilisee as being important to the latter. Once the goal is seen by the mobilisee as important for himself, the degree of his cooperation will depend upon the kind and degree of sacrifice---in time, effort, money or social standing—that he would be called upon to make. There has to be a certain mutuality between the degree of importance of the goal, the end-result, and the degree of sacrifice that an individual is called upon to make.

In discussing mobilisation in a national context the evaluation of a goal as "important for himself" is done not in a narrow personal or material context, but often at an ideological and idealistic level. Thus, youth as a potential mobilisee group, may not look for immediate material benefits for the particular individuals making up the group. They would rather think of 'youth' in the abstract as a potential beneficiary or sometimes not even of youth alone but of the 'nation' as a whole benefiting by the movement into which they are being mobilised. This balancing between the effort required and the result expected is also not a simple one. It is influenced by variations in temporal perspective and the value attached by individuals to short-term and long-term goals. It depends upon the relationship that binds the mobilisee to the mobiliser. The nature of this relationship may be such that its continuation is satisfying in itself and may considerably add to the value of the goal to be achieved. This is the type of relationship that exists between a charismatic leader and his followers.

From a sociological perspective an analysis of the process of mobilisation would raise questions about the social factors that determine the substantive nature of the goals set up by the mobiliser and the extent to which these goals are likely to be shared between him and his followers in a given society at a given stage of its development. Applying this to India as well as other developing societies, we would look out to see whether there is anything about developing societies generally and the Indian society in particular that would tend to define the nature of goals pursued by the mobiliser and the chances of these goals being shared by the potential mobilisee group—the youth of India.

It is obvious that in most developing societies the health and education needs of youth require prime attention. These needs must be addressed through formal programmes of schools, colleges, public hospitals, etc. But, there is also a great need for informal programmes of health ad personality building through sports, athletics, swimming, hiking, etc. These activities would need to be taken up by NGOs and individuals that can provide special leadership. In most advanced societies, such leadership groups exist. We need to consciously develop them in association with schools, sports clubs, boy scout and girl guide groups, etc. To begin with, this may be easier in the urban areas but over time they can reach into the rural areas as well.

It is, of course, true that human behaviour is conditioned by personality factors as much as by societal factors. The specific goals pursued by the mobiliser and the extent of their acceptability or otherwise would depend upon the individual personalities of the mobiliser and the mobilisee. In so far as personalities are the result of factors which are unique to each individual, the sociologist would have little to contribute to an analysis of mobilisation based on personality variables. However, to the extent that the distribution of personality characteristics is also governed by social and cultural characteristics, the sociologist or the social psychologist would be interested in examining these possibilities. Specifically, a sociologist may be interested in asking whether in the area of personality analysis there are sociological factors that determine patterns of autonomy and group dependence in the particular society under study.

Other dimensions of personality of interest to a sociologist are those of identity and alienation and the distribution of the achievement orientation in the population. To the extent that individuals in a society tend to be group dependent one would expect them to be responsive to a pattern of leadership which draws its sanctions from group consensus and adopts an authoritarian but paternalistic pattern of leadership. On the other hand, in cultures characterised by the predominance of autonomous personalities, the interaction patterns are likely to be characterised by open discussion, confrontation and use of authority which is direct and which recognises and respects the conscious choice exercised by the individual. Such authority may derive its sanction either from a democratic or an authoritarian polity but in either case it will be unequivocal in its objectives and conformity requirements. On the other hand, a culture which promotes autonomy is also likely to facilitate alienation of the individual from the group. If, for some reason, members of the youth group in society are so alienated, i.e., not identified with the goals and objectives of the older generation in the population, it will reduce the possibilities of goal convergence between the mobiliser and the mobilisee.

Apart from goals and personality systems, there is the element of programmes through which and in terms of which the goals are to be attained. At the level of programmes two types of questions may be raised by the mobilisee. Are the programmes 'rational', i.e., can they be seen to be the appropriate means for achieving particular goals? And, is the implementation of programmes efficient? Efficiency is influenced partly by available technology and resources and partly by the personality systems involved in the implementation process. The perception of particular programmes as rational is also a function of the cultural and personality systems. Rationality and efficiency are interlinked, especially when the term 'rationality' is used in an economic sense and the maximisation of output becomes the evaluation for both these concepts. However, in non-economic areas, rationality tends to be judged merely in terms of whether a particular practice is in conformity with a prevalent value. For example, all human beings should be treated as equals is a value; there is no result or output criterion that can or need to be used to justify it. Rules for admission to an institution or for employment in it which are in conformity with this value are rational. In this sense, rational only means consistent with certain values. Further, rationality like efficiency is also linked to the state of knowledge in a given field at a given point of time. What appears a rational way of treating disease at one time may appear irrational when the knowledge base has changed.

In so far as rationality is linked with values and knowledge at a given time, the perception of a particular programme of action as rational and relevant depends at least partly on the ability of the mobiliser to communicate this rationality and relevance to the mobilisee in symbols and in terms that are meaningful to the latter. It is often said that results speak of themselves. They may, but results follow after a programme have been implemented whereas a good deal of speaking and interpretation is necessary before the programme is launched. Besides, in many areas of human life, results are ambiguous and a lot depends on how they are interpreted. The success of the mobilisation process is contingent on this ability to interpret and communicate with the mobilisee.

The question of efficiency relates not so much to value as to technology. In examining the efficiency of programmes we may have to ask whether the end-result obtained is of the quality and quantity desired. In programmes involving and dealing primarily with human beings an important determinant of efficiency is the adequacy of the organisational tool used in implementing the programme.

The discussion so far has been abstract, if not abstruse. It has sought to identify the elements that are important in an understanding of the process of mobilisation of human resources. The elements identified are: the broad social context in which mobilisation is attempted; the goals of mobilisation; the personality systems of the mobiliser and the mobilisee in so far as they may be said to have certain socially determined characteristics; the programmes of action, their relevance, seeming rationality and organisational efficacy; and, last but not the least, the communication process between the mobiliser and the mobilised group. Needless to say, these factors are not established in neat and separate identities; there are areas of overlap between them. What is regarded as a generalised observation about the personality system in a particular society is also a fact describing the social context in that society; similarly, the communication skill of a mobiliser is as much a part of his total personality equipment as any other aspect considered separately in the discussion of the personality systems of the mobiliser and the mobilisee.

Having identified some of the important elements in the mobilisation process, we may now turn to a discussion of these in the specific context of developing societies.

SOCIAL CONTEXT IN DEVELOPING COUNTRIES

The most important fact about developing countries is that they are poor, not only in a relative sense but also in an absolute sense. Substantial segments of the population of these countries suffer from malnutrition, lack of education and health facilities, lack of adequate clothing and lack of adequate housing. Most of these countries were former colonies of advanced western nations and have gained their freedom only since the World War II. Having freed themselves from the political hegemony of the European nations, they now find themselves under the economic domination of the most advanced nations. Their present preoccupation, therefore, is to earn their economic freedom, to achieve economic growth and be in a position to raise the standard of life of the people in material as well as non-material terms. They have all verbally accepted the goals of democracy, socialism and secularism to varying degrees and with varying time perspectives. They are, however, agreed on the immediate need for achieving economic development. The decade of the 1950's saw an almost exclusive emphasis on the goal of economic growth whereas the decade of the 1960's has seen an acceptance of the need to broaden the concept of development to include the expansion of social services like health, education, housing, urban planning, etc. The change in nomenclature from development to social development indicates a gradual shift in perspective, but even now the acceptance of the 'social' dimension is only because it offers a plausible explanation of and an excuse for why the development efforts of the 1950's did not show results. It is only recently that the relevance of politico-economic implications of development in terms of a change in the structure of power and the structure of the distributive mechanisms in society are beginning to be appreciated.

In all these countries youth constitute a large proportion of the populations. A fuller appreciation of the situation of youth in developing countries is sought to be developed based on data limited to India. In India, the age group 0-24 accounts for 59 per cent of the total population and the age group 15-24 contains 17 per cent of the total. The population between 5-24 years of age is 240 million, i.e., 44 per cent of the total. Of this latter population of 240 million, children and youth constitute 184 million, i.e., nearly 76 per cent, who have no formal education of any kind though 39 million, i.e., 16 per cent of them are literate. This means that only 40 per cent of the youth in the country are literate, and 24 per cent out of these have had different levels of education though, of course, they may not all currently be enrolled in schools and colleges. Thus the vast majority of youth in 1971 comprised both uneducated and illiterate.

One would expect that youth who are not in schools and colleges are probably in employment and that their employment is probably the reason for their not being in schools and colleges. This is not so. Restricting the analysis only to male youth between the ages of 15-24, it is found that of the 47 million young men, 31 million are in the workforce and about 11 million are full-time students leaving a balance of only 5 million young persons who are neither in the workforce nor in educational institutions. (The statistical data are taken from 'Youth and National Development', Directorate of Non-Formal Education, Government of India, 1975.)

Most of the Indian youth, like the rest of the population, reside in rural areas. The 31 million male youth (15-24 years), who are in the workforce, are mostly engaged in agricultural occupations and are thus inhabited in villages; on the other hand, most of the 11 million student youth in the age group

15-24 are probably urban residents. The rural-based students are known not to continue their education beyond the primary school level, and even among the urban students those who continue into high school and college are more often than not children of fathers who are in the white-collar occupations. Thus, while there are no figures readily available, one expects urban residence and middle class parentage to be associated with student youth and rural residence and agricultural worker status to be associated with non-student youth. This social dichotomy of the youth world is important to bear in mind in considering problems of mobilisation of youth in India and probably in other developing countries as well.

Thus, the gross poverty of the people, the general paucity of financial and capital resources, the immediacy and urgency of finding solutions to the problem of poverty, the large proportion of youth in the population, the relatively small proportion of youth in educational institutions, the existence of an unascertained number of unemployed, non-school-going youth, the two separated worlds of urban, white-collar, higher-educated youth and the rural, cultivating, uneducated youth----these are the broad features of the relevant social context against which youth mobilisation has to take place in India, and may be, in the developing countries as a whole.

SOCIAL BACKGROUND OF THE MOBILISER

Who are the mobilisers in these developing societies? It is difficult to generalise, but in all countries which were formerly colonies and which earned their freedom after 1945, the ruling class is made up of two groups: the rural landowning gentry on the one hand and the urban industrialists, businessmen, bureaucrats, professionals on the other. In a sense, it is individuals drawn from this ruling class that is seeking to mobilise youth for national development. But, this ruling class is not one homogeneous group, nor are its various segments internally unified. In countries which follow a single political party system, it is the party that is the mobiliser; in other countries where more than one political party is in existence, the mobilisation is attempted by all of them separately as well as by the government agencies for youth welfare, rural development, etc. Since most of the parties are drawn from the same socio-economic group and since they find themselves under similar situational pressures to seem to work for the majority, who are poor, the scope for the development of sharp options is limited. The manifestoes of the political parties differ more in style than in substance. They also differ in the degree of priority to be given to the urban or the rural sector, and in the emphasis to be given to industry or agriculture. The dominantly urban professional-bureaucrat groups consider themselves modern and describe the landowner-small shopkeeper groups as traditional, but often the two are separated from each other only by one generation.

In such a situation loyalties often get organised on personal and personality considerations rather than on ideological grounds or grounds of basic conflict of interests. The groups whose interests would conflict with those of the ruling elite are often not organised. This may be true even in countries where a single-party system of political authority exists. The single party may more often be of the right than of the left. This background of the mobiliser tends to influence the style and pattern of the youth mobilisation effort in developing countries.

THE GOALS OF YOUTH MOBILISATION

Given the social context of developing countries one would expect that the rationale for youth mobilisation is self-evident. Since youth constitute almost 60 per cent of the society, social development should mean the development of youth. The mobilisation of youth is really the mobilisation of people for their own development, for the removal of their own poverty, for the betterment of their own standard of living, and for their own better education and better health. But this is not how the situation is always perceived. That youth of a country should be mobilised for purposes of development is a fairly common theme in all countries—developing as well as developed. But, surprisingly, youth are not always seen as participating in an essentially self-help operation; the common image is one of putting the energies and the talents of some outside group to the service of the people. The reason for this image is not hard to find. The youth whose energies are sought to be tapped are the student youth of these countries and as already mentioned, the world of these student youth is different from the world of the majority of youth in the country as a whole. Therefore, in the concept of youth mobilisation, there is, in many countries, this element of the privileged serving the less privileged. Of course, this element would be present in any effort to mobilise one section of the community to serve the whole community but it gets somewhat accentuated in the case of youth mobilisation which is restricted to student youth.

It should be said at once that governmental programmes for youth do seek to include non-student youth as well as student youth, but for several reasons the activities for non-student youth are at best symbolic. The non-student youth are too widely dispersed in the urban as well as rural areas to be easily accessible, there is no organisational base from which they can be contacted and, moreover, they are mostly busy working for their own livelihood to be able to participate in service activities. On the other hand, student youth living in urban areas are found in clusters of educational institutions and are not overly busy with their studies. There is also the fact that not being very busy and being somewhat insecure about their own future in terms of middle class aspirations students can be occasionally restive. Once restive, they can also be articulate and very demanding in terms of their own needs. Mobilising students for 'service' is thus at once a diversionary move and a way of using available manpower resources for social development. A further point in favour of youth mobilisation is that this is something that all 'progressive' or 'radical' movements have done in all countries that have seen rapid change. From a purely political point of view the unmotivated, frustrated student is ready to be mobilised and nearly every party in a developing country wants to mobilise them for party ends either to embarrass or to sustain a government.

The concept of youth mobilisation has thus become very murky. It has confused between youth and student youth and its focus is blurred between various manifest and latent objectives it is supposed to serve: objectives serving the interests of individual youth and objectives serving the interests of political, religious and other organisations. The goals of youth services and youth mobilisation need to be defined more clearly. If youth are to be mobilised for purposes of social development, an exclusion of rural, non-student youth from the category of those who are served or those who are mobilised, cannot help in attaining the objective. Rural youth must not only become objects of service, but must also be mobilised for community service. Movements which have helped to effect rapid social change have sought to embrace all youth---students and workers, the very young and the adult, the rural and the urban---in their sweep.

PATTERNS OF MOBILISATION

A look at recent history in the developing countries suggests that there are two different patterns of youth mobilisation which have been followed in these countries. These patterns seem to depend largely on the strategy for change adopted by the governments of these countries. For want of better terms, the two strategies may be labelled as 'revolutionary' and 'constitutionalist'. In many countries of Asia, Africa and South America, there have been civil wars---armed struggle for power between different groups within the country. Sometimes these groups have been neatly polarised as standing for well-defined politico-economic approaches, sometimes not; but, in either event, wherever there has been an armed struggle for power, the youth of these countries have been 'mobilised' in a somewhat literal sense. Civil wars can be confusing in terms of identifying friends and foes, unless they have been born out of or result in the crystallisation of clear ideologies. Revolutionary struggles—whether of the fascist or socialist variety—depend heavily on youth. The youth participating in such struggles have to be provided with a relatively unified set of ideas—the ideals of the revolution—which legitimise their violence. In the absence of these ideas violence would be brutalising for the individual and would tear a society apart.

Revolutionary mobilisation insists on discipline and tends to subordinate the identity of the individual. The emphasis is on the collective: the party, the nation. Revolutions require a simplification, sometimes an oversimplification, of issues. Those who engage in revolutionary activity must clearly demarcate good from bad, friend from foe. Revolutionary mobilisation leans heavily on authority—a defined organisational hierarchy and a line of command. It demands organisational commitment and, at the lower levels, a suspension of critical judgment. The revolutionary leader relies on charisma rather than on the authority of office. Depending on the nature of the revolution and the degree of success it has attained, it may result in a complete change in the power alignments in the country or in a strengthening of the earlier power structure. If a new group or class comes to power at the end of the struggle, it will have to set itself to the task of liquidating or otherwise neutralising the youth who were in the 'enemy' ranks and then converting the rest of the society to its way of thinking by using its revolutionary cadres. In this process again, the conversion of the younger sections of the population must get priority for they can then be used for consolidating the new power structure.

Revolutions provide scope for idealism, action and merging one's identity in a larger whole. They attract youth. Revolutionary leaders welcome and rely on the young. They see youth as natural allies in change. Even children of the well-to-do sections and the aristocracy may respond to the idea of change for the sake of change. Also, since revolutionary movements—even if they are not based on class ideology—need to generally broaden their support, they may be willing to accept partisans from different strata including the lowest. Revolutionaries may make their manifesto more radical than they may be willing to sustain after they achieve power.

The pattern of youth mobilisation of the 'constitutional' or 'democratic' variety is very different. Here, the goals of social development are pursued through legal and legislative channels. Violence as a means is renounced though, in certain situations, the state itself may use violence to ensure conformity to law even if it is iniquitous. As explained above, the leadership is drawn primarily from the modernised middle and upper class groups in the urban areas who, while they may be genuine in their efforts at development, are not touched by a sense of immediacy. Such a leadership seeks to avoid division, polarisation and splitting up of the society into sharply differentiated interest groups. These leaders want to contain militancy in their own ranks and are afraid of fanning the spark of anger among youth. In any case, the youth they mobilise belong largely to their own social group. The established bureaucratic and organisational channels do not reach down to the low and deprived groups. The mobilisation is more metaphorical than real. It is always visualised as mobilisation of the better-off urban educated students in the effort to serve the deprived segments of the population. If the students take their mission seriously, they often find themselves running into conflict with the traditional segments of the well-to-do and the slow-moving officialdom that works with their assistance. To the extent that the student youth is partly drawn from the poorer, working class sections of the society, they are themselves in need of 'service'. Parts of the youth programmes are, therefore, oriented to the youth themselves.

The modern urban elite are gradualists. They regard youth work and youth mobilisation as a part of the process of spreading the democratic message and extending the area of participation. But, if social development does not take place or if it is delayed, then this leadership finds itself under pressure from its own youthful following which may grow cynical about what it is asked to do and restive about the good things of life they are themselves denied or are afraid they will be denied by the time they enter adult life.

This is admittedly a rather negative assessment of the pattern of youth mobilisation in the democratic, 'soft' states of the developing world. But it is not untrue in its essence nor specially exaggerated. This is a part of the broader problem that the liberal-democratic polities are facing in handling the whole developmental task. Has liberalism a chance to survive in the developing world? Or, will it give way to alternatives of the extreme right and the extreme left? The answer will depend upon how genuinely 'liberal' the ruling elite are. Are they able to see that the values of freedom, equality and rationality are indivisible? That a structure of laws which permits equality and freedom, and which treats every citizen as equal in the context of the legislature and judiciary, is not sufficient to ensure either of these to the poorer segments of the population unless the state can also provide full employment and a more equitable distribution of national resources? Liberalism in the 19th century was based on the assumption that if the citizen was given education he would gain access to the door of opportunity. This was true of the industrial societies of Europe with an expanding economy and an expanding empire to support the high standard of life of the European working class. In the absence of such an empire, the developing countries cannot ensure that their poor have access to opportunity and cannot fully mobilise them in the developmental process unless their basic needs are met, even if this involves a measure of 'distribution of poverty'. Such redistribution will call for self-discipline, particularly on the part of the middle and upper income groups in terms of their own priorities of expenditure. But this is the price that a 'free' society will have to pay if it values its freedom. Freedom cannot be defended in a society where the well-to-do will not share the sufferings of the poor. Democratic societies have shown the ability to unite and mobilise as nations during periods of war. Is the war on poverty less consequential? Such a programme will appeal to the idealism of youth; it will also reconcile the duality between the goals of 'service' and 'self-development' which are today placed before our middle class youth. In the absence of such a wider commitment, service will appear as condescension and will not elicit a response from the rural youth who also must be involved in the process of development.

Another aspect of the youth mobilisation effort in developing countries, which have a plural democratic structure, is the large number of independent groups that seek to mobilise. In itself a multiplicity of youth agencies need not be discouraged in a democratic system, but where the preoccupation of these agencies is immediate political advantage, they have only the consequence of disrupting youth movements.

One way of meeting the situation is to develop a youth programme under governmental, as different from the ruling party, auspices. Such a programme can be operated through universities and colleges. The students of colleges who would work in urban as well as rural areas would mobilise youth in the community to join them in organising services for the community.

An attempt will now be made to discuss the programmatic and the organisational form youth mobilisation takes in one country of the democratic, developing world, viz., India.

PROGRAMMES OF YOUTH DEVELOPMENT

The Government of India's publication entitled *Youth and National Development* (1975) lists four programmes providing for contribution of youth to development. These are: (i) National Service Scheme for university students, (ii) National Cadet Corps in universities, (iii) Student Service Institutes, and (iv) National Service Volunteers Scheme.

Of these, the last two are largely experimental and limited to a few projects. Of the other two the National Cadet Corps (NCC) is by far the larger one since it covers as many as 6,50,000 junior students and 3,60,000 senior students. It is also the older of the two programmes. But though it is listed as a programme providing students with an opportunity to contribute to development, its primary aim is "to develop qualities of leadership, character and comradeship" which would be of assistance in the defence of the country in periods of emergency. So it is not really a development-oriented programme in the limited sense of that term though it is admittedly a programme that could serve the needs of the country in certain areas. It should also be mentioned that this programme is organised in close collaboration with the three wings of the armed services. It has the advantage of being well established---it was in fact established prior to independence, is able to count on well-trained personnel borrowed from the armed forces as also from within the universities and has a well worked-out curriculum and set of activities. But it is not a development-oriented programme.

So, that leaves only the National Service Scheme (NSS) as the major development- or service-oriented programme for youth on the national scene. Like other programmes, it is limited to student youth and is financed from public funds. The scheme was launched in 1969-70 and covered 40,000 students in its first year; by 1975-76 it was expected to have involved 2,00,000 students in its activities. The scheme is still not universal and even with strength of 2,00,000 would cover only about 5-7 per cent of the students in colleges and universities.

While there are no absolute standards that can be specified about what proportion of students should be mobilised in any development-linked programme, it is obvious that the total coverage of the NSS is rather small. It is a new programme and still in many ways in its early stages and therefore the numerical coverage need not be a criterion for judging it.

In the first three or four years of its operation the government allocated on an average Rs. 120 per student per year. Since the students were expected to put in approximately 120 hours of work during the year, the cost of the programme may be said to have worked out at one rupee per student per hour of work. The actual amount disbursed to students in cash was much smaller since about 30-40 per cent of it was spent on administration, training and evaluation at the university and college levels. Since the students worked as volunteers---as did most of the teachers---the remaining amount was just adequate and used mostly to cover expenses like out-of-town transportation, food during camping periods and small contingencies. During the year 1975-76, the money provided per student was reduced by half. While this need not be a major point of criticism, it would be important to know whether (a) any effort has been made at costing student effort and assessing the benefit derived by the community as a result, and (b) whether the government is willing and able to set aside any appreciably larger funds to provide for expansion of the programme to twice or thrice its present size in terms of student coverage. If not, on what basis was it decided to cut the per student cost and on what basis are suggestions being made "to make it (NSS) universal for all university students?".

The nature of the NSS programme as it manifests itself in specific activities is well conceived in so far as its educational and personality development goals are concerned. The community service that students undertake, whether in rural areas, urban slums or social work institutions, certainly brings the middle class students face to face with aspects of life which they would have had little opportunity to see in their own lives. The opportunity to work with the poorer and needy sections of the population helps them understand the statistical and descriptive data on the subject in their textbooks; the problems of people eking a livelihood from agriculture come alive in a new way. In many cases the experience shakes the students out of their preoccupation with themselves and motivates them to seek ways of helping others.

The work undertaken under the NSS is varied. Students have set up medical centres and recreation centres, undertaken literacy and blood donation drives, organised immunisation and sanitation drives, mounted campaigns against famine, dirt and disease, done manual work to dig wells and build roads and participated in over a thousand longer duration camps devoted to study and service.

It cannot, however, be seriously claimed that the student effort has significantly contributed to the developmental efforts of the country. The fault does not lie with the students. There are indications that students are interested in the work they do and more of them would be willing to join if work was serious and absorbing. It is due to the fact that student effort is difficult to coordinate in a manner that will enable them to make a difference in the fight against any specific problem. Students have only so much time to give; it is available in small units per day for most of the year and then in longer units for a short interval during vacations. Their competence in most cases is of a somewhat generalised character; it is not specialised or professionally focussed, so that most of the time the help they can give is of the lay variety. While they can perform manual work, they are not physically fit to do this over long periods.

The main problem, however, lies in the lack of seriousness and the consequent absence of organisational effort that goes into the programme. While, on the one hand, there is light talk about making the programme universal, there has really been no effort to think about the implications of engaging student youth in programmes of national development. If student effort has to feed into ongoing developmental programmes careful planning and coordination at the national, state, district and block levels would be required between the development agencies and educational institutions. Specific projects requiring bulk labour inputs in short periods of time or small but sustained inputs over longer periods of time would have to be identified. The types of skills and competences required from students would have to be analysed. If necessary, the academic programmes and calendars of colleges and universities may have to be reorganised so that students are available when and where the projects require them. Projects may have to be classified in terms of whether they require students to work in large numbers, in small groups or singly; student groups may have to be organised not by the institutions from which they come, but on the basis of a mix of skills and abilities the projects require.

All this involves careful planning, detailed coordination and considerable organisational effort. Currently, there is very nearly an absence of any organisation except at the local college level and, sometimes, at the university level. The colleges and the universities have no links with the development agencies and if there is such a linkage it is limited to single projects at a time. Even at the college level, there is no full-time functionary who can plan the projects of student involvement. Even if 100 students enrol for the NSS programme it involves a great deal of planning; universal coverage would mean anywhere from 800 to 2,000 students per college. Obviously, no amount of 'dedication' on the part of college teachers can meet the requirements of advance planning. If student activities are not carefully planned, they prove not only wasteful and infructuous, but also tend to boomerang in terms of demoralisation and a more general loss of faith in the intentions and abilities of the older generation. Students tend to feel that they are being treated like troublesome kids who have to be somehow kept busy by being given something to do.

The fact, however, is that once their imagination and abilities are challenged, students can contribute a great deal in terms of labour and talent. In the limited, experimental form of the NSS, students have functioned in many roles. They have functioned as teachers in literacy programmes, as organisers of campaigns, as facilitators and channels of contact for the villagers with the urban bureaucracy, as advocates who have interceded on behalf of the underprivileged within the community, sometimes unwittingly, as models and elder brothers, as information communicators, etc. In some cases, as students of particular disciplines like English, Mathematics, History, they have been able to give professional advice and services.

If the NSS is to go beyond its experimental stage and become a programme for mobilising student youth in programmes of development, there will have to be a change of perspective on the part of government. It will also call for greater organisational effort in establishing linkages and this in turn will call for more staff at the college and university levels to devote time to planning and coordination. Thus, even on the basis of voluntary service by students, the financial allocations will have to be considerably larger per student than at present. Even more important, it will require a basic change in attitude towards student participation. Such participation must be welcomed not because it keeps students busy, but because it is expected that students will make a substantial contribution to the developmental effort of the country, and such participation will strengthen their social commitment. By widening the area of social communication between different segments of a highly stratified society, they will also deepen the roots of democracy. There can be no youth mobilisation except as a part of the total effort at national mobilisation.

13

Development Planning and the Cultural Context: The Indian Experience

Throughout history India has been characterised by the contemporaneous existence of a number of religions, languages, techno-economic systems and, in this sense, of diverse civilisations. In its long history there have been periods when one particular civilisation has been dominant in a great part of the country and though it has never completely replaced earlier civilisations it has tended to control variously the political, religious or economic centres of power in the complexity that Indian society is. In this sense, one can identify the pre-Vedic period, the Vedic period, the pre-Islamic Hindu period, the Muslim period, the British period and the current, post-colonial period of a politically free India which is economically and ideologically strongly influenced by countries of the First and the Second Worlds. In each of these periods the relationship between the dominant civilisation and the earlier civilisations has been of various degrees of conflict and accommodation. Whereas the economic and political institutions have necessarily reflected and followed the dictates of the currently dominant civilisation, in the social, religious and metaphysical systems of belief, the earlier civilisations have enjoyed greater

---

Paper presented at the Workshop on New Focus in Development Studies convened by the Institute of Social Studies, The Hague, May 18-22,1981.

continuity. In another sense, one could say that subtle changes and accommodations, and newer integrated forms arose at the social and philosophical levels, whereas there was more direct confrontation at the overtly religious level and there was often a complete surrender to new influences in the economic and/or political spheres.

It is difficult to delineate clearly what Indian civilisation is as of today. The difficulty arises not only because of the complexity and vagueness of concepts like civilisation and culture and a lack of uniformity about what is exactly intended or referred to by these terms but also due to the simultaneous existence of different value systems and goals among different segments of the Indian population: the rural and the urban, the educated and the illiterate, the Hindu and the Muslim, the liberal and the radical, those who are involved in the modern industrial urban-commercial nexus and those who are outside it, and so on. The different value systems are not necessarily always in conflict, but they are not fully reconciled to each other either. In a sense, this is true of every country. The value consensus is always relative.

One can begin with the value framework of the urban, educated segment which in many ways is the socially dominant segment in present-day India. This is the segment most influenced by the builders of modern India beginning with Raja Ram Mohan Roy in the 19th century through Jawaharlal Nehru in the 20th, who in their turn were influenced and challenged successively by evangelical Christianity, liberalism, Fabianism, communism and the post-Second World War demands of political equidistance from conflicting ideologies. Christianity challenged the inegalitarianism of the Hindu social order with its promise of equality, its directness and simplicity, and the worldly opportunities that conversion to Christianity offered to the poor and the outcaste. Evangelical Christianity generated internal pressures for change among the Hindus. This challenge was reinforced at the intellectual level by the new philosophy of liberalism. Liberalism emphasised the concepts of the dignity of the individual, equality before law of all citizens, the value of science and the increasing control of man over the environment, of the importance of modern education and the goals of a parliamentary democracy. It initiated the first efforts at improving the status of woman. Liberalism and evangelical Christianity did not reach the proverbial common man directly, but through a series of religio-social movements that were stimulated by them or rose to meet the challenge posed by them. In course of time, the nationalist movement as it developed in India virtually absorbed its major premises and communicated them to different segments of society in the form of a promise to create a society which would be free from caste, class and religious discrimination.

Liberalism contained the seeds of an egalitarian message, but the egalitarian message came through more clearly in Fabian writers who influenced the Indian elite in the 1920's and later through the socialist-communist movements as they developed in the post-independence period. Under this influence, the emphasis was not on equality before law, but on equality of life-chances. There was also an emphasis on the inevitability of conflict of interest groups on the role of the state in regulating the national economy and the need for organising the workers as a means of achieving a more equitable distribution of the wealth produced. The socialist and communist movements have also tried to interpret their own activities in the context of the global framework of ideas provided by their international counterparts.

NATIONALIST MOVEMENT

It was mentioned above that the liberal message reached India in the 19th century and found a fuller expression in the nationalist movement as it developed under the auspices of the Indian National Congress. A platform which promised a society free from religious or caste-based discrimination---and in this sense, secular and egalitarian---was essential to forge and maintain unity. These liberal goals are reflected in the kind of constitution that India gave itself wherein the goals of a democratic, secular and egalitarian message were spelt out. From one point of view they symbolise the socio-political goals of the Indian elite in the middle of the 20th century. Even then, there were differences about the exact connotations of the words 'secularism' and 'equality'. On balance, it would be fair to say that the 'equality' that the constitution spoke of was social and civic equality and not economic equality. Egalitarianism in the economic sense was never clearly spelt out, though there were demands for such a clarification from the socialists within the Congress and the communists outside it.

The Indian political leadership has found it necessary and expedient to remain ambivalent on this issue. The sources of this reluctance to accept the socialist-communist interpretation of the idea of equality have been both political and philosophical. One can probably understand this better by focusing our attention on the thought of the most important leader of the Indian National Movement---Mahatma Gandhi.

MAHATMA GANDHI

Mahatma Gandhi was a political leader, a man of great moral stature and one who while sensitive to all noble ideals from wherever they were derived, remained totally Indian in his mental responses, in the cultural symbolism that he used in his speech and action. His emphasis on simplicity, austere living, the purity of means, fasts and the need for self-purification was very much a part of the Indian tradition. Gandhi had certainly been exposed to and absorbed western liberal influences; the young socialists and communists in fact considered him a leader of bourgeois nationalism, but above all, he was a humanist. He absorbed the liberal influences but he went beyond liberalism in the sense in which Thoreau, Russel and Tolstoy went beyond the middle-class liberalism of the 19th century. He was acutely conscious of the importance and meaning of freedom for the individual. He accepted the claims to human equality in the civic and social sense and he indirectly conceded the morality behind the concept of an equitable share for everyone in the wealth of the community. This is seen in his view that the wealth of the rich man does not belong to him, but is held by him as a trust on behalf of the community. But, he found the socialist doctrine unacceptable on a variety of grounds: it was based on an assertion of rights rather than duties; it recognised open class conflict as necessary and desirable; and it tended to emphasise the material values in life and de-emphasised—if not, denied—the spiritual and religious values. He sought to approach the problem of gross inequalities in society by condemning the process of mechanisation and industrialisation which made these possible. He was, of course, aware that inequalities existed even in the pre-industrial society, but he probably thought that they were held in check by the control that the community and the social bond exercised on the individual. If he disliked accumulation of productive resources in a few hands, he also disliked the accumulation of political power in the hands of a few leaders or of a monolithic political party. Politically as well as economically, his vision of the ideal society was one made up of a large number of autonomous and locally self-sufficient communities. He also seemed to look forward to a time where the power of the state would wither away. He eschewed violence as a way of bringing about change, though he recognised the need for organisation of the weak. But, the weak must work for change through the mediacy of love and a change of heart in the perpetuator of inequality. He saw that conflict of interests existed, but he wanted it resolved without dividing the society into enemy camps and through a process of moral persuasion, self-sacrifice and willingness to suffer for the "assertion of truth" through non-violent means.

It is more than likely that had Gandhi lived to see the constitution that was finally adopted he might have found it unacceptable, for all its liberalism and idealism as reflected in the directive principles and the statement of fundamental rights. He would have found it too centralist and too much of a monolith in which the people in the villages had little direct share. It is also more than likely that had he lived he would have found the strategy of the successive plans of development unacceptable. It was a strategy based on large-scale state initiative, large capital investments, greater and greater industrialisation and international dependence and, generally, a strategy which seemed to lead the nation to the development of a strong modern, industrial urban sector and to a relative neglect of agriculture, rural industry and the subordination of the villager. Gandhi died within a few months of independence and though many of his followers in the Sarva Seva Sangh, the All-India Spinners Association and a large number of other Gandhian organisations raised voices of protest or dissent, none of them was strong enough to affect the decision-making process in government. This decision-making process was firmly in the hands of the educated, urban middle class in the ruling party as well as in the governmental bureaucracy. Their model of development was the model of economic growth through industrialisation followed in the most industrialised countries of the world—the UK and the USA.

INDIAN DEVELOPMENTAL EXPERIENCE

The middle class leadership was strongly nationalist and sensitive to the dangers of domination by foreign capital and of a total dependence on imported technology. This led to the promotion of scientific and technological research which, it was hoped, would soon enable the country to stand on its own. But several factors have slowed the pace of progress. The relative neglect of agriculture in the initial years of planning and the rapid growth of population led the country to a heavy dependence on food aid; the Pakistan and the China wars led to an increase in defence expenditure which inevitably cut into the funds available for development; while industrial technology within the country has continued to grow it has not been able to make up the gap between the pre-Second World War technology of India and the post-Second World War technology of the West, and has led to a dependence on foreign know-how and foreign collaboration in important segments of industry. While India has won and maintained its political freedom, it has not been able to materially modify the terms of trade between the developed countries and itself. Much of the foreign aid received has had to be utilised to purchase foreign capital goods and foreign know-how though this tie-up between aid and trade is somewhat relaxed through the aid operations of bodies like the World Bank, the International Monetary Fund and the regional banks. There is also a persistent effort made by India and other developing countries to extract concessions from the industrially advanced countries through the discussions at the successive meetings of UNCTAD. These efforts have so far not been largely successful. The efforts by the petrol producing countries to wrest an advantage by raising the price of a crucially important commodity in which they have a near monopoly have placed a greater burden on the developing countries than the developed ones because the latter have successfully passed on a good part of the increased burden to the developing countries which buy their finished industrial goods.

But, the Indian experience in development cannot be understood only in terms of the relationship between the developed and developing countries though this relationship provides the important world context in which most developing countries have to function today. The smaller developing countries like South Korea, Taiwan, Hong Kong and Singapore have been able to show substantial economic growth within this world economic context, largely by accepting the rules of the game as dictated by the developing countries and by the multinational corporations. But, the larger countries----large in landmass and population—have not showed similar gains. The failure, however, has to be understood both in terms of the intra-national as well as the inter-national forces at work. The Indian experience is one case which might help understand the problems.

The model of development that India opted for has been described as the model of a 'mixed economy'----an economy which provides for private ownership of capital, for an open market and yet for state enterprise and state intervention in regulating the economy. The intervention of the state was expected to ensure that the social justice aspects of development were not lost sight of in the pursuit of the goals of economic growth. While the right to private ownership of capital and the right to make profits from economic activity are recognised, the state is expected to regulate the economy in a manner that the interests of the urban, industrial worker, the lower middle-class white-collar worker, and the agricultural producer are safeguarded through a complex system of direct supports and controls of prices, fixation of minimum wages, a machinery for handling industrial disputes, a policy of fitful physical controls over the distribution of essential commodities, through price supports for agricultural product and occasionally through a policy of monopoly purchase of certain commodities by the state. In order to be able to support increased responsibilities for state investments in the basic or heavy industries sector as also to mobilise resources for defence, social services and social welfare services the state has had to pursue a policy of high rates of individual taxation. In the pursuit of its socialist objectives the government has also tried to introduce land reforms through a specification of maximum limits on landownership and an abolition of the system of tenancy under a class of absentee landlords.

A combination of private enterprise—presumably intended to foster entrepreneurship through the prospect of profits in industry—and of state regulation—presumably intended to control the rapacity of private capital and ensure a more even sharing of the benefits of growth—has led to the growth of an enormously complicated system of licensing and permits which concentrates power in the hands of the bureaucracy and the politicians and is difficult to operate under the best of circumstances and is otherwise ridden with red-tape and rampant corruption under less propitious conditions.

The net result of all governmental policies and actions so far has been the laying down of a large and varied industrial infrastructure which enables India to be counted among the industrialised countries of the world and the conversion of India from a food deficit country to one with large food reserves. India has also among the largest pools of scientific and technological population. These could be considered to be the gains of development, but these have not benefited the people. Over the past thirty-five years the percentage of the population living below the poverty line has increased from 45 to 52 per cent; while there is surplus grain in government warehouses, there are segments of the population in rural as well as urban areas who have no money to buy the food. The industrial potential is not fully utilised for want of demand; in relation to the developed world Indian industry is also becoming fast obsolescent and may not remain competitive despite lower labour costs. Any adoption of newer technology involves the import of know-how and import of capital goods which create new burdens of foreign payments. Besides, the newer technologies are more and more capital intensive and less and less job creating. The new industry therefore is unsuitable for the developing countries in both ways—in their demand for capital and in their inability to use the available manpower. Industrialisation today does not create jobs for all those thrown out of the agricultural sector let alone those who are being added to the population every hour, every day.

In the agricultural sector the great achievement has been an increase in the total production of food crops—first, wheat and now rice. There is also an increase in the production of eggs and milk though it is doubtful whether these have kept pace with the increase in population. At any rate the poor who cannot buy enough cereal to meet their requirements cannot afford to buy the milk and the eggs.

In agriculture, the efforts to achieve a more even distribution of landholdings have failed. The developmental strategy of increased use of irrigation, fertilisers and the new hybrid seeds has called for employment of resources which are available only with the large and medium sized landowner and which a small and marginal cultivator cannot afford. In the wheat granaries of Punjab, Haryana and Madhya Pradesh and in rice-bowl of Andhra Pradesh development has led to capitalistic forms of agriculture and an increasing pauperisation of the former tenant-cultivator and the landless agricultural labourer. The agricultural wage rates have gone up, but it would appear that the small cultivator has been squeezed out of the agrarian economy.

Thus, the number of landless in the countryside as well as the total load of full and partial unemployment has increased. All efforts at development—in most developing countries—seem to have increased inequalities. This is a direct consequence, particularly in agriculture, of the maldistribution of productive resources.

The intra-national experience of developing countries is matched by their experience as members of the international community. The world development decades have led to greater inequalities in the living standards of the rich and the poor countries. This is despite all the efforts at international aid whether on a bilateral basis or through world bodies. In fact, some political economists would argue that it is because of the forms of developmental aid that the 'developing' countries are becoming increasingly 'underdeveloped'.

Critique: One

The development experience so far---1947-1980---seems to have led to a sharpening of the controversy in India on the path followed for achieving the goal of well-being and plenty for all. Some would argue that the attempt to achieve growth through a planned, state-controlled econcmy has failed and that the country would do well if government were to relax various types of controls and allow a freer hand to private entrepreneurs and industrialists; this would reduce corruption and the operation of a black economy and the forces of competition would bring down the prices and raise the quality of the product. In course of time the benefits of the free economy would reach all segments of the population. However, there is no agreement about how far the state should relax its regulation. Industrialists who would like the urban-industrial sector to be given greater freedom would still favour a better distribution of land in rural areas and an introduction of tax on agricultural incomes to compensate for the reduced collections resulting from lower taxes on urban corporate incomes; further, while industrialists would like the freedom to enter into collaborations with international firms, they would still like government to retain protection against competition from imported products of industry. In fact, those who are already engaged in production of particular types of industrial machinery would not like the import of more recent technologies which would make their own method or product obsolete.

The argument for freedom from state interference is therefore usually an argument for selective controls where particular groups of industries---those based on foreign collaboration and imported know-how, indigenous capital and somewhat older know-how, and of medium size and scale---are arguing in their own particular interest.

This criticism of the path of development is in a sense not a criticism of the fundamental approach of a mixed economy adopted by the country so far. It is a criticism of particular strategies or particular combinations of control and freedom adopted from time to time by government. It is doubtful whether the Indian entrepreneur has either inclination or the vitality to face the rough and tumble of a free and competitive economy which is a part of the stereotype of 19th century capitalism. In the 20th century such competition is allowed—even in developed countries---only as between national entrants. There are no free international markets except between favoured partners and even these economic transactions are allowed only so long as national economic interests are not seriously threatened.

Critique: Two

The second response to the Indian developmental experience is to point out how this 'failure' was inevitable and indicative of the fundamental contradictions which were bound to be generated by an essentially capitalist strategy. This focuses on the failure of the Indian government to ensure a redistribution of productive resources, particularly in the agricultural sector, the futility of setting up an industrial infrastructure, which apart from facing the danger of rapid obsolescence, is unlikely to be fully utilised since the vast majority of the country's population has no money to buy its product, the inevitability of the development of inflationary pressures in an economy wherein the distribution of commodities is left to the vagaries of a market process, and the problem of regulating the national economy without regulating incomes and without restricting private property or private profit. This perspective carries the criticism of unequal exchanges beyond the national boundary and shows how, given the existence of a system of international stratification, any economic exchange between the developed and developing countries is bound to be exploitative and how the 'aid' strategies of developed countries are often part of their economic strategy of finding market for their surplus consumables, the products of their capital goods industries and the products of their industrial technological research. From this perspective development is a transitive verb where one country is trying to 'develop' another country and only succeeds in 'underdeveloping' it.

This criticism of the Indian developmental experience is a part of the larger critique of the development strategies adopted in the Third World countries. Its analytical framework is Marxist, but as modified and adapted to an understanding of 20th century international political economy by a group of Latin American social scientists. The prescriptions emerging from this criticism would be the adoption of immediate measures of redistribution of productive resources in agriculture and industry, and the narrowing of income disparities and regulation of commodity distribution through state intervention; the specifics of how these results are to be obtained are not always spelt out and one would assume that there is a wide variation in the degree of 'coercion' that the state would be expected to exercise in achieving the goals depending on the position that an individual critic occupies on the individual primacy-state primacy continuum. In the eyes of some, the very idea of individual freedom or civic freedom smacks of an outdated liberalism since there is no such thing—neither in the capitalist state nor the communist state—in the 20th century.

Critique: Three

There is a third response to the Indian developmental experience. This response focuses on the fact that thirty years of efforts at planned development in the country have only led to an increase in the number as well as proportion of those who live below the poverty line. This is because, it is argued, the goal of development, or, of an affluent society, is itself fallacious. The goal should really be to remove poverty, to work towards a non-poverty society and not towards a consumer oriented, highly industrialised, high energy using society. There are a whole set of studies and value preferences behind this critique. To begin with there is a realisation that life on this earth cannot be supported at the high levels of average energy and product consumption characteristic of the developed countries of North America. The publication of *Limits to Growth* underlined the finiteness of our energy and other resources. The Latin American scientists and some of the publications of the United Nations and the World Bank have pointed out the great disparities in the levels of consumption of people living in different countries. Writers like Schumacher and Ivan Illich have sought to provide a socio-economic philosophy for a life of limited, material wants and a life not dominated by large, overarching, economic and business organisations at the national and international levels.

The Gandhian and Sarvodaya thinkers in India, who had even earlier criticised governmental developmental plans for their overemphasis on industrialisation and their neglect of agricultural and rural industries, have now found a new support in all the literature that has been published since the 1970's underlining the increasing pauperisation of large segments of the population within the developing countries and of the developing countries as a whole in relation to the developed ones. The literature has also emphasised the material compulsions for the world to accept a simpler, more austere style of life in the interests of conservation of resources. This has given a new meaning to Gandhi's vision of a society composed of locally self-sufficient communities in which the scope for exploitation would be limited and the opportunity for participation by the individual in the community's decision-making process would be maximised.

The goal of a self-reliant, participative community made up of self-denying, non-acquisitive individuals does indeed seem attractive when pitted against the crassly materialistic, inegalitarian, competitive society of the First World or the highly ordered, and partly state dominated society of the Second World. But how is such a society to be brought into existence? Further, even if the goal of 'development'—interpreted as the pursuit of insupportably high standards of material and energy consumption—is given up, how do we achieve the no-poverty goal, i.e., the goal of freedom from want for every member of the society?

Even if we wish to achieve only a no-poverty situation—and not a situation of affluence—we would need to increase the total production of food and of other necessities and, of course, achieve a better distribution of these commodities.

SEVERAL QUESTIONS ARISE

First, a question of technology. What kind of technology will help us achieve an improved standard of living? Often, the phrase 'intermediate' technology or an 'appropriate' technology is used as an answer. But, what is the definitive characteristic of such a technology? Gandhi had answered this question by saying that it must be a technology that uses only the simplest machines and does not use power other than the power of the human limb or animal limb. He argued in favour of the use of hand-spun, hand-woven cloth, the use of hand-driven grinding wheel and the animal-driven oil expeller. His argument was based on the need to be rid of dependence on a technology imported from other countries, a technology which is likely to give rise to squalid urban concentrations and a technology which by concentrating productive resources in a few hands was bound to be exploitative. But if we wish to raise standards of living to acceptable levels of well-being for all we would need to change our technology. An improved technology is not a once-for-all phenomenon. It is a dynamic phenomenon which would need to be promoted and kept continually under observation for its 'appropriateness'. What are the criteria of such appropriateness? And, how is the dynamism of technology and of the search for knowledge to be maintained in a non-acquisitive, non-competitive society which distrusts the machine?

Further, even if we wish to be rid of the affluence or consumer orientation in society, we would still need to maintain an adaptive and an achievement orientation. What is our motivational model of man in the new society? Are we working towards some kind of a stasis where a balance between human needs and productive technology is to be achieved, towards a society where individuals free from poverty will work for some non-material goals? What is the level of material need satisfaction that is visualised? Is this level to be determined by each individual for himself or is it to be socially determined?

Again, is the goal of a no-poverty society to be pursued only by the underdeveloped and developing countries or is it a universal goal for mankind? If it is to be universally applied who will ensure---and how---that the First and the Second World countries which will have to make the most sacrifices in terms of their existing standards of living will accept this goal? The no-poverty society cannot obviously function like Aldous Huxley's *Island*---except in a few idealistic communities and for limited periods of time.

It would seem that a vision of the simple, small and locally self-sufficient community of the pre-industrial period does not offer a practical or even a desirable goal. The rural, small communities of old were marked neither by equality nor by individual freedom. The scale of exploitation may have been small, but that was because of the small scale on which the technology of production and distribution operated. With that scale now irreversibly changed the solutions may have to be sought not in a return to the past but in new modes of social and political organisation.

If developing countries decide to go alone along the path of a localised, small community which has accepted voluntary poverty, they will only continue to be dispossessed of whatever they might otherwise lay claim to by way of territory and resources.

SEARCH FOR A NEW SYNTHESIS

This does not mean that simplicity in living and self-denial have no place in social life. They are, on the other hand, important values for ordering individual as well as social life. Specially in developing countries where the total resources available to the community are small and where the first priority must be to eradicate the poverty of half the population, these values have a critical importance and their practice must be further strengthened by a scrupulous avoidance of any kind of ostentation. Even where a country and a people are affluent, simplicity in personal life will remain an important value, but simplicity should not be the beggar's choice. The Indian civilisation recognises and emphasises the nobility of altruism and of self-denial but it does not make the mistake of assuming that human beings can ever be wholly and consistently motivated by these values. Even Gandhi, who recommended non-possession and 'Christian poverty' as qualities to be cultivated by his ashram colleagues and co-workers, did not expect that this virtue would be practised by society at large.

Human life requires that the claims of the ego and alter ego, of the self and of the community be reconciled. The human being is inevitably caught between the opposites of love and hatred, acquisitiveness and sharing between perceptions of what is right and what is pleasurable, and between the short-term and long-term perspectives of what is desirable. The Indian ethos has sought to tell the individual how he might reconcile these claims in his own life by the pursuit of appropriate goals in the four major aspects of life—socio-religious, economic, familial and spiritual. The Indian ethos is neither dominantly ascetic nor materialistic; it recognises the claims of both and seeks to provide a proper place for them in the life of the individual.

Even at the level of the group or the community the Indian ethos has led to a continuous search for new syntheses of divergent thought and a reconciliation of divergent interests. It has not denied the existence of conflict, but has sought to reduce it and to contain it through new social mechanisms. The divergence of thought and philosophy is not denied, but an effort is made to seek unity in diversity. The essential evanescence of the social manifestations of life is not denied, but an effort is made to seek continuities in the midst of the endless flux.

The implication, therefore, is that faced as we are with the problems of development and the undesirable consequences of the developmental effort so far, we should seek to tame the process and not give up the developmental goals altogether. We need distributive justice, but we also need increased production if we have to gain freedom from poverty. We should not think in terms of small, locally self-sufficient communities. We should rather think in terms of a global community which, with the utilisation of the best that modern technology can provide, makes an acceptable standard of life and the goals of freedom and individual autonomy possible for all. The newer means of spatial and verbal communication should make individual autonomy and individual participation possible in large regional organisations of the world. This calls for the building of new institutional structures which go beyond our present concepts of nationality and allow for easier flow of ideas and commodities between countries without the exchange being exploitative of the poor. This is not easy and particularly from the point of view of the developing countries, can be full of pitfalls. The weaker nations will necessarily feel insecure in the face of this challenge, but a withdrawal into a shell, or into the past, is not an option to be followed except, may be, temporarily as a strategy.

At the national level, the secular, democratic and egalitarian society visualised by the makers of Indian Constitution still has great relevance. The egalitarian dimension was vague to begin with and the modalities of achieving this goal have now been found to be far from adequate. The phenomenon of an increasing proportion of the population being driven below the poverty line year after year has been effectively underlined by the socialist critique of Indian developmental planning who have also indicated why without a meaningful redistribution of productive resources reversal of the trend of pauperisation cannot be achieved. This is where the future of the Indian experiment in democratic planning will be determined. In the meanwhile, the Gandhian plea for an urgent expansion of the labour intensive sector, their particular emphasis on generating rural employment, their criticism of high living and simple thinking by the well-to-do, and their vision of a policy in which the individual citizen can become a participant in the decision-making process in more than the merely formal sense have highlighted other areas that need attention. Another underlying theme in much of the criticism of national developmental planning---though it has not been explicitly mentioned in the above account---is the futility of development planning which is narrowly focussed on economic parameters.

The focus on poverty has helped to bring the human being back into planning as the ultimate and only justification for the entire exercise. It is realised that human well-being cannot be regarded as a by-product of economic growth. It is also being recognised that human well-being ensured through services and equitable distribution is an essential condition for the success of economic planning.

With all these provisos and modifications planning is still necessary. Development will not simply happen. Without planning the internal inequities will only increase. The task of scholarship is to lay bare the machinations through which inequalities might increase in spite of planning.

Also, at the international level, some lessons are clear. While it is true that the population of the whole world cannot expect to live at levels of affluence characteristic of North America or North Europe, the way to redress the balance is to go on working for a more equitable distribution of world resources and for a greater regulation of the world production and trade system to serve the interests of the developing countries. The interests of these countries are not served by a rejection of that system, together with a rejection of the knowledge and technology base which have made it possible. The efforts will have to continue through education of world public opinion, a stronger organisation of the poor countries, and negotiations and confrontations in international forums. The inefficiency of the United Nations Conference on Trade and Development (UCTAD) and the lack of progress in the recent talks on the sharing of sea-bed resources are certainly a warning against any starry-eyed, boy-scoutish enthusiasm for the role that world bodies can play in promoting a more constructive relationship between the developed and the developing countries; but, for the present, attempting to establish such a relationship seems to be the only way open to developing countries.

Within the country again the weaker sections would need to be awakened and organised. In a democratic polity the voter must exercise his judgement and it is the function of those who would plead on behalf of the poor to educate them to do so. Freedom—whether from foreign rule or from poverty—has to be won. Gandhi has shown that it can be done by refusing to cooperate with those who would withhold freedom. His methods which were effective against a foreign government and in the achievement of a political goal must now be tested for gaining social and economic objectives at the national and international levels.

References

Dasgupta, S., "Facing the New Year: A Plea for a New Approach to Human Well-Being" in *Human Well-Being*, New York: International Council of Social Welfare, 1979. The paper effectively presents the case for a no-poverty society.

Gandhi, M.K., *India of My Dreams*, Bombay: Hind Kitabs Ltd., 1947. Compiled by R.K. Prabhu. It contains several extracts from Gandhi's writings outlining the society of his 'dreams'. Includes one essay entitled "Every Village a Republic".

Hiro, D., *Inside India Today*, London: Routledge and Kegan Paul, 1976. It is a lucid analysis of the Indian experiment in development planning.

India: Treadmill or Takeoff? A survey in the *Economist*, Vol. 278, No. 7178, 28 March-3 April 1981.

ILO, *Poverty and Landlessness in Rural Asia*, Geneva: I.L.O., 1977. The slim volume contains four papers on the rural poverty in four of the Indian states. It has additionally papers on Pakistan, Bangladesh, Sri Lanka and China.

Joshi, L., *Vaidik Sanskriticha Vikas* (The Development of Vedic Civilisation), Wai: Pradnya Patheshala, Rev. Edn., 1978.

14

National Goals and Mass Media Communication

The national seminar has been planned—as the brochure indicates—with eight broadly conceived themes which are expected to be discussed from seven different perspectives in as many sessions. Obviously what I have to say cannot possibly cover all the themes nor all the perspectives. What I will attempt to do is to briefly outline how one sociologist would spell out the issue relating to media communication in the context of national goals.

It may be permissible to say that in broadest sense the national goals as enunciated by Indian Constitution are those of creating a democratic, secular, egalitarian society. Some choose to use the word 'socialist' in place of egalitarian, but taking the reality and the experience of the past 38 years it might be truer to say that our polity is at best oriented to achieving an egalitarian rather than a socialist economic order. These goals, however imprecisely defined, provide the value framework within which the more immediate, substantive goal of economic and social development is sought to be achieved.

When we think of mass media communication in relation to national goals, we are looking at the former primarily as

---

Talk delivered at the National Seminar on 'National Goals and Mass Media Communication' organised by the Indian Academy of Social Sciences in Delhi.

instruments of achieving social and economic development within the value framework of democracy, secularism and equality. This way of visualising the relationship between mass media and national goals suggests that mass media are the 'independent' variable and national goals the 'dependent' variable. In other words, mass communication—in this model—is expected to subserve the purpose of achieving national goals.

FUNCTIONS OF MASS MEDIA

It is expected that mass media can help achieve national goals by performing certain functions for the society they serve. The UNESCO report on communication and society, entitled *Many Voices One World* (p. 14) identifies eight different functions for mass media as under:

(1) The function of *disseminating information* so that the recipient of the message is able to understand and react knowledgeably to the world and to the complex of social, economic, technological and political conditions around him.

(2) The function of *socialisation* through the provision of a common fund of knowledge which enables people to operate as effective members of the society in which they live (socialisation also involves the communication and inculcation of an agreed set of values).

(3) The function of *motivation* through the promotion of immediate and ultimate aims of each society and the stimulation of personal choices and aspiration, through the fostering of individual or community activities, geared to the pursuit of agreed aims.

(4) The function of *promoting debates* and discussion through the provision and exchange of facts to facilitate agreement or clarify differences on public issues.

(5) The function of *education* through the transmission of knowledge so as to foster intellectual development, the formation of character and the acquisition of skills and capacities at all stages of life.

(6) The function of *cultural promotion* through the dissemination of cultural and artistic products.
(7) The function of *entertainment* through the diffusion of drama, dance, art, literature, music, sports, etc., for personal and collective recreation and enjoyment.
(8) The function of *integration* through the provision to all persons, groups and nations access to the variety of messages which they need in order to know and understand each other and appreciate others' living conditions, viewpoints and aspirations.

But this very concept of someone or some agency using mass media to achieve certain goals may not be consistent with one of the values sought to be realised, viz., democracy which, in the area of communication, minimally implies the right to free expression in addition to the right to information. Further, in the democratic value framework, the mass of people should not be conceived merely as recipients of a message. They should also have the opportunity to participate in the process of formulating and transmitting a message.

Two policy issues arise----one relates to the freedom of the communicator, i.e., the right to freedom of opinion, and the other relates to the availability or access of communication media to the common man for the twin purposes of seeking as well as imparting information or ideas. Mass media, particularly broadcasting media as against print media, tend to convert the mass of people into receivers of the message and provide them little opportunity to be originators of the message.

The Universal Declaration of Human Rights seems to imply that the receiving and imparting of information will be governed by the value of truthfulness and will, in its turn, help to arrive at the 'truth'—of an event, a social phenomenon or a concept. This in turn is expected to lead to mutual understanding and integration. Free communication is one way of ensuring truthfulness and, therefore, also the credibility of the media.

SOURCES OF CONSTRAINTS ON MASS MEDIA

For the social scientist, this raises a question. Since mass media are seeking credibility, what are the social, political, organisational or ideological constraints that might vitiate their efforts at approximation to truthfulness in communication? The social scientist cannot assume the existence of a totally 'free' communicator nor a totally unbiased receiver of the communication. It is, therefore, important to identify the types of constraints and influences that will affect the origin of the message as also the receiving and interpretation of the message.

As social scientists we may not dwell at length on the physical technological factors that influence the transmission of a message and its reception, though even the physico-technological factors, e.g., the hardware aspects of communication determine whether or not particular modes of communication are available to the sender as well as the receiver of a message. The less developed and developing countries have less access and control over modern mass media, particularly in so far as they involve extensive news gathering and dissemination of news from and to different corners of the world. The discussions at various meetings of non-aligned countries have emphasised this fact and efforts—so far largely ineffective—are being made to develop a communication network which would be available for projecting the point of view of the poorer, the less developed countries of the world. As compared with major broadcasting systems the print media lend themselves to an easier and wider distribution in terms of ownership and control. Even in the developed countries, while every country may have its own local newspaper, they cannot have a comparable radio or television system. This situation is of course a result of the combined influence of technological, economic and political factors. But, even when the economic and political factors are controlled, the technology gap accounts for the great difference in the ability of nations to control the flow of information in terms of its content as well as direction.

Our discussion, however, should focus more meaningfully on the social, economic and political factors that influence the access to and control over mass media by different sections of a community and the manner in which mass media tend to be used.

GOVERNMENT AND MASS MEDIA

We may begin by examining the relationship between government and mass media. Here, the major policy issue and the dilemma arises out of a professed commitment to free communication and the expediency of controlling the message. There are three or four major patterns of relationship between government and mass media.

One pattern is that which obtains in communist countries, where the state finances and controls the mass media as well as the messages communicated. This applies to newspapers and other print media as well as to broadcast media. This pattern also obtained in fascist countries, of which we can take German communication network under the Nazis as a prototype.

The second pattern is the one where government does not own the media network nor does it directly control the message. The pattern is found in the USA where neither the print nor the broadcast media are subject to direct government control.

A third pattern is the one where both types of state-media relationships are found to coexist. An example would be the simultaneous existence of the BBC and the ITV networks in Britain. The BBC is largely state financed and the ITV is commercially financed. Despite state-financing, the BBC has generally been kept free of direct state control. Its autonomy is sought to be ensured by its being provided with an independent corporate board of control, though in special circumstances the government retains the right to direct the network not to broadcast certain messages. The image of the BBC's autonomy has been maintained largely by the fact that the British government has generally abstained from interfering with the working of the BBC. There was, of course, the recent instance when government dissuaded the BBC from broadcasting an interview with an IRA leader. There is a recent book by a former BBC official which makes out that the BBC has never really been totally free from government interference and that successive Prime Ministers have sought to influence its coverage at certain critical points.

The print media in Britain, as in USA, are not government owned nor government controlled. India has sought to follow the British pattern, but not with great success. The broadcast media are wholly government owned and are closely supervised by government in their operation, particularly in their news broadcasts. The print media are not government owned but, at various times, government has sought to influence newspapers in their editorial policies through adoption of discriminatory practices in the supply of newsprint and the patronage offered through governmental advertisements. Once, during the emergency, the government also exercised direct censorship of the press.

It is obvious that the extent of control exercised is determined by the type of political system that obtains in a given country and by the stage of politico-economic development at which the country is. It is equally clear that almost every government occasionally finds itself embarrassed by the freedom of the mass media though, given their political systems, they may or may not be able to do much about it.

In the British and American contexts where the right to freedom of thought and expression of individual citizens are fundamental concepts of their polity, it is difficult for the state to interfere with the media despite the fact that the modern form of investigative reporting can place an incumbent party in a very difficult position. It is only on grounds of national security that governments in these countries can persuade mass media to keep anything from being published or broadcast. Even here, on many occasions, the editors of newspapers have not agreed with the government on what constitutes a risk to national security. In fact, media reporters who have ferreted out state secrets can yet count on judicial support against being required to reveal the source of their information.

In communist countries, the state and the party, both, effectively control all the mass media and use it for selective news release, ideological indoctrination and mobilisation of public opinion in support of state action and policies. In order to keep the people from being influenced by foreign media, governments in these countries have at certain stages of their development and to various degrees prevented foreign newspapers and periodicals from reaching the people. They have also sought to control the activities of foreign correspondents in their countries by imposing restrictions on their entry into the country and freedom to travel and gather news about people or events. Private citizens are discouraged from establishing contact or communication with foreigners generally through systems of surveillance. This effort at blocking out news of other countries from reaching the people or news about the country from reaching the world outside is what has commonly been referred to as the iron curtain or the bamboo curtain by the mass media of non-communist countries.

The efforts of governments to regulate the message that reaches the people through mass media are somewhat constrained by the need to maintain credibility of the media in the eyes of the people. If the message communicated by the media is at total variance with the experience of the people, the latter will cease to believe the media altogether and then the utility of the media as agencies of mass mobilisation will decrease. The need for credibility makes it necessary to maintain the appearance of the existence of free communication. There are also technological limitations on what can be kept from the people in the modern world. The radio broadcast medium, which the government of the country uses to transmit its own messages to the people, can also be used by foreign broadcasting systems to provide other messages through programmes beamed to particular regions and countries. The Foreign Services Division of the British Broadcasting Corporation (BBC) and the Voice of America (VOA) often serve as alternative channels of obtaining news about their own countries to people who live under political regimes that overtly censor national mass media. Under these circumstances, the communication of the foreign-based broadcasting system may gain greater credibility just because it is different from what the local government controlled media broadcasts. The receptivity of the audience to foreign sources of information increases as the confidence of the people in the veracity of their own media decreases. This can often be an indicator of the morale of the people of that country and the degree of consensus that exists in the country and generally or on particular issues.

The relative confidence that people have in national media as against foreign media is delicately balanced. While they may suspect that local media publish or broadcast what is acceptable to their government, they also suspect the message of the foreign media of being motivated and biased in other ways. People in countries where news is censored listen to the BBC or the VOA not because they believe them to be wholly truthful or unbiased, but because these agencies have the advantage of giving the other story. If the people and the government are united in their purpose, they may see divergent, outside messages as motivated and against national interest. On the other hand, if government attempts to totally prevent any but its own message from reaching the people, there is a likelihood that a rumour network will develop and clandestine channels of communication will gain greater credence than they might otherwise merit.

We have so far restricted our discussion to the linkage between the political system and mass media. But this does not mean that where mass media are free from direct government control, they are free of political or other bias. If mass media are influenced by governmental policy, they are also influenced by centres of economic power.

MASS MEDIA AND MARKET ECONOMIES

In communist countries the government exercises both political and economic control; it has a decisive role in regulating the economy as well as the media. In market economies, economic power—the power of the big business houses—may seek to influence both the government and the media. But, the influence of business houses cannot be as direct or open as that of government. When government strictly controls media, as in communist countries, it is supported by an ideology that does not recognise the legitimacy of the existence of competing ideas. On the other hand, market economies in democratic countries are based on the ideology of the freedom of the individual and the freedom of the media.

Economic power is exercised in two ways—indirectly through differential support of the different political parties which are seeking to gain control of the rein of government and directly through control of media where private ownership of media is possible, as in the case of the print media network in India. But, even where ownership of a newspaper is in private hands, the control exercised by the owner on the message communicated through his paper cannot be as comprehensive, detailed, persistent or direct as in the case of government. For, in comparative terms, while government is a monolith, a single entity, the market economy is not a single entity; the market economy is made up often of competing groups who are united, if at all, only as an ideological category. Business houses get together as Chambers of Commerce, but even then beyond arguing that the burden of taxation should be reduced and that the government should adopt protective policies in favour of local industry they may find that they have little in common.

Even on the question of providing tariff protection to local industry the industrial houses and the trading houses may not always agree. Among the industrial houses themselves there can be differences of opinion between those which have foreign collaborations and those which are built on local technical know-how.

When one speaks of the capitalist control of mass media it becomes meaningful to do so in two or three different ways. One of these is with reference to the pervasive influence of capital or money power in market economies on the political system itself through its ability to support differentially parties and persons with different economic ideologies. Through this means big business may be able within limits, to influence governmental policy making, including government's policy with reference to mass media. The limits are set by the fact that while big business controls the supply of funds to political parties, they may not directly be able to control the popular vote which puts a party in power.

The second meaning in which big business can influence mass media is through direct ownership of such media, wherever that is possible. In the USA, as stated earlier, all media are owned privately. In Great Britain, there is a coexistence of government and privately owned media in the field of television broadcasting, whereas the radio network is managed by a government-owned but autonomous corporation and the print media are privately owned. The business house which has controlling interest can pick and choose its editorial staff and through this broadly lay down the business as well as the editorial guidelines for the particular newspaper or periodical. Newspapers play a great role in building up the images of political leaders and parties and to that extent they exercise influence on the politician as well as the public. But, where newspapers are privately owned, they can be owned by people belonging to different political persuasions. To that extent they exercise a mutual constraint on each other.

The third way in which big business control of the media can make itself felt is in the area of ownership or control of news gathering and news supply agencies. While most individual newspapers or broadcasting houses have their own correspondents, news gathering has become a specialised task requiring heavy capital investment and those who control such specialised agencies wield great influence on what is supplied to the media and in what manner it is presented. This is the point that was referred to earlier when a reference was made to the control exercised by North American and West European news agencies over the flow of information from and to developing countries. Their coverage of international news can make subtle differentiation in presentation of news items from communist countries, developing countries of the Third World and countries of the western world.

Our discussion so far has been focussed on the right of the media to free communication and how this freedom might be constrained by political and economic factors. These constraints might take the form of direct censorship and/or control of the news gathering and news supply processes. This might be done for reasons of national security for reasons of party interest or for reason of ideology—whether the ideology is capitalist or communist. In the course of the discussion we had occasion to refer to the need for credibility—the need to ensure credibility of the message---as a counter-constraint on the efforts of political or economic interest to control and regulate the media.

CREDIBILITY AND THE PUBLIC

While we speak of the 'public' in the singular as though there was one undifferentiated mass of people, in reality there is not one public but several publics differentiated by age, sex, religion, nationality and socio-economic status. In a differentiated society—and every large society is differentiated—a single message from a controlled medium cannot possibly maintain its credibility.

Credibility of the message of mass media depends partly on the public's own perception or experience of events in the world around them, but it also depends upon the extent to which the public has access to information and has available to it divergent points of view, divergent interpretations of events based on an agreed set of data. In the absence of free availability of information—whether about persons or happenings—the public may accept a version that is presented to it through the controlled media or may begin to depend on other channels of informal communication—rumours, word of mouth messages or messages received through clandestine channels. Whether the people accept the message of the controlled media or believe in messages received through other channels will depend on their faith in the sender of the message. Credibility of the message in this sense depends on the credibility of the sender of the message. It also depends upon the public's own predictions, and its needs to feel secure in its existing set of beliefs.

In this sense, free media create and also are dependent on the existence of a free critical public. This public—whether readers, listeners or spectators—must articulately respond to the news and views presented to it. A free press or communication depends on the existence of two-way communication, which in turn depends upon the existence of a significant number of discriminating readers/viewers/listeners.

Such a discriminating public does not arise in a day. It is at once the necessary condition and the consequence of the existence of an open polity, open press and system of education that promotes the ability to form judgement and a willingness to express it.

All judgements by their nature are, in the last analysis, value-based. These values are partly based on verifiable knowledge, such as values relating to health, hygiene, civic responsibility, etc., but there are others which are in the nature of ideals, such as the concept of human freedom and equality. In this sense liberalism is as much an ideology as communism is—one built round freedom as the central value. Yet, neither freedom nor equality can exist without the other. Free mass media and communication channels are in this sense the necessary means as well as ideals characteristic of an open and egalitarian society.

From this perspective, the right to freedom for the media and the right to information for the public are central issues in the formulation of a national policy with regard to mass media and in the role that the media are expected to play in national development. A dilemma arises when freedom is seen as in opposition to equality. The unequal distribution of political and economic advantage in society poses a threat to the freedom of the media and the right of the citizen to information.

Similarly, the unequal distribution of knowledge, wealth and military prowess between nations creates a threat to the freedom of the media or the free flow of information. National governments may tend to restrict free flow of information—outward or inward—on grounds of national interest whether economic or political. In the short run, these restrictions may be seen as desirable by the people generally and may even be voluntarily accepted by the media themselves, but in the long run they will be seen as counter-productive in so far as they keep the people ignorant of what the reality is.

OTHER ISSUES IN DEVELOPING A MEDIA POLICY

Freedom is, however, not the only issue in the formulation of a media policy nor is freedom affected only by inequalities of wealth, political power and armed might. There are other issues too. One of the more important of these relates to establishment of priorities, at least relative emphasis, between the different functions that mass media are expected to serve.

The first function of mass media is said to be the communication of information. Mediamen speak of the emergence of communication gaps between countries, communities, and people. We have seen how political and economic factors may give rise to the development of such communication gaps. But, in a multilingual country like ours, language can be another major source for such a gap. If information and ideas have to be communicated to different linguistic groups, the message of the media must be available in all the major languages of the country. The medium of newspaper is fully developed from this point of view and TV the least developed. But even the newspapers experience a total inadequacy in the availability of information supply in the regional languages. Despite the establishment of Samachar Bharati the supply of news in Hindi is not comparable to that of the English news agencies. Besides, the resources available to regional (even Hindi) newspapers are not comparable to the English newspapers. While most national English dailies have editions of sixteen pages, the Indian language newspapers are rarely larger than six to eight pages. While the space given to editorials remains the same, the space available for news-based articles is severely limited in the Indian language newspapers.

The space available for news-based articles is important because that is where exchange of views takes place. They are the major agency for educating public on important national issues. Such space also decides how much opportunity informed readers----as different from editorial staff----will have to communicate their views through central page articles, middle page articles, etc.

The size of a newspaper depends upon its economic viability which in turn depends upon its readership and the advertisements that it commands. Government may have no direct role to play in either of these, but the fact remains that Indian language newspapers are restricted in their coverage of news and communication of views by the limited space available to them. This is critical in a country where the broadcast media are wholly owned and controlled by the government. Such news as they broadcast is carefully screened and projects primarily the government's points of view. Even where discussions take place on matters where government has a declared policy dissent is carefully kept out or kept within acceptable limits.

PRIORITISATION BETWEEN ENTERTAINMENT AND EDUCATION

Another issue arises from the twin demands of entertainment and education. This is not a major problem with regard to newspapers because newspapers are not primarily a source of entertainment. But, with regard to periodicals and in respect of the broadcast media, the relative time given and the quality of entertainment and education programmes becomes important. Between Akashwani and Doordarshan the former has more time and a larger proportion of programmes which are informative and educative, in the form of news bulletins, discussions, talks, farmers' programmes, health-based programmes, youth programmes, etc. The purely film music and film personality-based programmes are kept largely reserved for the Vividh Bharati network. Doordarshan also had a larger proportion of educational programmes before the era of the sponsored programmes began. Apart from the film-based and film-related programmes which already existed, the sponsored programmes have added a large number of serials whose entertainment and educational potential is often doubtful. Sponsored programmes have helped extend the broadcast time from two to an average of six hours per day, but like the commercial film most of the sponsored programmes offer entertainment of a dubious value. As though to salvage the situation the Doordarshan fills up blank spots with repetitive quotations from Mahatma Gandhi and Jawaharlal Nehru or with didactic messages of its own.

REGIONAL AND NATIONAL PROGRAMMES ON DOORDARSHAN

The development of the national network on the Doordarshan has been a mixed blessing. The national newscasts are better and more comprehensive, but the rest of the fare served on the network does not compare favourably with what the local stations were able to offer earlier. The country-wide classroom programmes are an exception.

This throws up another issue of TV media policy, viz., the relative time and encouragement to be given to regional language and national programmes. While the national programme with the use of the Insat-B has certainly extended the area coverage of Doordarshan, this extension has cut into the prime time available for regionally produced and regionally oriented programmes. This may be justified on grounds of national integration, but it has discouraged local initiative and one is not sure whether sponsored programmes which take up a good part of the network time achieve national integration any better than the commercial film.

As, at present, in the absence of really informative, artistic or genuinely entertaining software, the national network seems to be fulfilling the gloomy prophesies of some who were afraid that the it would only serve as a channel for an extension of the commercial film and the projection of political personalities in power. The coverage of the Asian Games still remains the only major achievement of the network.

I am aware that tastes differ and what I like need not necessarily appeal to others. But, if education, mobilisation of public opinion and national integration are among the accepted goals of mass media, they seem to receive at present fairly low priority even after granting that many of these goals could be achieved through entertainment.

CHOICE OF TARGET AUDIENCE

Another issue relates to the choice of audience or audience mix for whom the programmes are broadcast. Initially, when the radio and television stations had local coverage, their audience was understandably the urban middle class since this was the group that owned radios and TV sets. The introduction of transistors in the 1960's and now the establishment of the national network for the TV have considerably changed the situation. The listening and viewing audience is wider but the media message is still from the urban middle class to the urban middle class; the rural sector is covered by short stints of farm and agriculture-related programmes and sometimes by studio-bound folk dances and folk music. Even the urban working class gets a special half an hour per week set aside for it. It is doubtful whether isolated programmes which are thus prepared for the rural or the urban working class audience can really achieve much. The participants in these programmes are so obviously playing a 'role', one is not even sure that they are drawn from among these groups. An honorable exception is the 'Gyandeep' programme on the Bombay Doordarshan where a real movement seems to have developed involving lower middle class and industrial working class families who organise themselves into Gyandeep Clubs. They plan, produce and participate in the programmes. These programmes achieve a combination of education and entertainment. They may not appeal to the connoisseur of art or drama but they are obviously satisfying and meeting a real need of this audience which participates creatively in formulating its own message. Some of the programmes organised as a part of 'Sunder-Maze Ghar' (again a Bombay Doordarshan production) have the same quality of a clearly identified audience participating also in the formulation of the message. The programmes achieve the goal of education effortlessly. In a different way Kamaleshwar's suspended programme, 'Parikrama', achieved the goal of educating the urban middle and upper middle class about the life of the other urban dwellers whom they often meet in their daily lives but do not know or understand.

A somewhat 'highbrow' programme, based upon interviews with established writers, thinkers, poets, playwrights, and artists, entitled 'Pratibha and Pratima' has again the advantage of a clearly identified target audience. The programme continues to occupy a very prestigious position among the programmes telecast by the Bombay Doordarshan.

Considering some of these programmes one wonders whether the locally produced programmes do not have an edge over the national network so far as their ability to raise social awareness and elicit understanding are concerned.

One can go on raising and discussing other individual issues relating to media policy. But, within the confines of a single paper, such a discussion will necessarily be superficial. What I have done so far is to raise first of all the question of constraints on the freedom of the media to communicate information and the freedom of the individual to have access to such information. This issue is critical from the point of view of both democracy and equality which are two of the three basic values of our polity. Later, at a different level, and very briefly, I have discussed some of the other issues relating to Indian mass media. I would now like to move towards a conclusion of this talk by returning to more general discussion of the social scientists' perspective in the study of mass communication.

MODELS OF ANALYSIS

Social scientists have utilised two models in the study of communication and the media. One of these is provided by the American political scientist, Lasswell. It sets out the parameters of its analysis in the simple question: Who says what to whom with what effect? The source of the message, the content of the message, the audience to which the message is addressed and how effectively the message is communicated or received are the four major areas of study. Some students of communication consider this framework to be simplistic and at best useful in analysing the intra-system processes. They argue that it neglects the larger socio-political-economic context within which it takes place. According to them, a more meaningful and penetrative understanding of the functioning of mass media is achieved by probing the power nexus in which media operate---power in all its forms, viz., economic, political, religious or social. Class interests and class relations are, according to them, the key to an understanding of the way mass media function.

To my mind the two frameworks are not mutually exclusive. The question 'who' is the sender of the message can be answered in terms of status hierarchy based on caste or class, but it can also be answered in terms of the categories of age, sex and cultural background of the communicator. Answers obtained at both the levels can be meaningful depending on the problem to which we are seeking an answer. The fact that the communicator represents the government or the capitalist class may be more important than the fact that the communicator is a male (chauvinist) or old (outmoded) or a city dweller or a heretic or a believer in an analysis of the message of the communication. Similarly, the effect of the message need not be analysed in terms of the power nexus though that is a meaningful dimension; it can also be analysed in terms of credibility persuasiveness and the result it achieves in changing an established pattern of beliefs or practices.

The two frameworks of analysis are mutually supportive. One can be used to spell out the implications of accepting certain national goals like democracy, socialism and secularism for developing national policies and programmes of mass media communications. The other can be used to see who and what message, communicated in what manner, is likely to achieve the desired goals of making the recipient more work oriented, more socially committed, more accepting and respectful of people who are different from him, more rational, more able to think for himself, etc.

In my talk I have suggested a few of the directions along which such analysis can be undertaken. The questions I have raised have focussed primarily on freedom and control of mass media. This is an important dimension of analysis for the democratic structure and democratic functioning of our polity.

But similar questions can be raised in respect of the goals of equality and secularism. In each case we would need to examine how far the institutional structure is favourably situated for promoting these goals and to what extent the message is likely to strengthen these values.

It is possible that at the institution level we arrive at a broad conclusion that the framework within which the media functions are not supportive of the goals we have set for ourselves. Then two types of questions arise: first, what are the modifications needed in this structure and second, what can be and what has been achieved within the limitations of this structure. This latter issue would involve undertaking an analysis of significant exceptions wherein despite limitations imposed by institutional framework programmes are able to convey messages which are supportive of the professed goals of equality and secularism, at one level, and of messages of family planning, civic consciousness, national integration or environmental conservation at the other. The achievement of these latter, more proximate goals, is as important for national and social development as the pursuit of the broader, more pervasive national goals. It would also be important to analyse ways in which the generality of programmes fails to communicate messages supportive of the goals or, in fact, convey messages which conflict with them. Similarly, communication studies could seek to analyse why programmes which seek to convey supportive messages fail in their objective. This would involve studies of the message, the modes of communication, the compiler of the message and of the psychological barriers that may exist in the minds of different sections of the population, constituting the audience, which make them non-receptive to the message.

15

The Cultural Perspective in Social Work in India

There are at least five distinct approaches adopted by persons engaged in the broad field of social welfare in India and the approach of professional social work is one of them. It is not only the newest of the five approaches but also the only one which has been clearly influenced by ideas and methods developed outside the country. Both these facts provide an important context in understanding the attitudes of non-professional workers and the general public towards professional social work.

It would be useful to identify and briefly describe the five approaches so that their mutual relationships are better understood. These are religious-traditional, liberal-reformist, secular-missionary, ethical-revolutionary, and liberal-professional. This is in no sense a typology. It is at best an attempt to identify the more important value premises from which the five approaches seem to emanate. There is no suggestion that the value premises of the five approaches are either irreconcilable or mutually in conflict. It happens that they have so far continued to function largely independently of each other. In a sense the numerical order of each approach also represents the sequence in which they made their appearance though as is probably only to be expected in the large diverse

This paper was written in 1966.

society that India is, they all continue to function contemporaneously even today.

THE RELIGIOUS-TRADITIONAL APPROACH

The religious-traditional approach is typified largely by individual charity directly benefiting the needy as when the giver doles out food, foodgrain, clothing, etc., to a mendicant or a beggar. Sometimes, the donor may enable a church, temple or mosque to undertake charity on his behalf, sometimes he may create a trust or an endowment for charitable purposes. The inspiration is religious and the mode of expression of concern for the fellow-being conforms to known, traditional channels. In Hinduism, as in most religions, an act of charity counts as a deed of merit and confirms a benefit on the giver. The benefit is counted in religious-spiritual terms. At the more sophisticated level religion enjoins that acts of merit must be undertaken without expectation of reward. Nonetheless meritorious deeds help raise the tally of good deeds in the final reckoning.

In the religious-traditional framework characteristic of Indian religions the sufferings of an individual are usually put down to his own past actions whether in this life or in a previous life. The suffering may evoke sympathy and helpful response but will rarely raise questions as to whether it could be attributed to an external factor. These are no doubts raised about the justice or equity of particular social arrangements. The social order as prescribed in the scriptures is God-given. The needs perceived are on the one hand physical and on the other spiritual. The suffering individual has to be given bread, clothing, shelter or some physical relief and to be guided to the religious path. The social and psychological dimensions of need are not clearly perceived in this approach.

A good part of the assistance provided within the religious-traditional context does not require an intermediary to mediate between the giver and the recipient. The setting up of a service to provide water to the thirsty wayfarer, the setting up of a rest home for travellers, the building of platforms where load carriers could rest their burdens, the distribution of food to the poor at fairs and temple doors, the regular feeding of young students, etc., are actions that do not call for specialist workers. And, even if a worker is required, his work does not call for training.

The dominant values of the religious-traditional approach in India is comparable to the values governing similar approaches in other parts of the world. The dominant value for the giver is the attainment of religious merit. This is acknowledged and supported by the recipient who invariably invokes God's blessings on his benefactor. There is, however, another component of this value framework which probably is not equally characteristic of the Judaic and Christian faiths. This is the component of a sense of redundance or futility on the part of the giver and a corresponding sense of fatalism on the part of the recipient. Since the sufferings of an individual are a consequence of his past actions and these consequences are inescapable, there is not much that one can do to help oneself or another person who is suffering. If you help, you do so because it is your duty to help, but without the conviction that your efforts can really solve a problem. This accounts at least partially for the passivity with which Indians are said to accept human suffering.

However, modern interpretations of the theory that actions have inescapable moral as well as material consequences and that these consequences may be experienced not only in one life but also other lives to follow question the imputation of fatalism and passivity to it. They argue that this theory instead of encouraging passivity really emphasises the fact that man is the master of his own destiny.

THE LIBERAL-REFORMIST APPROACH

The liberal-reformist approach, which dominated the period from 1875-1920 in Indian social history, manifested itself mainly in two forms. In one form it led to large-scale pamphleteering, public speaking, editorial writing, and other modes of educating and organising public opinion. These were the days when educated men and women organised themselves into associations devoted to several newly discovered reformist goals and worked for social change and new social legislation. Education was considered important both as an end in itself and as an instrument of change. Religion and certain social customs were subjected to rigorous criticism. The spread of education, the abolition of child marriage, the abolition of *sati*, the removal of the prohibition against widow remarriage, the banning of polygamy, and the prohibition of unequal marriages (between doddering old men and teenaged young girls) were issues that were seriously debated and canvassed. In religion the issues centred round the image worship, the caste system, and the wide variety of superstitious practices. The entire period was marked by great religious and social movements, though these movements were largely confined to the educated middle income groups of society. Undoubtedly, and almost inevitably, the reformist movements also succeeded in generating counter-currents of orthodox, revivalist opinion. And, these latter also organised themselves into groups though largely they fought a losing battle, at least at the ideological level.

The other way in which the liberal-reformist approach expressed itself was through the establishment of institutional services, namely, schools, hospitals, orphanages, homes for destitutes, widows and women in distress. Initially, many of these institutions were started by foreign financed and staffed Christian missions, but in course of time other groups—religious as well as non-religious—took the lead. Among these latter were also individuals who were influenced by the reformist and revivalist thought currents of the time. Unlike the arena of intellectual discussion the field of service provided scope for joint work to many who otherwise disagreed on ideological issues.

Liberal thought in India has emphasised a particular complex of ideas—democracy and democratic procedures in political and social organisations, the value of education, science and knowledge, and a limited acknowledgement of the need for rationality in public life. The source of liberal ideas adopted in India is to be found in the 19th century liberalism of Britain and the channel for their communication was provided by the new system of education introduced in India by the British about the middle of that century. Democracy brought with it the idea of equality—an equality largely based upon the goodwill of the privileged, but still strong enough to have generated a movement for the betterment of the status of women in society. The idea of equality did not, however, spread to question the basis of the caste system or of untouchability until much later, in the 20th century. Democracy was viewed largely as a political concept as well as a set of the procedures for the conduct of formal public life. The proponents of liberalism often practised the caste system in their individual lives. If the concept of equality was accepted in a limited way, so was the norm of rationality. A few liberals allowed their rationality to modify their basic religious positions and question or negate the existence of God. Most tended to limit the application of rational norms to the areas of knowledge and education and economic and political life.

From the point of view of social work this meant that while the acceptance of democratic and rational values developed a certain new sensitivity to problems heretofore neglected, this sensitivity was largely restricted to one's class and caste. The problems of the poor, rural populations, traditionally underprivileged caste groups or outcaste groups did not receive the attention that they deserved. The discussions about caste disabilities were largely related to legal norms and use of public facilities; it is doubtful whether many of the social reformers and social workers had visualised or worked out the implications of a 'casteless' society in their own individual lives. But, within the safe limits of a predominantly middle class liberal philosophy, the social reformers and workers had a clearly conceived programme of action, both at the levels of legislation and service organisation.

Apart from the physical needs of food, clothing and shelter, the social worker now saw the need for education. The attitude to the recipient was characteristic of oldworld charity. But, there was an absence of the religious emphasis. The motivation of direct religious-spiritual benefit for the donor did not have the same central role in the somewhat impersonalised agency of an orphanage or a widow's home. The donor was removed from the recipient and, besides, there were now many small donors instead of one single benefactor. A full-time functionary was now required to operate the services. Often, this functionary was a voluntary worker.

THE SECULAR-MISSIONARY APPROACH

Another type of social worker, however, appeared on the scene at this time. He was comparable to a missionary belonging to a holy order, except that the order to which he belonged was not always a religious one. Apart from the Christian missions, there were at least two near-religious orders----one created by the Arya Samaj and the other by the Ramakrishna Mission. But, there were also several secular organisations established during this period which drew to them young, idealistic men who wished to dedicate their lives to public or social work. Often, the same persons devoted themselves to both types of work. Besides, when social and legislative reforms were one of the main avenues of work, the line between the political and purely social spheres of work could not be a sharp one.

The inspiration of these men who committed themselves to a life of service was often religious but there were among them some who were sceptics and agnostics, if not atheists. At any rate their immediate objectives were clearly social and this-worldly though altruistic in the best sense of the term. The emoluments that these men received were meagre and admittedly lower than their education and ability would have otherwise commanded. Sacrifice and simplicity in personal living were important components of their life and self-image. Except in the case of the workers of the Ramakrishna Mission, they were not required to remain celibate. They were expected to devote their entire time to one or two areas of service of their choice.

The emphasis on simplicity and sacrifice linked them with the asceticism of religious mendicants and provided a continuity in tradition, but this was the first time in India, with the probable exception of the Buddhist order of Bhikkus, that organisations of committed men were set up with social service rather than the pursuit of individual salvation as the dominant goal. Sacrifice and simplicity in personal living had an important function in the general scheme of things. Apart from incidentally linking the workers with the tradition of holy or religious men, these requirements helped them in establishing their bonafides. It gave them the necessary status and authority in the community to play a leadership role. They had no sense of being 'employees'. They followed the rules and discipline set by their own group. When they collected funds, it was for their organisation and its several causes. The transparent simplicity of their personal lives made it clear to the community that the material support given to the organisation was put to maximum social use.

The theme of sacrifice, simplicity and asceticism is a recurrent one in the Indian social work scene. Sacrifice and asceticism are attributed to a definite spiritual significance. The man who is spiritually involved is marked by his non-attachment to worldly things. Also, the continual exercise of seeking detachment----through sacrifices and ascetic vows----is supposed to help the progress of the soul towards salvation. The Indian mind responds in admiration and deference to any person who has mastered his physical needs. It is the contribution of the Arya Samaj, the Ramakrishna Mission, the Servants of India Society, the Servants of the People Society and other such organisations that they put this charismatic appeal of asceticism and personal simplicity to the service of contemporary social objectives and causes.

These social workers, or 'social servants' as they called themselves, had been influenced by the liberal-democratic thought of the time to which they belonged and thus retained their link with the liberal-reformist approach which has been described above. The fact that they were the first set of workers devoting themselves full-time to organising services of various types and the fact, further, that many of them had developed a healthy respect for the collection and study of data relating to the problems they tackled linked them effectively with the professional workers who were to come later. On the other hand, their emphasis on limited personal incomes and simple living brought them closer to the older religious missionary on the one hand and the later Gandhian workers with their ethical-revolutionary emphasis on the other.

THE ETHICAL-REVOLUTIONARY APPROACH

Mahatma Gandhi's was a complex personality. Besides a statesman, politician and strategist of the freedom struggle, he was journalist, social worker, educationist and feminist. His major impulses, however, were deeply religious and ethical in the sense in which Ruskin, Thoreau and Tolstoy could be called religious. They did not conform to any traditional, institutionalised religion of his days though he was unrivalled in his mastery over the subtle religious symbolism of the people whom he led. He was devout by temperament, believed in fasts, austerities and the moral-spiritual value of silence but he attacked the concept of pollution by touch, fought against the iniquities to which women were subjected, sought to do away with religious ritual, argued against the gradation of occupations as being high or low, and stood firm in his faith in the dignity and freedom of man. He was concerned basically with the nature of relations between man and man whether as between ruler and subject, employer and employee, trader and customer, or relations within the family. Over a period of time he had worked out his concept of an ideal social order.

The programmatic details of Gandhi's concept of the new social order are not immediately relevant for this discussion. Economically, he thought in terms of a primarily peasant economy leading to local self-sufficiency. The programme of *khadi* (hand-spun and hand-woven cloth) and cottage industries had an important part in this economy. Politically, he conceived of locally self-governing communities with national and state governments retaining the minimally necessary residual powers. Socially, his vision of the ideal society allowed for the maximum possible individual freedom and equality. His world is dominated by moral and not by legal norms. He speaks of the duties of the individual rather than his rights. The individual, according to him, owes it to himself to develop his potentialities to the maximum possible extent so that he can be of better service to his fellowmen.

For Gandhi the role of the social worker, or 'social servant', is to help bring about this ideal social order. Indian freedom and economic development were justified only as part of this vision of universal freedom and development. It was the compulsion of moral logic that drove Gandhi into the political struggle. He expected the same logic to motivate his workers. If they were so motivated, they would not only be social workers, social servants or missionaries but also the promoters of a silent revolution. They would have a picture of the society they were to create. This society could not be static because freedom and equality are not static concepts.

Gandhi spelt out clearly the values and the discipline by which his workers were to abide. These values are listed as the eleven rules of a resident of his ashram (colony or settlement). The rules are: non-violence, truth, non-stealing, continence or general personal restraint, non-accumulation, bodily labour, non-attachment to pleasures of the palate, elimination of all fears, religious tolerance, swadeshi (commitment to use only locally manufactured articles) and removal of untouchability.

In this list of rules there are clear echoes of the values of austerity and simplicity in personal living: the rules of continence, non-accumulation of personal wealth and non-attachment to bodily pleasure reflect these earlier values. But Gandhi laid an equal emphasis on three other values, those of truth, non-violence and elimination of fear. Truth was a dynamic concept in Gandhi's life. It meant not only the telling of truth and the eschewing of lies or untruthfulness, but a positive pursuit of all the consequences following from the perception of truth. A man devoted to truth could not stand by and be a witness to injustice and untruth. He had to fight untruth and fight it not by inflicting pain but by his own willingness to suffer. In this sense non-violence was not a passive, negative concept but a tool of social action. It called for great physical and mental courage. A coward could not be truly non-violent. If one is afraid he is likely to acquiesce in perpetrating injustice. One cannot be truthful and yet be a silent witness to injustice. Gandhi's non-violence required a weapon and this he forged and called 'satyagraha'----the weapon of insistence on truth through readiness to protest and non-cooperation with untruth and through readiness to suffer, if necessary, for this protest. It was his conviction that such purposeful suffering brings about a change of heart in the perpetrator of injustice.

This is hardly the place to discuss the validity or invalidity of Gandhi's methods or moral assumptions. What has been said should be enough to indicate the nature of his basic concern and the goals that he set for himself and for his workers. The concrete programmes that Gandhi placed before his workers covered all segments of life. He usually made a distinction between the political struggle for the country's independence and the movement to bring about a change in the social and economic conditions in which people lived. He asked his 'social servants' or 'constructive workers', as he called them, to concentrate on the latter. The economic programmes consisted of propagation of khadi and village industries, the social programmes consisted of removal of the disabilities of untouchables, tribals, women and all socially underprivileged groups. In his own life he displayed great sensitivity and responsiveness to the feelings of individuals who worked with him, but his programmes of work were concerned with the problems of large groups rather than individuals. He felt that though serving individuals in their sufferings and problems was important, he could not attend to them himself. He had respect for persons like D.K. Karve who worked patiently to build up single institutions over many years, but he did not undertake or directly promote such work himself. The one exception to this general rule was the special attention he gave to the problems of leprosy patients. This to him was a social as well as a moral problem. He could not bear to see the injustice and inhumanity of the normal social attitudes towards leprosy patients and made it a point to personally nurse and serve one of his followers who suffered from leprosy. Another of Gandhi's followers, Baba Amte, has now developed one of the most thorough-going and progressive institutions for the rehabilitation of leprosy patients. However, the general emphasis of Gandhian programmes has been towards tackling the larger social and economic problems of the entire community or section of the community rather than problems of handicapped individuals or individuals in special need.

Gandhi's followers have followed the same path after him. They have established an organisation called the Sarva Seva Sangh Association for the Service of All, under the guidance of Vinoba Bhave, who is commonly regarded as Gandhi's spiritual heir. The workers of the Sangh have actively participated in the land gift and village gift movement. This movement was conceived as a typically non-violent solution to the problems of iniquitous land distribution and of landless agricultural labourers. Many others have continued to work in the field of village industries, basic education, urban slum improvement, etc. But, despite Vinoba's great appeal and influence among the people, there is a vague uneasiness among the workers. While the people can be aroused to a new consciousness of their responsibilities and motivated to make substantial gifts, it has been found difficult to consolidate the gains so won. The concept of lokshakti, or the collective will of the people, is an effective one for generating a movement, but it does not seem to bring about lasting changes in people's ways of thinking. Also, not everyone has the charismatic appeal to generate this enthusiasm for a cause.

Recently, there has been considerable searching for ways of working among people which might bring slower but stabler changes. There is an appreciation of the need for systematisation of skills and techniques. This rethinking is born not out of despondency but a genuine appreciation of the problems faced in the course of work in several experimental projects in Dandakarnya, in Wardha, and in many of the gift villages.

The contribution of the Gandhian social movements has been that they have brought dignity and self-respect to the common man. They had succeeded, by the time India became free, in making the Indian village and the villager a matter of central concern to all interested in national growth and development. They had been instrumental, through the active participation of women in various types of work, in so advancing their cause that without a feminist battle, they had earned political and legal equality with men in all matters. They had succeeded in agitating the issue of untouchability and winning the battle at the intellectual level so that it is no longer respectable even in the villages to defend the practice of untouchability. Gandhian social movements had prepared the ground to make it seem natural that India should accept a constitution which embodies the goals of social justice and social equality. The liberal and the socialist movements had certainly contributed greatly to the development of this new consciousness but neither of them had the capacity on their own to reach the millions of illiterate peasants of India's remote villages. Gandhian movements alone had the capacity to do this. The changes sought to be brought about by Gandhi were revolutionary in their significance because they questioned the legitimacy or morality of the traditional attitudes in matters of caste, sex, ownership of property etc. Yet all this questioning was done by men who conformed to the traditional concepts of goodness and virtue.

THE LIBERAL-PROFESSIONAL APPROACH

The above discussion provides the varied context against which the professional approach in social work in India must be discussed. It may be helpful to bring together the main points of the above discussion in the form of a table which identifies the value framework, the attitude to society, the mode of need-definition, the methods and tools characteristic of each of the four approaches. This is attempted on the next page.

When the concept of a social work profession was introduced to India in the late 1930's, it had already developed its distinctive approach in the USA, the country from which the concept was imported. Those were days when a strong case work tradition existed and the term 'social work' was used synonymously with case work. One would have expected that social work in India would follow the model and develop along the same lines. Actually, despite the general validity of the impression that Indian professional social work has been greatly influenced by the American pattern, there are important differences. Both these similarities and differences need to be understood if one has to understand the peculiar position in which professional social work in India stands in relation to the other approaches that have been discussed above.

Approaches to Social Welfare and Social Work

	Religious-Traditional	*Liberal-Reformist*	*Secular-Missionary*	*Ethical-Revolutionary*
1. Dominant values	Charity, pursuit of individual salvation, ensuring the spiritual well-being of ancestors, etc.	Democracy, humanism, rationalism, etc.	Service, democracy, humanism	Humanistic, spiritual, ethical
2. Orientation to existing social structure	Unquestioning conformity	Reforms in social structure	Revivalist conformist or limited reform	Raising basic issues, redefining traditional structure in its social, economic and political aspects
3. Types of level of needs perceived	Primarily individual physical needs for food and clothing and the religious spiritual need of promoting individual salvation	Primarily the needs arising out of 'unfair' social arrangements	Needs of individuals who suffered from existing social arrangements, physical needs, need for education and vocational rehabilitation	Primarily needs of groups and communities affected by varied discriminatory practices
4. Organisation, methods and tools	Direct charity or charity through temples, mosques, etc.	Educational and legislative measures	Establishing of 'orders' with full-time staff to give leadership in community, establishing of residential institutions	Establishing an 'order', use of religious symbolism: *Satyagraph*, *Lok Shakti*, etc.

The similarities are obvious and they are not necessarily all superficial. First, following the American pattern, social work education in India was designed as a two-year graduate programme. It followed the pattern of a combination of class work, field work and research. The professional social worker in India is given broadly the same value framework as in the USA. This framework, based as it is on a liberal-humanistic set of values, does not conflict with the values articulated by the educated elite and as reflected in the Indian Constitution. The principles of acceptance of the dignity of man, right and duty of man to seek development of his potentialities, and right of the client to self-determination gain easy acceptance, at least at the intellectual level, with the Indian student in the same way as with the American student. The professional social worker in India has learnt about the same social work methods, viz., case work, group work and community organisation, as his American counterpart. His teachers exhibit the same ambivalence about accepting social administration and social action as methods of social work as, I believe, the American teachers do. What is more, the Indian students often read the same textbooks as the American students and if they have not discussed the same cases in the classroom it is because the case records are not available with the same ease! So much for the similarities.

The differences in professional education between the two countries, however, are also important. Historically, social work education in the USA has been methods-centred; in India it has been more oriented to fields of work. Quite early in its development in India, social work education developed specialisations or concentrations in terms of such fields as labour welfare, family welfare, rural welfare, etc. The different methods were taught with an even emphasis as necessary equipment to all the students. This difference reflects a greater preoccupation with the problem to be tackled than with the professional function to be served by the worker. If all the schools of social work in India are taken together, the teaching of methods of social work and a clear identification of the social work function in various fields of work still remain somewhat weak. The emphasis has been on a descriptive understanding of problems and a programmatic handling of them.

The reasons for this situation have been many. To begin with, many of the early teachers in schools of social work had training in the social sciences and not in social work. Most of the teachers who are currently teaching were taught by those social scientists who were naturally stronger in the description and analysis of problems than in the methods of handling them. When they thought of solutions, they turned to overall programmes of work which modified the environment than to the need to work with the client. The relatively early absorption of schools of social work in the universities has had the same consequence of emphasising the social science information part of the equipment of the social worker more than the methods of social work. In a written three-hour examination the knowledge of information is tested more easily than the knowledge of methods. Besides, a heavy loading of the curriculum with social science topics which have a higher status and are conventionally accepted, gains easier passage for the social work courses in various academic bodies of a university.

Apart from the particular combination of academic circumstances, the fact that most of the problems sought to be tackled in India have been problems of large masses of people and not of a few individuals, has led to this emphasis on the need to modify the environment rather than the individual. This emphasis is natural and not necessarily to be regretted, but to the extent that this approach is adapted it becomes difficult to identify or emphasise the professional function of social work as it has so far been conceived. The problem tends to be defined more in terms of the paucity of material resources and the solution seems to lie in the development or procurement of these resources.

It can be argued, with perfect legitimacy, that the development of material resources and their proper handling also involve the problems of motivating individuals and communities, enabling them to assess the nature of their problem and the extent of their own resources, and helping them to develop the organisational resources to fully utilise the material supplies that are available. This could be a professional social work function, but social workers and social work educators have not thought about the problems and systematised their knowledge in the area. In the meantime, revenue administrators (in the area of rural community development) and doctors (in the area of family planning) are attempting to organise these programmes. The programmes tend to be looked upon essentially as programmes of distributing material supplies. There is still a need for a clear statement of the nature of contribution that social work can make to these programmes. The area of labour welfare, which is among the oldest fields for which schools of social work equip their students, is subject to other strains but following basically from the same source, viz., the failure to identify the special contribution that social work can make to the solution of social problems.

In the field of labour welfare the social worker entered as a person in charge of worker amenities, safety programmes and labour community work where workers were housed in factories. They were drawn into the field of industrial relations because with the spate of labour and industrial legislations industrial managers needed someone who could keep them informed of the legal implications of their actions and policies. Some of the managers turned to formally trained lawyers and some to social workers. Social workers were happy to accept the opportunity because it made them more valuable to management and offered better career opportunities. In course of time, as the younger industrial managers became aware of the concept and need for personnel management, they again looked around for possible sources of supply of personnel managers. Some of them turned to graduates of schools of business management and some to social workers. The social workers accepted this opportunity as well. The curricula of schools of social work have naturally sought to keep pace with this changing and expanding role attributed to social work. On the whole, one would say that the schools have done as competent a job as they could be expected to. In the process, however, the overall concept of what social work is has become even more blurred.

The work situations in which social workers are engaged are so varied in India that an effort to conceptualise the professional function anew is called for. The Association of Schools of Social Work has been struggling with this problem for some time without making much headway. The question that social work education and social work practice face in India is whether social work has a specific professional contribution to make in such diverse fields as family planning, community development and personnel work in industry. One facile answer is to say that social work is concerned essentially with problems involving human relations and wherever such problems arise social work has a contribution to make. But, at this level of generality, the entire area of application of the social and psychological sciences, from pedagogy to public relations, will have to be treated as the area of social work practice.

Thus, professional social work in India faces a dual challenge in the problems that it is called upon to handle: first, the mode of definition of the problems of material supplies, and second, the varied and entirely new situations in which social work is being asked to make its contribution. The challenge is not fully met and there is often a lingering doubt in the minds of social workers about the validity of the social work methods in the Indian situation or at any rate about the primacy given to case work in the methods of social work. There is a conflict about whether social work in India can afford to be concerned with individuals when the problems are really problems of large masses of people and not of single individuals or groups. There is a temptation to define every problem as a problem of the environment and not of the individual. Even social workers who begin by speaking of community development soon discover that they have really been thinking of enhancing the material resources of the community and not of developing the human potential, or the capacity for organisation and self-help among the members of the community.

The accumulated pressure of the tradition of the liberal-reformist and the ethical-revolutionary movements is also in the direction of finding global solutions in which the individual is taken for granted. There is a demand for forging the tools of social action which is expected to somehow solve a totality of complex problems.

Basically, it is necessary to recognise that the problems of people living in an underdeveloped economy cannot be defined primarily as problems of emotional adjustment though these problems inevitably exist. Yet social workers can make a contribution by pointing out that there is nothing like a mass problem except in so far as it is a problem of a mass of individuals and that there is no way of tackling problems except by working with individuals—may be large numbers of individuals and sometimes in groups. It is possible that to some extent these problems can be tackled by the use of mass media; where this is the case, social workers must make way for social educators. But much work has to be done with individual communities and the individuals in these communities and social workers can draw on their skills in promoting programmes from this point of view.

Increasingly, the professional social worker in India will be called upon to take up preventive and developmental functions rather than clinical and curative functions. In some respects his role will be closer to the role of the extension agent and the social educator than the role of the physician and the nurse. In meeting the demands of this role he will need to know at least as much of the society and culture in which he works as of the workings of the mind of the individual. An understanding of the processes of social change at the level of the individual as well as the group must form a part of his basic orientation.

DIFFERENCES BETWEEN THE PROFESSIONAL APPROACH AND OTHER APPROACHES

If the reality of the work situation introduces certain strains and demands on professional social work in India, the value framework characteristic of the tradition of social work in the country introduces certain others. It was mentioned above that so far as the basic liberal-humanistic value framework of professional social work is concerned it does not give rise to any major conflicts or differences. However, there are certain other aspects of the professional approach, real or imputed, that create difficulties in mutual understanding between the professional and the other approaches in Indian social work.

The first of these arises from the fact that for most professionals their work is also a source of earning their livelihood. They may be dedicated to their work, but somehow in the Indian tradition of social work there is an assumption that dedication can only be established by not drawing a salary for the work that one does. The Gandhian social workers and the religious or secular missionaries have always been maintained by their orders or organisations but it has been claimed that the maintenance allowances given to them are low to begin with and do not progressively increase as would a salary with a specified scale. The fact that a person draws a salary is by itself interpreted to mean that he is primarily interested in the monetary reward, in his career and in the improvement of his material prospects. Professional social workers, on the other hand, do not grant that dedication to work is inconsistent with a desire to improve one's salary. They find no need to be apologetic about making a career in social work. And, sometimes, they may turn round and ask whether all the traditionally oriented social workers are really making a sacrifice and whether they are not making a virtue of necessity since they could not expect to earn any better salaries even if they gave up their 'vow of poverty'.

This problem is not restricted to the understanding between professionals and men belonging to missions or orders. It extends also to voluntary social workers in the community. The volunteer leaders share the reservations of the 'missionaries' about professional social workers, though, over the years, there has been some change in attitudes.

Another assumption about social work is that social workers must live a simple life. Considering the average salary drawn by a professional social worker one would have assumed that this condition should not prove difficult to fulfil for the professional. But, the word 'simplicity' has many meanings. For many Gandhians it means the wearing of hand-spun and hand-woven cloth. For the religious missionary it means the wearing of the saffron robe and the observance of several austerities. Actually, if the standard for simplicity is set by the poverty of the Indian peasant, none of the social workers can claim to live simply.

There is another, and a somewhat more fundamental, criticism voiced by thoughtful Gandhians against the professional approach. They contend that the practice of social work as a profession largely depends on the existence of a basic consensus in society about ends and means. Where such a consensus exists social work can legitimately focus on the problems of adjustment whether of individual or groups. But where, as in Indian society, two of the basic characteristics of the 19th century liberalism, viz., a belief in a free, competitive economy and a *laissez-faire* state, are being attacked, the social worker can take no system of values as given. He has to participate in the process of arriving at a consensus. He will, therefore, have to possess a value framework of his own—a framework which may sometimes require him to act in ways which affect certain groups in society adversely. The nearest American example to this situation would be the problem of the liberal, white social worker working with Negroes in the southern states. In India, a close parallel would be a social worker concerned with the problems of untouchables in rural areas. The legal position in both cases is clear but the battle is not over at the level of practice. How does the social worker function? Further, what happens on issues where even the legal position is not stabilised and where the ideological issues will not necessarily be settled through the ballot box? Does the social worker have any function as a professional in such a situation? Or does he wait until the issues are settled? The Gandhian position is clear. The Gandhian worker has a social philosophy and he considers it his duty to enter the fray, however non-violent he may conduct himself and help in achieving the kind of a society that he considers just and ideal. The profession of social work has been equivocal in this respect.

The issues involved need not be politically changed. Even at the social-cultural level dilemmas arise. What stance does the social worker assume where a client who shares the values of the social worker in matters of marriage and sex morality finds herself in conflict with the values of the sub-culture in which he lives? Gangrade has described the case of a village woman who seeks the help of a social worker against the sub-culturally sanctioned advances of her brother-in-law *(Indian Journal of Social Work*, January 1964).

In many of the countries which are in the process of industrialisation and modernisation the process of value integration is far from complete. Do the existing values of professional social work have sufficient positive content to guide the social worker? Or, will the social worker tend to give a passive interpretation to the concept of self-determination and let the client fend for himself?

INDIAN CULTURAL VALUES AND PROFESSIONAL SOCIAL WORK

Notwithstanding the differences between the professional and other approaches to social work in India, there is a growing respect for the contributions of the professional approach. These contributions cannot be said to be typically Indian. In fact, it may not be incorrect to say that professional social work in this country has not developed any special Indian identity. It is not even certain that it should necessarily be expected to do so. In so far as it is a science-based practice it should have a cross-cultural identity based upon science.

It is this aspect of the professional approach that commands recognition. This is the approach which is firmly rooted in available knowledge of human nature and human society; this is the approach which has taken the first steps towards an analytical understanding of the problems it tackles and has sought to develop a methodology for tackling them. It has over the years developed some methods of transferring the knowledge and the skills from one generation of social workers to another, retaining all the while the possibility of this knowledge and the skills being modified by subsequent experience and observation.

The professional social worker in India has been responsive to the challenge posed by the experience gained in the field and the criticism of some of its methods voiced by other types of workers. Recently, some of the professionals have become more introspective and searched for a continuity between the values of Indian culture and the values of the profession. There are at least three doctoral dissertations—two written by Indians and the third by an American—on this theme. Dr (Mrs) Ammu Menon Muzumdar (Columbia) has studied Mahatma Gandhi's contribution to social welfare in India. Dr Frances Yasas (Catholic University) has studied Gandhian values and professional social work with special emphasis on the dignity of man. Dr (Mrs) Viaya Rao (Philadelphia) has studied the teachings of the *Bhagwat Gita* and their implications for social work. Additionally, Dr (Miss) G.R. Banerjee has written from time to time articles in the *Indian Journal of Social Work* about social work and the concepts of *karma* and *karma yoga* in Indian thought. Recently, there was also an extended dialogue between professional social workers and the Gandhians. The report of this dialogue identifies the points of concurrence and difference between the two approaches. The efforts of most of these scholars and discussions have been to show that there is no basic conflict between professional social work values and Indian cultural values and further that in many instances the cultural values can be said to support and strengthen the professional values.

The dialogue between the professionals and Gandhians brought out clearly that if social workers wished to accept the responsibility of working for a change of values and resisting social injustice in whatever form it may express itself they could usefully borrow two important concepts from Gandhian thought, viz., *satyagraha* and *lokshakti. Satyagraha is* the weapon of non-violent resistance to evil. It may take the form of non-cooperation, picketing or civil disobedience. The weapon has potentiality for good as well as evil. There is a danger that if it is used unscrupulously it can become a form of political blackmail. Its use can be justified only in extreme situations where the law of the land does not provide for the possibility of change through persuasion and resort to the ballot box. The concept of *lokshakti* refers to the will of the people and to the capacity to rouse it and mobilise it for action. Where law allows the freedom of expression, the social worker must develop this ability to touch the active centre in the people among whom he works.

But *satyagraha* and *lokshakti* are not mere tools which can be picked up and used at will. They involve a whole set of attitudes. Gandhiji, as was seen above, had laid down rules for his non-violent soldiers. Surprisingly, the rules did not emphasise one quality of mind that he himself possessed and invariably displayed---the quality of love and freedom from hate. He insisted that his worker must be able to keep his mind free from hatred and be able to think of the well-being of his opponent. This calls for a maturity of mind and a capacity not to retaliate even when provoked. A social worker can find this ability useful in working with individual clients as well as with groups and communities. The worker who does not retaliate against the aggressive feelings of his client keeps the relationship open and allows for a rapproachment. The quality which enables a worker not to retaliate and to evince a positive concern for the latter's well-being introduces a dynamic element in the worker-client relationship. It may, of course, be that this non-retaliation or turning of the other cheek will give rise to feelings of guilt in the client and the professional worker may have reservations on this score.

Another value which is greatly emphasised in Indian thought is the value of work without expectation of reward. The word 'reward' refers not only to personal reward in money, fame, power or religious merit but even to the reward of success in one's efforts. Man, according to the *Bhagwat Gita,* has the right only to perform his duty and not to expect the fruit thereof. There is a certain stoicism involved in this attitude and many a social worker has ploughed his lonely furrow with this philosophy as his sheer anchor. This philosophy in turn is based upon faith---faith in God, in the moral law or in a final arbitor of man's fortunes.

The professional social work value of limited involvement gets support from the Hindu emphasis on detachment. A detached attitude is said to contribute to clarity of perception and helps not only in gaining one's spiritual freedom but also in the development of the capacity to be of help to others. The Hindu is told that he can expect to gain such detachment only through freeing himself of desire, anger, fear and hatred. Sacrifices and austerities are only exercises on the path to attaining this detachment and steadiness of mind.

Often, detachment can lead to passivity in attitudes and this is one of the pitfalls to be avoided. Vivekananda, Tilak and Gandhi---the three great modern interpreters of the *Bhagwat*

Gita----have emphasised action. Detachment, according to them, does not mean inaction. In fact, action in the service of others is for them the best form of religious action. The paths of knowledge, devotion and discipline of the body must lead to the path of action in the service of man.

It need hardly be said that these values of Gandhian and traditional approaches in social work are not a part of the professional curricula followed in the country. They cannot be easily integrated either. These values proceed, in the last analysis, from certain supra-rational assumptions regarding the nature of man and the purpose of human existence. Professional social work is firmly committed to rationality in action. The individual professional, however, is not entirely rational and he is inevitably influenced by his upbringing and the beliefs of his culture.

The more sensitive are aware of these influences and the recent introspection on the part of professionals, which was referred to above, is a part of their response to these influences. It is a matter for consideration whether these values have a cross-cultural significance and whether they can be integrated into a professional ethic without reference to the religious assumptions from which they proceed.

16

The Scope of Social Work Practice

One of the issues which social work in India seems to be confronted with is that of establishing its identity as a profession. It may seem surprising that such an issue should be raised at the end of more than forty years of professional social work education and practice in India. But I believe that social work educators are still seeking clarity on the role and function of social work in our society at the present stage of development.

The identity of a profession depends on our being able to answer at least two important questions: (i) What are the special skills provided by the profession? (ii) Which are the client groups whose problems are sought to be tackled by the profession? The answers to the two questions are interdependent. One cannot speak of skills except in relation to problems and clients. Yet, this is precisely what social work educators have often tried to do.

The answers generally given by social work educators to the above two questions are: (i) the skills of social work consist of case work, group work, community organisation, welfare administration and social action (sometimes, they add the skills of research and teaching); and (ii) the clients of social work are

---

Paper presented at a Seminar on Four Decades of Professional Social Work Practice and Education in India, held at the Madras School of Social Work in 1976.

all those whose social functioning is impeded because they are unadjusted, handicapped, poor or otherwise vulnerable sections of society. They then go on to elaborate the categories of handicapped or vulnerable sections of society.

The problem, however, is that social work postgraduates are often not available for meeting the needs of unadjusted, poor or handicapped individuals and groups at the field level. Unlike in some of the other professions, the individuals to be served by social workers are poor and cannot pay for the services which they need. While it is true that problems of social adjustment could arise even in the case of the well-to-do and that physical handicaps could occur in any segment of the population, the clientele of social workers is dominated by the poor because the poor constitute a substantial segment of our society. Moreover, poverty often aggravates other problems as well. The services have, therefore, to be organised on a charitable, low-cost basis. The whole cost structure for delivering welfare services is designed to be modest---so modest that persons who render direct service to the client are in most cases paid salaries which can only attract individuals who have passed the SSC or at best college graduates without any professional equipment. The postgraduate, professionally qualified person is not generally available for these positions. And, the administration of these institutional services, which could have offered an acceptable minimum salary to a professional, is often done by volunteers. From the point of view of social workers this situation is one of unemployment. In an economic sense there is a very low effective demand for the services they wish to render. For whom, then, are their services meant? It is not an accident that at times social work looks like a profession in search of a client.

This situation is, in fact, quite typical of some other professions as well which involve relatively heavy initial investments in education. The services of qualified doctors, engineers, architects, etc., are not available to the vast majority of the population since the latter cannot pay for these services. The poor utilise the services either of qualified persons or persons educated at lower levels and, therefore, at lower costs. Thus ayurvedic practitioners substitute for allopathic doctors; mistris and overseers substitute for engineers and architects.

There are, however, two differences. Doctors, engineers and architects find some opportunity for utilising their professional skills in the service of the better-off sections of the community by undertaking private practice or by serving the general population through employment in government or institutional settings. The social worker could also probably find paying clients for some of his services---family or marital counselling, for instance---but this area has not been sufficiently explored or developed. Many of the problems that are identified as problems needing a social worker's attention are typically problems of the economically deprived sections. Perhaps, at our stage of development, the problems of adjustment experienced by the non-poor do not become generally visible as problems needing specialised services. Even if they are visible, they cannot compete with the physical problems of deprivation and poverty to merit special allocation of resources. In fact, even the problems of adjustment of some of the physically and mentally handicapped individuals do not get identified as social work problems unless these individuals also happen to be poor and then very often it is only their problem of economic dependence that gets attended to.

Thus, the problems that social workers can tackle have not gain visibility among the better-off segments of our society and the services that social workers can give to the poor, the latter cannot afford to buy. By focusing attention upon this aspect of the relationship between social work and the social context, I do not intend to suggest that the professional social worker should seriously find out ways in which he can develop a practice by catering to the non-poor segments of society. To some extent this has already happened in the case of medical and psychiatric social work, school social work and industrial social work in which areas the client is not necessarily poor. But, the non-expansion of psychiatric social work, school social work and industrial social work underlines the problems of non-visibility of needs other than the needs of physical poverty and the difficulty of obtaining allocations for these programmes in a poor country. The intention here is to underline the paradoxical situations in which the profession is operating and the pressures that this situation generates. An understanding of this situation helps in appreciating some of the anxieties of social workers and social work educators and their efforts to cope with them.

One of the first consequences of the situation explained above is that most social workers with professional qualifications tend to look to the government for employment, though historically, welfare services have developed in the voluntary sector. Satisfactory employment in voluntary agencies is hard to come by. Not that employment in governmental agencies and departments is easily available; but because of the relatively greater emoluments in government jobs social work graduates would prefer to work in government rather than in voluntary welfare agencies. But, then, government recruitment procedures do not take cognisance of the special preparation needed for social welfare posts. The profession and social work educators have, therefore, sought again and again to get this recognition from the government at least to the extent of regarding a social work degree as a desirable qualification for recruitment to social welfare posts.

Another important area of employment for social workers---in fact, in many ways, a preferred area---has been social work education itself. While it is not known in what proportion social service agencies have grown over the past forty odd years, it is known that schools of social work have grown by forty times. Social work graduates prefer to work in schools of social work than in social welfare agencies. The fact is that the salaries of college teachers are better than the salaries of professionals working in the field, particularly those working in voluntary agencies. Of course, where this situation obtains and where schools of social work multiply faster than welfare agencies, it is obvious that the professional schools defeat the purpose for which they have come into existence. Their reason for existence is that they should promote the growth of services; what they achieve in a large measure is their own growth.

Another consequence of the lack of correspondence between professional education for social work and the ability of the welfare agencies to utilise their services is that social workers try to co-opt new fields of work as areas of professional practice. Personnel management and industrial relations can be taken as an example. When labour welfare was identified as an area of concern to social workers in the 1930's and 1940's, industrial labour was a relatively unorganised and also unprotected segment of the workforce. Activities undertaken for ensuring their social well-being and satisfactory conditions of work were a matter of humanitarian concern and endeavour. One could say that even today a part of the activities of a personnel officer in a factory continues to be oriented to workers' welfare. But, the social worker who enters this field has his eyes set on other positions, functions and rewards. He does not wish to limit himself to what may be called 'industrial social work'. The functions of labour welfare have given place in his priorities to personnel functions, industrial relations and managerial functions. Social work educators have struggled to cope with this expanded role and in doing so have brushed aside questions of their own resources and their major goals. Are social work skills necessary or useful in the area of personnel management? Are the goals of social work coterminous with the goals of personnel management? Are industrial workers a 'handicapped' or 'vulnerable' group in the sense in which the term is used in the area of social welfare?

In the 1950's when community development and national extension service occupied the centre of attention, an attempt was made to find a meaningful role for social workers in those programmes. Many social work graduates would have liked to function as block development officers and a few of them did secure such positions. Some others accepted posts of social education officers and an equal number worked as the teaching staff of training institutions set up for the community development programmes. The social work profession could not find a meaningful role in which to exercise its professional skills of community work perhaps because at that time there was no understanding or acceptance of the profession on the part of the community.

In the 1960's, when the family planning programme was conceived and developed, the profession again tried to find out ways in which its members could participate in the programme. Some functioned at the field level as motivators, some participated in the training and researches centres and a few at the level of organisation and coordination.

In community development the posts of social education officers were abolished in many states. Similarly, in the family planning programme, the whole emphasis shifted from motivation through education, to motivation through material incentives and, later, to motivation through sanctions. The social workers remained a marginal group and their contribution could not make an impact.

In both these instances social work educators were faced with the problem that their graduates could not engage in the programmes as direct service functionaries and at the administrative and policy levels their special claims to expertise could not be established on the basis of special knowledge and/or experience.

The national enthusiasm for the two programmes----at least in the manner in which they were then conceived—has also proved too short-lived for social work educational institutions to make modifications and adjustments suited to the needs of these programmes.

The objective of discussing at some length the experience of social workers in the areas of labour welfare, community development and family planning is simply to point out that given the postgraduate level of training of social workers they have had to look for client groups other than the handicapped and vulnerable sections of the population There is nothing intrinsically wrong in this, provided the shift takes into account the consequent implications for the programme of education and for the broad goals of the profession. In the case of community development and family planning the overall goals of social work and that of these programmes may not conflict, though they are not identical. Social work can, therefore, function in these settings as though they were programmes of prevention of social problems and promotion of general well-being in which social work skills have a role to play. However, it is doubtful whether this is the case in the area of personnel management. At any rate, to work in any of these areas, they would need to have more in their cognitive and analytical equipment than they have at present. Also, the emphasis on present social work skills, particularly their therapeutic orientation, may not have the same relevance in this context.

Currently, there is a growing opinion in the profession that social workers and social work educators should address themselves to the challenge of social development. This view is held internationally and is a part of the shift from an exclusive emphasis on economic growth to a concern for overall development. Yet, the meaning of the term 'social development' is not clear. The term has been interpreted variously to mean economic growth with social justice, poverty eradication and minimisation of economic inequalities as part of the goal of development, emphasis on human resources development through a programmatic emphasis on 'social services' which are inclusive of 'welfare' services but extend also to cover health, education, housing, rehabilitation, etc. In its most limited sense social workers have used the term 'social development' as meaning simply development of social welfare services.

The popularity of the term among social workers is due to the fact that it generally fits into their concern for the disadvantaged in society and emphasises the value of equality. However, unless social development is defined clearly and understood in the context of what role social workers can play in bringing about such development, the term will be used only as part of a rhetoric without stating its programmatic implications for social work education. So far as the non-social work community is concerned, they use the terms social, sociology, social sciences and social work almost synonymously. They also fail to understand the difference between the skills of working with people which are at the core of social work practice from the generalised human relations and public relations orientation that many other professions also emphasise. Social workers accept this ambiguity partly because they are themselves confused and partly because they hope that they will thus co-opt a new client system. Just as at one time it was argued that social workers could be good block development officers or district family planning officers, it is now argued that they can become social planners, social researchers, integrated rural development officers, etc. Their claims to these positions are based on the premise that social workers have a social sciences base and that they have the skill of interpersonal relations.

Some individuals who have been trained as social workers may in the course of their occupational careers occupy one or the other of these positions and function very effectively. The question, however, is whether these have been consciously accepted as part of the professional roles of a social worker, whether the curriculum has been restructured accordingly and whether social work educators have equipped themselves as a faculty to teach the new courses. If broad social developmental tasks are to be taken on as part of the professional responsibilities of social workers, the curricular content in the social sciences will have to be wider and deeper. Their knowledge in the areas of developmental economics, organisational behaviour and the analysis of social systems will have to be extended at least to the extent to which the understanding of human motivation, psychological processes and abnormal psychology are emphasised in preparing psychiatric social workers. Is this a realistic goal for our schools? Can this be attempted in a two-year programme of instruction where even students without any base in the social sciences are admitted?

In two thoughtful articles----one by Sugata Dasgupta in a recent issue of the *Journal of Higher Education* (UGC) and another by P.D. Kulkarni, due to appear in the forthcoming issue of the *Indian Journal of Social Work*----the authors have spelt out in different contexts the complexity of the tasks involved in this new definition of the role of social work. Both of them, of course, consider that social work can undertake these new tasks. I have two reservations.

One of these arises from the unlikelihood of schools of social work as presently structured being able to cope with the responsibilities involved. If these are the tasks to be absorbed within the scope of social work practice, a different kind of educational programme and a faculty which is more genuinely interdisciplinary than the present faculties, are needed.

My second reservation is about whether the whole area of social development should be incorporated within the exclusive domain of social work practice. The distinguishing characteristic of social work lies not in its social sciences know-how or even in its skills in interpersonal relations, but in its concern for those in need of help—the deprived, the underprivileged, the unadjusted and the handicapped. Our interest in social policy is in terms of preventing this suffering and in promoting rehabilitation. Also, no single profession can expect to cover the whole area of social policy and social development expertly. Social development is a task to be jointly undertaken by many professional groups which have a common vision and understanding but whose individual contributions should be specialised and characterised by a high level of expertise. Those aspects of social development, which relate to the deprived and handicapped sections of the population, should be identified as their social concern by social workers and they should equip themselves adequately for this task.

On the other hand, the word 'handicapped' needs to be redefined to include not only the physically, mentally and socially handicapped, but also the large mass of the urban and rural poor. While there is probably not a great deal that social workers can do to create employment for the urban or rural poor, they can certainly help (i) in trying to bring existing services and facilities closer to the poor, and (ii) in encouraging and enabling the poor to take advantage of services provided generally in society or specifically for them.

In this context, the limited tasks for the social work profession would be as under:

(1) Meeting the needs of unadjusted, handicapped, poor or otherwise disadvantaged client systems at the direct field service level by operating special relief, rehabilitation and preventive programmes. These programmes may be addressed to individuals, groups and communities. The services may consist of direct material aid, counselling, environmental modification, referral or any of the additional supportive services.

(2) Modifying, augmenting, extending general community services to meet the special problems of the handicapped who can utilise and benefit from these services.

(3) Administering, financing or consulting in social welfare areas.
(4) Generalised advocacy on behalf of client groups through writing, lecturing, submitting of memoranda, etc.
(5) Undertaking social action within the limits of the law of the land on behalf of client groups involving various levels and degrees of political or community action.
(6) Teaching and researching in social welfare and analogous areas.
(7) Identifying new needs, services, and delivery systems.
(8) Planning and policy formulation in relation to the needs and services of existing or new client groups.

It is possible that while fulfilling the above tasks or beginning with the above tasks, some social workers may expand their abilities and skills to participate meaningfully in the more general area of social planning or social administration covering not only specialised client groups but also the total population. But, the schools of social work cannot place these broader activities as goals for their training programmes.

The eight tasks that are listed above for social work would require considerable efforts at faculty development on the part of the schools of social work. It would also be necessary to add and integrate social scientists----other than social workers----into their faculties. In the absence of such a wide-based programme of education they are likely to develop a narrow frame of reference which cannot help in equipping students to meet the challenge of their professional task.

The wider field of social development in all its aspects can at best be added as a tertiary area adjacent to the area of professional concern to social workers. In this perspective, social work practice may be said to have three types of foci and settings as follows.

(1) The *core area* of 'welfare' services directly oriented to handicapped sections of the population.

(2) The *secondary area* of social services in which social work skills can be practised either fully as in medical social work, school social work and personnel social work or peripherally as in the planning and administration of these services for 'handicapped' segments of the population.

(3) The *tertiary area* of general social planning where social workers have to call upon their resources as social scientists more than on their professional skills as social workers.

If social work education has to meet the demands for this wider range of settings and levels of operation, a conscious effort would have to be made to restructure its curricula and integrate the programmes from the undergraduate level to the Ph.D. level in a new way.

Since experience has shown that the postgraduate programmes of education in social work do not meet the field needs even of many urban-based agencies, the undergraduate programmes may have to be consciously enriched to equip students to take on responsibilities at least for preventive and generalised care services. It may then be expected that the clinical and guidance type of work with individuals, some types of group work, the whole sphere of community work, welfare planning and administration are attended to by senior workers with an undergraduate degree or those with postgraduate qualifications. The postgraduate programme would also have to be suitably strengthened in the areas of the social science and social policy. The teaching, research and social developmental tasks in the areas of social welfare and in the allied fields of social services could then be attended to by those who have equipped themselves for these tasks by experience or studies beyond the Master's level.

My concern in making the above points is not to establish a hierarchy of functions related to a hierarchy of levels of educational attainments. My objectives are three: first, to reaffirm that the primary client of social work is the unadjusted and the handicapped individual, group or community using the word 'handicapped' in its physical, mental, social and economic connotations; second, against too general and ambitious a statement of our professional tasks and capabilities so that we may not seem merely to say, "whatever you can do, I can do better"; and third, to point out that if, after due thought, we do decide to redefine or broaden the scope of our professional responsibilities, we must, as educators, undertake the sequential task of widening and deepening our academic base without sacrificing the present emphasis on self-awareness and the development of a professional self through supervised field work.

17

Social Work and the Eradication of Poverty

Poverty and social work have stood face to face with each other through the ages. In fact, at a time when the state took the position that the individual was responsible for his own well-being and the individual suffered or received according to his deserts, it was 'social work', expressing itself as charity or performance of religious duty, that sought to minimise the suffering of the poor and the disadvantaged. If, today, we seek to define anew the role of voluntary welfare agencies in tackling the problem of poverty, it is because of our changed concept of the role of the state, our changed perspective on the nature of poverty and our sense of uncertainty about whether private welfare agencies can cope with a problem of this nature and magnitude.

In feudal and peasant societies the vast majority of people eked out a subsistence livelihood and only a very small minority lived in luxury, with a middle group of courtiers, businessmen and priests living in relative comfort. In these societies inequalities in living conditions as well as in opportunities for individual advancement were considered normal and were explained by the principle of being born to a particular station in life. With most of the population living at

---

Paper presented at a plenary session of the Indian Council of Social Welfare in 1977.

bare subsistence levels, poverty was identified as a problem only in its most object form where the individual did not possess the barest necessities for survival. Such a problem of abject need was sought to be tackled through systems of extended kin support, through individual charity, motivated and supported by religion and through organised religious channels. The king, i.e., the state, did not normally intervene to provide direct relief except during periods of mass suffering as in famines, floods, earthquakes, etc. Even where the state did intervene, as in the case of the English poor laws, it sought to use existing religious and charitable institutions for alleviation of suffering and the law did not accept the principle of total responsibility of the state.

The implicit as well as explicit assumption in pre-industrial societies was that a healthy adult who wanted to earn a livelihood could do so by doing some type of work or the other. And, in the pre-industrial societies, in which populations were small and not all the land had as yet been inhabited or cultivated, it was probably true that a man could sustain himself either by directly engaging himself in a primary occupation like agriculture or fishing or by learning a trade and selling his wares. Employment was not so highly organised and restricted and productive activity did not call for major capital outlays. The problem of extreme poverty in the sense in which the society of those times understood it, was a marginal one and the institutional framework of that society was able to cope with it to a large extent.

In industrial societies, the structure of work and employment has undergone considerable change: the proportion of workers who are employees is higher than the proportion of those who are self-employed. The worker is less autonomous, though he is legally 'free'. Every job created in the economy requires increasingly larger investments of capital. In this context, the status of being employed or unemployed may be a consequence of factors beyond the control and competence of the individual. He could not therefore be held individually responsible for his state of poverty or indigence.

Yet, throughout the early period of industrialisation and through the 19th century, the ruling philosophy was one of individual responsibility for one's own condition of material well-being or deprivation. The state accepted no blame or responsibility for the well-being of the individual citizen. At the same time, the structure of support through extended kin relations, religious institutions and the system of poor laws, was found to be increasingly inadequate in meeting the problems of social dependence even in the rural areas. With the breakdown of the agricultural economy, the rural poor migrated in large numbers to the newly developing towns and cities. Some of the migrants found ready employment and the rest added to the desolation of the 19th century urban life. It is in this context that voluntary agencies—some of which were religious but others secular—came to be formed, to provide relief and care to the orphaned, widowed, handicapped, aged, unemployed and other needy segments of the urban population. The services provided by these agencies were primarily ameliorative. There was no attempt, at least in the initial stages, to provide preventive or rehabilitative services. No basic questions were raised about the social order which precipitated these problems. The services were offered as charity and there was no acceptance of the right of the individual to be provided work and security.

Gradually, first in response to humanistic impulses and later under the compulsion of Marxist thought, the success of the Bolshevik revolution and the gathering strength of the trade union movement, the responsibility of the state towards the welfare of the individual came to be recognised. Even prior to this major shift, the scope of services for different categories of socially dependent individuals had widened to include preventive, curative, rehabilitative and promotional services of many kinds. This had been the result of advances in the knowledge of human behaviour, genesis of social problems and scope for strategies of prevention and rehabilitation. The total resources available to the community for organising these services had also increased manifold as a result of industrialisation and growing world trade which favoured the industrialised countries. Today, in the western nations—whether capitalist or socialist—poverty in the sense in which we understand it, viz., lack of the basic commodities of food and clothing, is almost unknown. Even where such poverty occurs as in some remote pockets or during periods of war or economic recession, it would be regarded as a direct responsibility of the state. Voluntary agencies exist at least in the non-socialist countries and they play an important role in providing complementary services to tackle the correlates of poverty at the social and psychological levels and try to ensure that the services to which an individual is entitled from the state reach the individual concerned. They also provide new services which enrich the life of the community in other ways. One may say that the role of voluntary agencies in respect of poverty has diversified depending upon the meaning we give to the word 'poverty'. In socialist countries this role of providing complementary services is fulfilled by citizens' organisations, workers organisations, organisations of socialist youth, etc., which are not state agencies but are at the same time important elements in the political structure of socialist society. These agencies are vital channels for mobilising citizens behind governmental programmes and they also serve as agencies for ensuring that the citizen gets what is due to him from the state.

In India, and in developing countries, generally, the situation is different. Poverty even in its physical sense is not a marginal phenomenon. It is universally present. The state has declared its commitment to egalitarian ideals and should in principle accept the responsibility for providing minimum social security to all its citizens. But, the ability of the state to mobilise resources to meet this kind of a commitment seems to be severely limited. The problem of mobilisation of resources is an economic one but even more a political one. The economic aspect of the problem lies in the need to provide motivation to provide enterprise to invest in business and industry, whereas the political problem lies in the inability of the government to state clearly the terms on which private enterprise will function in a mixed economy and then to enforce these terms. Such resources as the government is able to mobilise through direct and indirect taxation are allocated on a priority basis to investment in laying down the infrastructure for industry, transport, communications, etc. Social services are given a low priority and within social services social welfare has a still lower priority.

It is in this context that we have to examine the role of voluntary agencies in the eradication of poverty. It is possible to take the position that nothing can be done in the present politico-economic context and sit back and wait for the 'great leader' to appear who will provide the magical solution to all our problems. It is also possible to say that the only solution lies in political action and that we should mobilise opinion and people for a total revolution. The first of these alternatives is not really a plan of action. It is a plan of cynical inaction and no one who is motivated by social concern can advocate it. The second could be a path to change but it is not a path that is open to voluntary agencies, especially, if the revolution involves use of violent means. Voluntary agencies therefore have to find a third path---a path of constructive action---which will (i) ensure that the programmes and services that the government has initiated for tackling the problems of the deprived segments of our population are fully implemented and reach those for whom they are intended, (ii) continue to exercise pressure on the government to widen the scope of its services for the poor, and (iii) mobilise resources outside governmental channels to provide services for groups for whom the government has little to offer.

Let us begin with the first of these three strands of activity. It has been stated earlier that our government has no programme of social security covering the entire population. In fact, it does not have a programme of income maintenance even for the lowest income groups in the population. Yet, there are some programmes which if fully implemented would provide some measure of economic security to a substantial section of the rural poor. Some of these programmes are: (i) rural works, (ii) guaranteed employment during emergencies, (iii) economic assistance to scheduled castes and scheduled tribes, (iv) the khadi and village industries programme, and (v) programmes of assistance and credit to marginal farmers and agricultural labourers. These programmes do not bear an apparent similarity to the social security provisions of the developed countries. But, if they are fully and properly implemented, they would have the consequence of providing additional employment and additional income to the low income groups in rural areas and would in this sense serve as measures of security. The financial provisions for these schemes are not large enough to cover the entire population of the potentially needy, but the more important fact is that even the existing provisions are not fully utilised and, where utilised, the benefits do not always reach the groups for whom they are intended. Can voluntary agencies help ensure the full and proper implementation of these programmes? The task is not easy and the difficulties are many. We need to examine some of them.

The first of the difficulties is that at present voluntary welfare agencies as we know them have no place in the implementation of these schemes. In most of them, particularly in schemes of rural works and guaranteed employment, the exclusive responsibility is with government departments and committees of the Panchayati Raj set up for this purpose. This is as it should be. But, at the point of implementation, it should be possible to associate voluntary agencies with these programmes. The somewhat questionable record of the Bharat

Sevak Samaj in the management of government sanctioned schemes is known and it is necessary to learn from this failure of a voluntary agency in mobilising public cooperation in the implementation of government sponsored programmes.

The following are a few of the precautions that should be exercised in developing a relationship between governmental and voluntary agencies for implementing such programmes. First, it should be seen that no single, monolithic organisation comes into existence which has exclusive responsibility for public cooperation in different fields and different states. There should be separate organisations to cope with different types of problems and services. Within limits, there is probably an advantage in having organisations which specialise in working in different fields and in different geographical regions. But large, single organisations which take up exclusive responsibility may be found to work undemocratically and will have a certain tendency to bureaucratisation built into them. Second, the organisations that emerge for this work, while they work in collaboration with government agencies, should not be identified with the government and must remain NGOs in the true sense responsive to the local community. To the extent that they get identified with government they will cease to enjoy an independent role and cannot therefore contribute anything new to the government's own pattern of work. Third, the objective and scope of the work of voluntary agencies vis-à-vis the above mentioned economic programmes should be clearly spelt out. The temptation to function as agencies for contracting out government work must be avoided. The voluntary agencies may collaborate with statuary agencies in planning and administering programmes and may promote the development of workers' organisations or agriculturists' organisations which can benefit by government programmes of subsidy or support. It is in fact the latter promotive role that would be the special contribution of voluntary agencies. Most government programmes suffer because (a) the personnel available for new developmental work is limited, and (b) the procedures of government scrutiny and sanction are such that the uneducated and unorganised sections of the rural community cannot cope with them. Voluntary agencies should seek to provide a corrective by giving organisational leadership and assistance.

The question, however, is whether voluntary organisations are themselves equipped for this work. It is obvious that the answer cannot be an unequivocal 'yes'. Their attitudes as well as equipment will have to undergo considerable change if they are to take up economically oriented programmes for the poorer sections of society. To begin with, the meaning attached to the term 'welfare' will have to be sufficiently broadened to include not only activities relating to socially and physically handicapped individuals but also 'normal' individuals and groups who are poor. The concept of services will have to include not only the provision of protective services and referrals, but also the promotion of organisational effort relating to economic programmes which will prevent destitution and ensure better distribution of services and goods through creation of employment. The problems of physically, socially and mentally handicapped individuals are not unimportant but social workers are not likely to be able to serve them if they cannot serve the economically handicapped. It is also true that this distinction between social, psychological and physical handicaps on the one hand and economic handicaps on the other is somewhat artificial, for those who are poor and therefore economically handicapped are also socially handicapped and even their physical health is likely to be impaired by long and sustained deprivation.

It is worth raising the question whether this exclusive concern of social welfare agencies for the problems of one set of individuals is not a device to escape responsibility for the vast majority of those whose problems are by definition treated as beyond the scope of social welfare. Even if this latter group is noticed they are approached with programmes and services which are at best in the nature of emergency relief and amelioration. The need for voluntary agencies involving themselves in programmes of employment creation is great. So far, most of the agencies that have taken interest in this kind of work have been the agencies of Gandhian persuasion. It is to their credit that they have repeatedly pointed out that those who will to tackle the problem of poverty in India must tackle it in rural areas. Most other voluntary agencies have worked in urban areas and their workers as well as clients are found both in the cities and towns. But, if these agencies genuinely aim at eradicating poverty, they must develop a rural base among the poor masses who live in the villages.

The urban tax-payer, the urban-based social worker and the urban dweller have generally taken the position—sometimes consciously and sometimes unconsciously—that the responsibility for solving rural problems lies with the government and they have done their duty once they have paid their taxes and rates. In fact, this is an argument often put forth by well-to-do individuals for not supporting voluntary agencies even in urban areas. This only reflects a class attitude. It is as false as it is suicidal. The higher standard of life and comfort that the urban upper and middle classes and the rural landowning peasantry enjoy would not be available to them but for the protection subsidies and facilities provided by the government. These are paid for partly out of the taxes that the well-to-do pay, but also largely through a system of allocation of national resources which is weighted in their favour. If they wish to retain a society which allows civic, political and economic freedom they would need to do much more than just pay their taxes. The more sensitive among them will have to create and maintain community support for a greater measure of discipline in urban levels of consumption and for a more equitable system of distribution. They will have to accept advocacy and exercise pressure on the government for providing more services for the poor both in rural and urban areas. They would have to be willing to develop voluntary agencies which will undertake on their own and in collaboration with the government programmes of rural development. This is not an easy task and yet it is a necessary task. If our democracy will not generate active social concern among its more advanced citizens and support a system of social and economic discipline it will have failed as a viable political structure for solving the problems of developing countries. To generate this concern and to make greater discipline acceptable is the second task of voluntary agencies. Voluntary acceptance of a responsibility for the well-being of our fellow citizens is the price of economic and political freedom of action. Social workers must identify and realise in their own lives the values of equality, rationality and secularism, the value of minimisation of personal consumption, the value of a social as different from personal ethic, the value of a national as different from a regional or caste identity and having done so they must canvass support for these values of a new age.

The third task of voluntary agencies is to continue and expand with a broader perspective the organisation of social and welfare services for the poor and disadvantaged to small towns and rural areas. The problem of poverty can be attacked in two ways----directly by increasing the real income of the individual and indirectly by providing him with the services that he would otherwise buy with his increased income. Both these tasks need performing. The path of raising individual incomes and thus widening the area of choice available to the person concerned is individually more satisfying but it is also likely to be more expensive and in any case likely to be further off in time for attainment. The path of providing community services which are available to those in need of them is likely to be more within reach of the available resources. It may happen that governments in developing countries do not have resources to provide fully even these services and the efforts of the state may have to be supplemented and extended by those of voluntary agencies. These services may be in the spheres of education, health, nutrition, recreation or special services for the handicapped sections of the population. By providing these services or strengthening and individualising them to meet special needs thus increasing their effectiveness, voluntary agencies will help lighten the burden of general poverty and make available to the underprivileged and handicapped the special assistance they need.

All these three tasks are important and worth performing, but by far the most critical of these from the point of view of tackling poverty is the task of ensuring the full and effective implementation of programmes of employment generation in rural areas. The performance of this task calls for a basic reorientation of social workers and social work agencies.

18

The Social Context and Crime

The study of crime has been approached from many different perspectives. Psychologists have sought to explain criminal behaviour in terms of personality needs and mechanisms. They have tried to explore on the one hand the motivation for individual acts of crime and on the other to identify personality types that would tend to find social deviance a 'satisfactory' form of adjustment to reality. Geographical explanations of crime have focussed upon climatic conditions as an explanation of the particular types of crime that are said to be predominant in particular climatic zones of the world. Students of human physiognomy tried at one time to explain crime in terms of racial types. The variations in the incidence of crime have also been related to economic cycles of prosperity and depression. Sociologists have approached the understanding of crime in terms of the socially structured sources of deviant behaviour in particular societies or in terms of the concepts of anomie, relative deprivation, and dissonance or displacement in the means-end relationship in human behaviour.

Modern criminological theory has rejected the racial or physiognomic explanations of crime, but has otherwise tended to accept a multidisciplinary approach in which each discipline

---

Presidential address delivered at the Seventh Annual Conference of the Indian Society of Criminology, Aligarh, December 28, 1977.

offers a valid but partial insight into the phenomenon of crime. The many explanations provide a base for a multipronged strategy for prevention of crime and rehabilitation of the criminal. It is realised that the term 'crime' refers to varied types of behaviour and a common explanation cannot apply equally to all the varieties of behaviour. Sometimes, the only common denominator for various types of crime may only be an imputed "tendency to deviate" from the norms of society. Such an explanation, however, does not further our understanding unless the tendency to deviate is itself shown to be an identifiable psycho-dynamic phenomenon. I am personally inclined to adopt a more eclectic view wherein the different disciplines are seen as providing insights into different aspects of the phenomenon of crime and have different spheres of applicability in any strategy of preventing crime or rehabilitating the criminal.

This paper is limited to analysing the structural source of two types of criminal behaviour in our society, viz., corruption and black marketing.

The words 'corrupt' and 'corruption' have a religio-ethical and legal connotation. In the former sense, the word 'corrupt' means depraved or decadent, in the latter it refers to the complex of behaviour involving the giving or demanding and acceptance of illegal gratification, generally in the form of money. Corruption in this sense exists in all societies as do other forms of criminal conduct. There seems, however, to be a difference either in the extent of its prevalence in different societies or in the level at which its prevalence begins to seriously impede normal social processes. In most developing societies corruption is a major problem and one of the major counter-active forces to development.

Corruption takes many forms and occurs in nearly every segment of social life. There is corruption in politics, in administration, in business, in education and even in religion. It may take the form of minor favours done out of turn for a *baksheesh* or tip or it may take the form of major and deliberate misapplication of rules in conferring a favour or overlooking a transgression. In the latter case, corruption may take the form of harassment followed by extortion. The gratification sought may be for personal ends or for ostensibly larger, social or political purposes. But, in all cases of major corruption, there is usually a misuse of authority, for without the authority there would be no leverage for demanding gratification. The authority which is misused is derived from office within a large structure, whether political, governmental, industrial, educational or religious. The other forms of authority, viz., traditional and charismatic, of which Max Weber speaks can also be misapplied. This happens quite commonly where 'Gurus' live a life of luxury at the expense of their credulous followers. However, our discussion here is limited to the misuse of authority flowing from office within formal organisations.

In order to understand the prevalence of corruption one has to understand the social context within which it arises. The social context in India, as in most developing countries, is a complex one. Economically, it is characterised by generalised poverty and subsistence or below-subsistence levels of income. In the midst of this poverty there is a small minority of individuals made up of large landowners, owners of industry and business and a proportion of successful professionals, bureaucrats and managers who are very well-off. There is also a somewhat larger group of lower bureaucrats, small businessmen, less successful professionals and workers in large, organised industries who keep themselves out of the sea of poverty represented by workers in unorganised industry, self-employed artisans, itinerant and partially employed workers, small landowning cultivator-tenants and landless agricultural workers. From the economic perspective the overall picture is one of poverty and gross inequality.

Socially, the picture is made up of a large illiterate population with a small school-educated and a smaller college-educated population. There is some relationship between education and economic standing on the one hand and education and involvement in the modern urban economy on the other. The urban middle and upper income groups are educated and their ideas of progress and modernity are largely derived from the western world. The intellectual framework is often an unorganised jumble of nostalgically selected Indian themes, western liberal idealism and a more recent strand of Marxist egalitarianism. It is this group that has provided ideational leadership in national politics, education and the relative modernisation of religious-ethical thought.

The Indian political structure is democratic. This is as much a consequence of the commitment of the political elite at the stage of independence to western liberalism as of the compulsions of the nationalist movement against a foreign ruler. The people could not be mobilised into a movement unless several ethnic groups which made up the colonial society could be assured of a share in decision-making and an opportunity for growth. Actually, a democratic polity does not necessarily guarantee an equal share to all groups though it is based in a sense on the assumption that there exists no major internal differentiation between different groups in a society. Democracy only provides for a majority rule and the presumption of equality is valid only in the exercise of franchise in so far as individuals behave freely and rationally in the context of an agreed set of values. If they are guided by primordial group affiliations of caste or religion, the democratic framework will not prove satisfactory and will not meet the aspirations of its members in the long run. But, where each of the several groups is small in relation to the size of an electoral constituency, the importance of group affiliation may be somewhat offset. In any case a democratic framework can be said to confer equal political rights on all its citizens, in so far as the word 'political right' is limited to imply the right to vote and the right to certain freedoms as a citizen. This is also true of the Indian polity.

Along with political rights the Indian political elite have also espoused the cause of economic equality. The specific content of this goal is not clear. The Constitution of India speaks of the right to equality before law and in a general way of social, economic and political justice. The state is also directed to ensure that the operation of the economic system does not result in a concentration of wealth into a few hands and to protect and promote the interests of the weaker sections of society. It is the political parties that in their manifestoes have spoken of their commitment to usher in 'socialism', 'Gandhian socialism' or a 'socialist pattern of society'---the exact content of which is not spelt out. But, there is no question that any democratically elected government in India, as in any developing country, will be under pressure to address itself to the problem of gross poverty of the majority of its population. The problem of poverty cannot be tackled merely by a strategy of economic growth unless the growth of the economy also means a better distribution of the economic gains between different segments of society.

Further, economic growth requires mobilisation of resources which implies a readiness to make sacrifices in the present for gains that will accrue in the future. In a predominantly poor society, the burden of such 'sacrifice' must also fall on those who have the necessary margin of excess to make the sacrifice. Thus, the democratic framework in a poor society compels the political elite to adopt an egalitarian, if not a socialist, stance. This, together with the demands of economic development, have led governments to adopt strategies of progressive taxation on personal incomes, discouragement of monopolies, nationalisation of major financial institutions, development of a dominant public sector in industries and the adoption of land legislation to fix ceilings on individually owned land. There are also efforts made to make limited supplies of essential commodities available through a public distribution system, control of commodity movement, freezing of prices, regulations against hoarding and profiteering and other measures. The egalitarian stance, therefore, is not merely verbal. It takes the form of legislative and administrative measures which are generally oriented to regulate the economy in such a way that ostensibly the interests of the economically weaker sections are protected and disparities do not increase. The state further recognises its obligations to the poor by way of providing increased opportunity for education and health and by a limited---rather very limited---recognition of their right to security of employment.

While a democratic polity thus generates some pressures towards an egalitarian public policy either through socialistic or social welfare measures, it simultaneously sets into motion other forces as well. A democratic framework depends upon periodic open elections in which different parties and individuals woo the electorate to secure a majority and a mandate to govern the affairs of the country until the following election. We have seen that the vote in such an election lies in the hands of a predominantly poor electorate that hopes for a redress of its condition of poverty. At the same time, the elections cost money, and money on a scale which none except the well-to-do minority or the corporate sector of the economy can find. And, if the poor electorate seeks its own ends, so does the rich community which directly or indirectly must provide the financial support for fighting the elections. The conflict of the opposite sets of demands does not take an open form. If it did it would not be harmful, for that is the logic of a democracy---the logic of settling conflicts through a process of accommodation of conflicting interests. But, the conflict is driven underground into illegitimate channels since it is not only the spokesmen of the rich but of the poor as well that have to be supported by the resources commanded by the economic elite. The fact is that fighting a national election costs a political party crores of rupees if it contests all the seats to parliament and the state legislatures and since the party cannot possibly raise funds of this magnitude from its own memberships, it must inevitably look to other sources where these funds are given openly or in a clandestine fashion, whether willingly or extorted by force.

The law seeks to prevent such dependence of political parties on large donations by limiting the expenditure that may be incurred by each candidate on his election, which includes printing of posters, support of volunteers, organising of public meetings, travel through the constituency, etc. But this usually only means that the declared expenditure of the candidate or his party is limited to the maximum that is specified. There is a general belief that the declared expenses are like the tips of icebergs, only indications of the vast mass that is submerged and therefore, unseen. The parliament by law also sought to prevent companies and business houses from donating large sums to political parties. Again, the belief is that this legislation only resulted in converting open, accountable expenditure to covert, unaccountable expenses on the part of corporate bodies.

The conflict between the two compulsions generated by the democratic polity, viz., the adoption of an egalitarian idiom and the helpless dependence upon the ability to procure large funds of money for operating the electoral framework, creates in a poor and illiterate country like ours a climate of ambivalence, if not of outright hypocrisy. At the organisational level it creates a split between the great charismatic leader who espouses the cause of the poor and the party boss who in the process of meeting the mundane requirements of the party machine, must soil his hands, refine his tools of political arm-twisting, and acquiesce in many acts which are only marginally legitimate and some which are wholly illegitimate and even illegal. The charismatic leader and the political party boss are not just two individuals, they are the two alternative phases of political organisation---the charisma representing the idealistic, if not romantic, phase and the party machine representing harsh reality. The charisma provides the idiom, the appropriate phrase and the forward-looking legislative programme; the demands of the party machine introduce the equivocation, the hyphens and the commas which can allow the law to be interpreted differently, to be left unimplemented or to be circumvented in different ways.

Those who provide the financial support seek to be compensated in many subtle and not-so-subtle ways. The settlement of their claims may take the form of convenient price fixation of commodities, the introduction, variation and removal of food zones, the variation of licensing policies for imports and exports, the redefinition of criteria of eligibility or otherwise for public borrowing or borrowing from public finance institutions. These are all political decisions taken openly and they are not necessarily malafide though they lend themselves to political manipulation at the level of the cabinet or individual heads of ministries. Governments ostensibly take decisions in these matters in public interest, but they could do so in response to other pressures communicated through the agriculture lobby or the large industry lobby.

I do not regard these interests, whether rural-agricultural or urban-industrial, to be illegitimate. It is the manner of their settlement that is legitimate or illegitimate. The hypocritical political style that has developed in the country and that seems to be a response to the situation of operating a wide-flung, electoral democracy in a poor, illiterate country, becomes the fountain-head of corruption.

Governmental decisions in several of the areas affecting large landed interests, industrial capital or trade and business are not necessarily illegitimate and they are certainly not illegal, but they set a style if and in so far as they seem to respond to covert, unarticulated pressures and are against the interests of the generality of people. The adoption of this style by individual ministers within their areas of competence can lead to a gross misuse of the discretionary powers conferred on them. Where the government or the party is openly responding to certain pressures, it has to keep within the limits of law as well as propriety; at the level of individuals these constraints do not operate with equal effectiveness. Even prior to many commissions appointed in the post-emergency period, there were at least half a dozen commissions that had been appointed to enquire into the alleged misuse of powers by particular chief ministers and ministers at the state level and several of these commissions had come to the conclusion that power had been used to serve illegitimate, personal ends by these elected representatives of the people. Problems begin when claims of individual creditors to political parties are sought to be settled by acts of favouritism at the cost of the public exchequer. Then, it is only a matter of time and the pliability of the minister's moral code before these actions become sources of personal gratification. Neither of these two sets of actions is legal or legitimate. Corruption at the level of the individual minister would not have been easy if those who seek favours were not conscious that they are treading well-worn paths and using old, established channels of communication which earlier had been used for illegitimate, though not for personal, ends when the minister as a party man sought to raise funds. The extent of corruption at the ministerial level is not fully known, but there is a general impression that it is widespread. Perhaps, the impression is erroneous but in its ill-effects the impression that people carry is more important than actuality itself. For, again, it is the impression that sets the style.

At the administrative level corruption is known to prevail, more particularly in certain departments of government where officers come in contact with monied clients either as assessees, contractors, businessmen seeking licences or offenders seeking to escape the consequences of their actions. In each case, the opportunity exists and in some cases it is said that an officer who does not participate in the system and accept his share of the spoils of office becomes a misfit. Corruption at the administrative level has no necessitous relationship with the larger political system except that a development-oriented state, which seeks to accelerate its resource mobilisation through high taxation and regulates the economy to serve social objectives of equity in distribution, inevitably finds itself engaged in a complex process of legislation and rule-making. Under certain conditions, each rule and new regulation has the potentiality of being converted into a leverage for self-aggrandisement and personal gain by the officers who administer these rules. These conditions relate not to the political system as such but to the lifestyle, the consumer orientation and the absence of social commitment of our upwardly mobile, educated middle class from among which the officers of government are recruited.

This middle class has not arisen out of the poorer segments of the population; it has emerged primarily from amongst the landowning agricultural castes whose members, even when they are poor, are separated from the artisan, the tenant-cultivator and landless labour segments of the community. The poverty of these latter groups or the economically marginal urban groups is an intellectual category, and not a matter of experience or even close observation to most of the professional and officer classes. They have been separated from it by their occupational class standing and segregated from it by their caste affiliation. This separation and segregation prevents the intellectual concern for the poor from becoming a commitment, it becomes a relatively impersonal matter of policies and programmes rather than an urgent action affecting the lives of people. Such a class of persons, whether in government or business, tends to be insensitive and often fails to see that their lifestyle, preoccupations and self-serving actions have grievous consequences for the mass of people.

This sensitivity cannot be generated by mere rules of financial and administrative propriety nor by the creation of vigilance cells, though both these measures may be necessary. It will probably come if the politicians were to set a better example but it is more likely that it will follow a process of education and organisation of those who are adversely affected by the corruption of the elite groups in our society. This process of organisation and education is difficult but without it the contradictions generated by our polity cannot be contained. There are those who in their impatience would suggest violent, revolutionary methods to end the problems. World experience does not show that bloody revolutions by themselves have solved any problems. At best, they may provide an opportunity, but the work of reconstructing a society gets done only by doing it whether with a revolution or without it. On the other hand, I do not think that the problem can be solved by only exhorting the rich to be mindful of their responsibilities to the poor. Such appeals have a value, but I think, it is equally important to teach and enable the poor to take responsibility for their own well-being and to protect it against expropriation by others.

In the meanwhile, corruption promotes, and is in its turn further strengthened by, the development of a black market. Black markets arise because people want to conceal their real incomes. This they want to do to escape heavy taxation, but, equally, because they have to incur concealed or inadmissible expenditures. Since the 'donations' given to political parties, the 'presents' given to ministers and administrators, the 'considerations' given to officers of law, the 'percentages' given to works department officials, the 'mamuls' and the *baksheesh* given to small fry cannot be shown as legitimate expenses for business, and are also too large to be absorbed in personal expenditure, the money so spent has to be earned and spent either without its making an appearance in the books of accounts or appearing in account books to be what in reality it is not. This cannot be achieved on any scale without the development of a well-organised 'parallel economy'. This parallel economy has to provide for the appearance and disappearance of money at will and may account for at least some of the vine-yards, agricultural farms, poultry farms and other such non-taxable rustic activities in which sophisticated, urban residents are found to indulge in as hobbies in their spare time.

The operation of a black market and a parallel economy involves a whole set of white-collar delinquencies beginning with tax evasion, corruption, falsification of accounts, breach of rent regulation, maintenance of false registers (for customers who may want to buy cars or scooters and other articles which are at any time in short supply), etc.

Money that is earned has to be spent; more particularly black money, since it cannot be easily saved or invested in an open way. This tends to exercise inflationary pressures on the economy generally and creates a demand for luxury goods. This, together with our fascination for anything made abroad, creates a heavy demand for foreign-made goods. This in turn accounts for the major smuggling operations in a wide variety of goods beginning with razor blades and cosmetics to transistors and tape-recorders, textiles and television sets. Smuggling provides a channel for the utilisation of black money both as investment and expenditure. Smuggling operations involve not only breach of customs rules and financial and foreign exchange regulations, but often a range of nefarious activities involving violence and murder.

Apart from exercising inflationary pressures on the economy, the need to spend black money generates a false sense of values and a general orientation to high living which makes the honest man of modest means feel apologetic about his very existence and conveys an impression to the young that so long as you succeed in achieving affluence---and sometimes only the external symbols of affluence---the means are unimportant. There is a pressure on everyone belonging to the middle class to live beyond his means and this pressure is accentuated by the lifestyle presented with fanfare by media men. Display of wealth and conspicuous consumption are emphasised. In affluent countries, where the general standard of living is high, this strategy of the mass media men succeeds in creating new markets; in poor countries they underline the great gap in the life of the poor, the not-so-poor and the well to-do. In the long run they may serve the purpose of raising aspirational levels, but in the short run where the opportunities for realising the aspirations are limited, they can give rise to frustration, resentment and serve as a quick resort to deviant forms of acquiring the externals of wealth. Thus black money originates in law-breaking and leads to law-breaking.

The operation of the parallel economy is probably the largest single factor responsible for a large number of urban crimes beginning with corruption, breach of all efforts at fiscal controls over the economy, smuggling and bootlegging to crimes against individuals. In some cases black money and smuggling get linked to large-scale drug trade and white slavery. In India, with prohibition being in various stages of suspended animation in different states, illicit brewing, smuggling and bootlegging continue to remain major avenues for employing and generating black money.

It is not the purpose of this paper to enlist in detail the varied types of white-collar crimes and trace their origins. The intention was to show what some of the structured sources of criminal behaviour are in our society, particularly in the areas of politics and administration, and to indicate some of their ramifications. This has been done by underlining the problems thrown up by our polity and to a lesser degree by our class and caste disparities.

19

Social Reform, Law and Social Change

There are several ways in which changes in social value and patterns of social behaviours may come about or may be brought about. Social reform is one such way and legislation is one important channel through which social reformers have generally sought to bring about social change. This paper is an effort to examine the relationship between social reform, legislation and social change.

Indian social reformers of the 19th and early 20th century seemed to have attached a great deal of importance to legislation as a means of bringing about social change. Legislative measures such as those abolishing the *sati pratha*, removing disabilities arising out of inter-caste marriage and restraining child marriage were urged for and enacted in the hope that these laws would abolish erstwhile social evils or facilitate some desired change. The Gains of Learning Act also made for a change in the law relating to rights of coparceners of a Hindu joint family to their individual incomes. Since independence the Hindu marriage and family laws have been further amended by enforcing monogamy, providing for divorce, giving daughters a share in ancestral property, and forbidding the payment of dowry at marriage. Some of the labour legislations also began as welfare legislations to protect the well-being of industrial workers.

Principal Pandit Felicitation Lecture, Law College, Pune, April 26, 1980.

Even the makers of Indian Constitution and members of parliament seem to have had the same faith in the legislative path to social reform and charge. The Constitution declared that untouchability stood abolished and when this was not enough, the parliament passed the Untouchability Offences Act and has now amended it to the Protection of Civil Rights Act, 1955.

The value framework for much of this reformist activity was provided by the liberal values of individual freedom, human dignity, social equality, rationality and democracy. The idea of 'equality' or at least of extending 'equal opportunity' to all groups in society was at the core of much of this activity; legislative reform was the particular tool of the reformers (in India as in England and other western democracies) for reducing inequality, extending opportunity or liberating the individual from the constraints of tradition or of the social group to which he belonged.

Several questions arise about this approach to social change through legislation. Have the new laws succeeded in bringing about change? If not, why? Who wanted this change? What were the assumptions behind this attempt to bring about change through legislation? What are the conditions under which legislation can facilitate social change?

Before turning to tackle any of these questions two observations are important. First, though all these various pieces of legislation sought to facilitate social change, they cannot really be all grouped together. They differed from each other in the rigour of their applicability. Some of the laws like the removal of caste disabilities in marriage were merely permissive. They did not prescribe or proscribe any particular pattern of behaviour; the law only permitted inter-caste marriage without any disability devolving on the individual marrying outside his caste. In this case, the law protected the individual against the possible danger of his losing his right to a share in the ancestral property of the family. The law could not, of course, ensure that the individual would not be socially ostracised or otherwise 'punished' by family and friends. But it protected him against loss of a certain social right. Where laws are merely permissive in nature, there can be no real question of whether or not they have 'succeeded' in bringing about a change. For instance, the permissive legislation on inter-caste and inter-religious marriage has not led to any substantial increase in such marriages. Yet, no one therefore says the law has failed in its purpose. On the other hand, the law of divorce is also permissive in the same sense. Yet, its enactment seems to have been accompanied by a substantial number of divorces having been obtained under the divorce provisions of the Hindu Marriage Act. Again, no one says, therefore, that the Act has succeeded in its objective. The judgement of success or failure with reference to permissive legislation seems inappropriate. It is probably more appropriate to judge them in terms of their timeliness or the need felt for them.

Some of the other laws mentioned above are directly prescriptive or proscriptive as in the case of the law for child marriage restraint, the law of monogamy or the law against the practice of untouchability. It is with reference to such legislation that the question of how successful the legislation has been in its objective of bringing about social change becomes pertinent. It is not the purpose of this paper to assess the success or failure of each of these pieces of legislation but generally to see what relationship between law and social change seems to have been assumed by social reformers when they sought the enactment of these laws.

At a very general level it is permissible to say that the proscriptive legislation against the evil of *sati* has succeeded whereas the legislation against the practice of untouchability—even in public places—has not fully succeeded. The law against polygamy has by and large succeeded but the law against child marriage is still flouted in many thousands of cases, especially among the uneducated, lower caste groups. What accounts for this relative success or failure? It will probably be conceded that both in the cases of the prohibition of *sati* and polygamy where the proscriptive law has succeeded the original practice was itself somewhat limited in geographical area and to a certain class of people. But, these practices were a characteristic, to the extent that they existed, of the upper caste, propertied groups. The social reformers of the 19th and early 20th century came from these very groups. They were able to communicate with and reach them through their newspapers, novels, dramas, lectures and all the media accessible to them. While the changes that they sought to bring about did involve a change of values and change of life-practices, they did not involve any basic conflict of interests. The expectation of the social reformers that a law would strengthen their hands and help them tackle a recalcitrant minority was well founded.

The legislation against child marriage has succeeded so far as the educated, white-collar groups are concerned, though it has made no dent among the uneducated, rural working class. The reason for its success among the white-collar groups lies largely in the prolonging of the period of education and occupational preparation and in the new norm of the middle class that a man must be able to support himself and his family before he enters upon marriage. The Sarda Act has had little to do with raising the age of marriage among this class. If the Act has not materially changed the attitudes of the uneducated rural segment, it is also because their occupational life has not changed much in terms of the average age of entry to the occupation or the preparation required for it. Most rural occupations are still inherited; a son begins to earn even as a child and the expectations of economic well-being are still modest. There is really no reason as far as they are concerned why marriages should not take place at an early age.

The lack of success of the untouchability legislation in rural areas and its partial success in urban areas has to be understood in terms of still another factor. So far as the practice of untouchability within one's own home is concerned, it is doubtful whether the urban home is genuinely and generally more liberal in its actual day-to-day practice, but it is true that at the verbal level and in public places in urban areas untouchability is less likely to be practised than in rural areas. This is due partially to greater education and, may be, to a real value change among some of the urban educated. It is also possible that the lack of education and the hold of tradition explain in some part the continuance of untouchability practices in rural areas. Of equal importance, however, is the economic importance of the practice of untouchability in rural areas. Belief in untouchability provides the legitimation for the oppressive employment practices of the landowners towards their landless labourers. Such a belief is probably not essential but that is the particular form in which the upper caste/class Indian in the village gives his farm servants the proverbial bad name which justifies his ill-treatment of them.

The chance of success or failure in achieving social change through legislation depends upon several factors. At least three of these can be identified from the above discussion---the degree of value change that reformers may have already succeeded in bringing about through their educational efforts, the supportive aspects of changes in the objective situation and the existence or non-existence of a threat to basic group interests as a result of change. There may also be additional factors which could be identified by a further examination of the success or failure of individual pieces of social legislation. Even without such an examination, however, it should be clear that legislation by itself is not the easy road to social change.

It, therefore, becomes important to ask why social reformers have tended to attach such great importance to legislative measures in support of their positions on various issues involving social and value change. Where the projected legislation is primarily permissive, the eagerness of the social reformers to work for its early adoption by the state or central legislature is understandable because such legislation does not require a person to do anything he does not wish to do. On the other hand, it extends the boundaries of freedom of individual action. Even such legislation can meet with considerable opposition as was experienced in the passing of the law permitting divorce and more recently in respect of the bill which sought to establish a procedure for child adoption open to all communities. But, in both these cases and in most others where law extends the options available to an individual, the social reformer's objective is clear and may appropriately be served by adoption of a particular law. This, however, is not the case where a new law proscribes or prescribes a particular type of action independent of the individual's own preference. What is the objective of the reformer in insisting on such legislation? What is his perception of the relationship between law and social behaviour? Does he believe that a change in law can in fact change social behaviour without any other efforts to change social beliefs?

There are several hypothetical positions which may justify the reformer's faith in the need for and efficacy of legislation. One of these—and the most illiberal one—is that he believes that people generally conform to law because they are afraid of the sanctions against its breach. The law, according to this position, emanates from the law-giver, the ruler: if a ruler promulgates a law and decides to enforce it rigorously, the desired consequences will follow. Now, there is no doubt that most of us at some time are tempted to break a particular law and desist from doing so because of the fear of sanctions that are likely to become operative. But, it is extremely doubtful whether most of us wish to break the law most of the time and are only prevented from doing so because of the punishment that will be meted out to us if we did. Besides, even if this proposition were valid, it would be inconsistent for a liberal social reformer to seek to enforce social change through enactment of laws because in the absence of a value change the process would be coercive and limiting of individual freedom.

Yet, the 19th century Indian social reformer sought to bring about social change through legal enactments issued by a non-representative foreign government. His own personal convictions about the 'rightness' of certain practices and values seemed to have blinded him to the inconsistency involved in his favourite method of social change. This is not to deny that he was actively engaged in educating people about what were right and wrong practices in terms of the new values that he propagated. But, his dialogue was at best with people of his own stratum. The non-literate segments of society were not a part of his universe of discussion though they were equally affected by the law. Thus, apart from the authoritarianism implicit in his method, there was also a certain paternalism in his attitude towards the non-literate segments of society whose interests he assumed could be safely entrusted to his own judgement. To seek to legislate a social change without a prior value change is in a sense to seek to use the authority and the coercive power of the state to enforce a new value framework.

It may be argued that in a democratic polity the reformer is justified in seeking to bring about change through legislation because if a law is passed by majority vote in a legislature, that itself is an indication that a value change has taken place. Even if this proposition were considered valid, it could not apply to the legislative process prior to independence----or at least, prior to 1938----since the legislatures of that period were not "representative of the people". They were in many cases nominated legislatures and even the 'elected' representatives were elected from limited constituencies.

But, one may raise a question about the validity of this assumption of 'representativeness' even with regard to the legislative process of the post-1938 and post-independence period. Can the fact that a particular law has been passed by a legislature be truly indicative of the acceptance and support of a majority of the people? If it is so indicative, what then accounts for the failure of the law against untouchability, the law against alcohol, the law against child marriage and other pieces of social legislation? Are we to regard them merely as administrative failures to enforce the law against a recalcitrant minority? Or, are they instances of the democratic process of legislation not truly reflecting the will of the majority? Is the breach of law an instance of an interested and powerful minority of individuals or groups setting aside the law of the land like any other criminal? Or, is the legislation itself an instance of an educated elite which dominate the legislature getting the legislature to adopt legislation for which there is no ground support? Both these possibilities exist and they may apply differently to individual pieces of social legislation, but they all highlight the dubiousness of the assumption that all laws passed by a democratically elected legislature necessarily have acceptance among the general run of people.

Legislatures in India and in most developing countries tend to be composed of the more educated, urban dwelling individuals drawn from the middle and upper-middle strata of society since they have the verbal skill, the organisational base and the necessary material resource (their own or lent to them by owners of urban industry and large, prospering landowners) to get elected to the legislatures. These legislators are influenced by ideas that they have drawn from their learning, their style of life and their international reference groups. In many developing countries these ideas are a mixture of social goals drawn from pre-world war liberalism, post-world war socialism and the personal goals of middle class comfort based on the style of life of the industrial west. The legislators have to mediate between this world of ideas and self-interest on the one hand and the reality of at least two other worlds—the world of poverty of the majority of voters and the world of successful cultivators and successful businessmen who support their political organisation on the other.

The representativeness of a liberal, democratic, legislative process seems to assume the existence of informed and organised opinion groups in society and also a basic minimum community of interests between various groups. Neither of these assumptions is likely to be fulfilled in developing societies which are often characterised by high rates of illiteracy, the division of the community into tradition-based ethnic groups and the prevalence of economic disparities which sometimes run parallel to ethnic divisions and sometimes cut across them. The problem of ethnic divisions may exist and also complicate the political process even in modern and developed societies, but in those societies the existence of relatively better informed, better organised opinion groups counters to some extent the chances of the legislatures being dominated by an interested power elite that unabashedly legislates in its own interests, or by a paternalistic liberal educated elite which, while often isolated from the rest of the community, still assumes that they know what is good for the community at large. In the absence of such articulate organised groups in the population, it is relevant to ask whether even 'freely' elected legislatures are representative or can be made to function in a manner responsive to public opinion except in the most formal sense.

This discussion raises a further question: Where does a law derive its legitimacy from? Several alternative answers are possible. From one point of view the legitimacy of a piece of legislation is derived from the correctness of the procedure adopted in enacting the law. In parliamentary systems, for example, a law has to be introduced as a bill, has to go through a certain number of readings in a representative legislature and has to obtain a required proportion of votes---usually a simple majority---before it can be regarded as having been passed, and therefore meriting its acceptance and endorsement by the head of state. Certainly, this is one aspect—the procedural aspect---of the legitimacy of the act of legislation. But, we have seen that such legitimacy, while it may be essential and necessary, is not enough to ensure acceptance or easy enforcement of the law.

Another perspective may be that a law is legitimate in terms of the intent of the legislator to benefit the people through this new legislation. This is often unconsciously the position taken by many liberal, reformist legislators. It has been seen that such legitimacy of intent is again not enough to ensure its acceptance by the people or its easy enforcement by government.

It would appear that the ultimate source of legitimacy for any given law lies in the existence of a consensus among the generality of people about what that law seeks to achieve as being desirable. The democratic, legislative process may be a way of ascertaining this consensus under certain conditions, but it cannot by itself bring such a consensus into existence. It is the function of social leadership---reformers, among them—to help different groups to identify areas of common interest, to show in what direction the "greatest good of the greatest number"—that hackneyed and yet irreplaceable expression---lies and to persuade them to make varying degrees of sacrifice of individual or group interest for the sake of the larger entity. What sociologists would call order arises out of such a consensus—an acceptance of some common values and ends and a perception of a commonality of interests. Success in the enforcement of law depends upon the existence of such a consensus. Order, which is indicative of the existence of such a consensus, does not follow the enforcement of law, it has to precede it.

It is obvious that 'order' in the police sense can be enforced for shorter or longer periods by use of large-scale physical force, but not in societies which have a 'representative' government in the parliamentary sense of the term. In such societies laws will need to be supported by a general acceptance of their legitimacy based upon the prevalent values of the time. They cannot be defended or enforced indefinitely by a display of force.

It is also true that while a consensus may have existed in a society about the legitimacy of certain earlier social arrangements, these arrangements may later come to be considered wholly iniquitous and unjust. For example, the social arrangements defining the differential rights of the aristocracy, the freemen and the serfs in feudal societies and the hereditary status definitions of our caste society may have found general acceptance at one time. But, once the idea of the divine right of kings and the rights of the nobility are questioned or once the idea of an individual's status in present life being determined by one's *karma* in a past life is disturbed, the whole edifice of social order built upon its foundations becomes shaky. 'Consensus' however vague the concept may be, is not a thing achieved once for all; it has to withstand change in the objective situation and also changes in basic values and ideas which lend legitimacy to particular practices. Bringing such a consensus into existence and maintaining it in new situations by absorbing new ideas and by evolving new social arrangements is the core task of social leadership, particularly the intelligentsia. The term 'consensus' is used here to imply an acceptance-----an implicit, unstated acceptance----on the part of the members of a social group of a minimal core of values and goals as also the modalities of reaching these goals for individual and group action. Order can be said to prevail in a group where generally most members conform to the prescribed modalities of action though they may not be able to argue about the validity of the goals or the relationships of social arrangements to the goals prescribed. In this sense, an ideology of free competition, ruthless individualism and an individual's total responsibility for his success or failure in life had a general acceptance in the early days of capitalist enterprise----acceptance on the part of those who succeeded as well as those who failed in the competition. It would be an error to assume that the capitalist ideology was thrust down the throats of the poor. In a period of economic expansion characterising 18th and 19th century Europe and even more particularly in America, the dream of success did seem too unreal even to those who had not succeeded all the way. If now, ideas of equal opportunity and of society's responsibility for individual well-being are to gain general acceptance, special efforts in that direction would have to be made. Every society has to provide mechanisms, e.g., familial socialisation, education, etc., through which young and new members are motivated to accept the stated social goals and the means. There has also to be a minimum level of integrity in the articulation of the goals and the implementation of the measure to achieve them. The minimal core of values, goals and prescribed modalities of action on which there is need for agreement covers among others the definition of life goals, the mode of allocation of social opportunities, the criteria of status allocation, the pattern of distribution of power in society and the modalities by which to bring about a change in social arrangements. The intellectual and the political elite in our developing societies have not shown clarity in perception nor integrity in pursuance of the new values and the new modalities of egalitarian society. The acceptance of any new set of values and instrumentalities is never complete, but it has to be sufficiently pervasive for a law to be effective. In its absence, law becomes a mere expression of pieties or a testimony to the hypocrisy of the law-maker.

It is true that the ideas of consensus and social order are vague and hard to define. They also may seem to run counter to the proposition that a society at all times is characterised by the existence of covert contradictions and conflicts between interest groups. They need not. Social consensus and social order must be conceived of in a relative sense so that in the same society at different points of time there may be a greater or lesser degree of value and goal consensus and order. One indication of order in a society may be the acceptance by its members of the prescribed modality by which changes can be brought about in social practices and social arrangements. One can conceive of a breakdown of social order when there is no agreement about how social change may be brought about or the agreement is lost because the changes proposed are so threatening to particular groups that procedural legitimacy does not ensure acceptance of new values, practices and relationships. The prescribed modality for bringing about social change may be one of several types: a papal bull, a new interpretation by the Supreme Court, a new law enacted by a legislature or the enunciation of a new theory and policy by the politburo. But, in so far as one speaks of social change, he must also concede the existence of a continuing social entity which is said to undergo change.

One implication of the proposition that order in society does not follow from the enforcement of law, but that successful enforcement of law depends upon the existence of order in society is that the social reformer should recognise the serious limitations of depending upon legislative activity as the sole or even major instrument of bringing about social change. While in democratic societies change in law is the accepted mode of bringing about change in social arrangements, the legitimacy attached by people to this modality of change is not wholly independent of the content of the changes proposed. These changes in practices, social arrangements and the values on which they are based would have to be legitimised first in the minds of the people. The people who need to be persuaded may be the illiterate majority (as, for instance in the case of the restraint of child marriages legislation) or they may be the power elite minority (as in the case of legislation restricting land ownership). But such changes in values and in belief systems must take place and must serve as an underpinning of a new consensus in society if legislative changes are to be effective.

It is the role of the intellectual elite from which group social reformers are generally drawn to help to develop this new consensus. In the Indian context the nucleus of values round which this consensus needs to be developed is already provided by the Directive Principles in the Constitution of India. The mistake that the intellectual makes is to assume that since these principles are already included in the Constitution, they are also present in the minds of the people. Our experience of the irrationality, iniquity and bigotry in our daily lives should be sufficient to inform us that the values of secularism and social equality are not yet incorporated into our thinking and that in some cases their verbal acceptance is a matter of immediate political convenience rather than of conviction.

The social reformer's preoccupation with legislation may be the result of several factors. It is possible that he realises that a change in law does not necessarily lead to a change in social practice, but he thinks that the adoption of a new law gives at least a certain legitimacy to the new point of view or the new value on which the law is based. In the case of permissive social legislation, this may be a valid, intermediary goal to aim at. It is, however, of no avail where the proposed legislation prescribes an obligatory path. In such cases, dependence on legislation is indicative either of the reformer's failure to understand the process of change and his belief that laws which run counter to people's beliefs can still be enforced, or indicative merely of the state of tiredness that an individual reformer has reached in his reformist battle. Further, given our legislatures, which are generally biased in their composition in favour of the educated elite, it is much easier and much less demanding to change a law than to change people's values, especially where the law does not directly affect any organised interest group. Working for a change in law does not require the reformers to communicate with the mass of people across barriers created by caste, class and education. It is enough if they can influence the political elite to the extent of getting a law passed. But, those who wish to bring about a change in deep-rooted attitudes and social practices cannot expect to succeed in their task through the legislative short-cut. Social reformers who have a commitment both to egalitarian and democratic values must on the one hand give up the solely legislative path to change, as also the seemingly brave path of change through violence and revolution. They must opt for the more time-consuming and demanding methods of education and organisation.

Here the term 'education' is used in its widest sense. It refers, of course, to formal education and to the opportunity it offers for communicating values and interpreting the implications of accepting certain values in day-to-day life. But, it also involves education of public opinion through all other means that are available to the reformer. The content of this education has to be not only a verbal communication of certain phrases and words, not even merely an intellectual appreciation of the interlinkages of these values and their relevance to social, economic or political philosophy, but a specification of their implications for the individual's personal and social life. It is this last that might help to some extent in minimising the conscious or unconscious contradictions in the lifestyles of most of us who claim to subscribe to secularism and equality but cannot live true to the implications of these values. Education in values cannot achieve any success if the educator's own life does not reflect them in his practice. There is need for considerable clarification of the social and personal implications of the values which we preach. It appears that in this respect some of the 19th century reformers who spoke of rationalism or dedication to national causes and some of the Gandhian and Sarvodaya workers who speak today of concern for the poorest of the poor have been more consistent in their personal and public lives than most of the present-day protagonists of liberal and socialist values who have been drawn from among the ranks of successful professionals. This calls for some self-examination.

The other aspect of education that needs some examination is to ask who this 'education' in new values is addressed to. So far, the social background of the reformers and the medium of communication they have chosen—primarily, the printed word---have automatically limited their public. Thus, very often, it is persons from the educated middle class. This dialogue may be necessary to reinforce convictions and to prevent the erosion of beliefs through cynicism or preoccupation with self-interest even in this class.

But among groups that need to be addressed by the social reformer one consists of those who are likely to be affected adversely by egalitarian social change. In some measure, every social change affects some group adversely. When women seek education or equality, it requires men to redefine their own role and status in the family; when untouchables seek social recognition and freedom from forced labour, it requires the upper caste, landowners to make new adjustment of self-interest. The previously advantaged groups have to be persuaded to accept the legitimacy of the new values and also the implications of these changes for their style and station in life. In the absence of this effort to move those who are advantaged to willingly accept modifications of the social order, there will be violence and conflict. While it is possible that conflict might become inevitable, the task of the reformer is to maintain channels of communication with those who are being asked to give up privileges and persuade them to accept the need for change.

Equally important is the task of addressing people who were previously disadvantaged and are expected to gain as a result of the proposed change. Here again, the Gandhian worker has a better record than most 'modern' liberals. How can we address and persuade those who are not 'educated', who do not live in cities or while they live in cities, do not belong to the organised, industrial sector? The need to establish channels of communication, the need to create and sustain structures through which the urban-rural, educated-uneducated, organised-unorganised gulfs can be bridged, is now all the greater. At present, the only channels that exist are political and economic. On the whole, both these channels have proved exploitative of the segments made up of the rural and uneducated groups.

The social reform leaders who sought to reach beyond the middle class in Maharashtra were primarily those who themselves came from the non-literate castes, such as Jotiba Phuley, Vithalrao Shinde, Bhaurao Patil and B.R. Ambedkar. But other social reformers have not been able to establish effective communication with the deprived groups of society. It is necessary that they find ways to communicate with these groups and that they communicate not only passively or condescendingly or paternalistically but communicate as with social equals. The message to be communicated to them consists not merely of the rights they should demand, but of how they must equip themselves through education and organisation in order that they may benefit by the new rights and 'services'. The potential beneficiaries need to know that they will have to invest efforts to benefit by opportunities that may become available to them.

Apart from directly 'educational' and 'didactic' channels of communication, it is necessary to forge new links through services. The organisation of services which will enable them to benefit by already existing services may provide one such link. Where words do not communicate or cannot convince, services oriented to the people's needs, inclusive of education, may succeed. The social reformer may find that social work provides a channel which, apart from giving him an opportunity to convey his message, also conveys his concern and readiness to translate his profession into practice. Social work also gives him the unique opportunity to listen and learn from what the potential beneficiary of his services has to say. The importance of service activity was realised by Ranade, Gokhale, Karve and Gandhi, though in the case of the first three the recipients of the service were largely drawn from the social groups from which they themselves came—the lower middle class, urban, literate communities. Gandhi consciously went beyond this group and sought to meet the needs of the rural and the illiterate poor.

The third important type of activity that reformers, or, at any rate, those who are seeking a change in values and social relationships through non-violent means, can adopt is the activity of conscientisation and organisation. Though conscientisation is a new term, it is basically education directed towards making the deprived people aware of what their condition is due to and what they can do about it. This task has been performed by various types of activist leaders from Jotiba Phuley, Ambedkar and Mahatma Gandhi to the socialist, leftist leaders working among industrial workers or landless peasants. There is a strident edge to this process of education and at least in some cases it is based on a social philosophy of conflict and confrontation. If conscientisation, organisation and social action have to fit into the kit-bag of a reformer and social worker, they will have to be rooted in the principle of social unity rather than in a strategy of dissension and conflict in society. This implies first adopting legal and constitutional methods in representation of grievances and a search for redressal; and where these have been exhausted, adopting *satyagraha*----self-denial and non-cooperation----but not the use of violence or coercion. The practice of conscientisation in the Gandhian context also means that the educative process must not generate hatred of other persons or classes who are considered responsible for the exploitation or deprivation against which the deprived groups are organised. This is not a matter of splitting hair, but of a basic difference in philosophy and approach to the task of education and organisation. It is an effort to seek social change without generating social hatred. Our polity grants the right of association. In the industrial relations field it also recognises the right to strike work, i.e., not to cooperate in the production process. It recognises further the right to picket and protest peacefully. These modalities of action can become part of a general strategy of containing social injustice wherever it occurs. But success in the use of these strategies requires education, organisation and self-discipline.

In this context, legislative change is only one and not necessarily the first or the most efficacious method of bringing about social change. The social reformer may use it to advantage if he has done at least the first important task of educating public opinion---the opinion of those who stand to gain as also those who may seem to lose as a result of the proposed change.

Index